The Political Buddha

Copyright 2018 Christopher Titmuss
All Rights Reserved
ISBN 978-0-244-08246-8

www.insightmeditation.org

Acknowledgements

I wish to express deep appreciation for the profound teachings of the Buddha (623 BC – 482 BC).

The Buddha inquired into every aspect of daily life. The Pali texts, which contain his teachings, encompass around 10,000 discourses. His teachings (known as the Dharma) address major institutions in society including the army, arts, democracy, education, entertainment, governments, law, medicine, religion, royalty and all of society, young and old in cities, towns and villages.

Drawing on the texts, *The Political Buddha,* looked into contemporary issues affecting our daily life and the influence of institutions upon us. The concerns of the Buddha apply as much today as 2600 years ago in northern India.

The Buddha spoke on the responsibilities of rich and powerful people, officials, priests and citizens. He gave 670 talks in the central park in Savatthi, the capital of the Kosala kingdom and sixth biggest city in India at that time. He spent more than three months a year there in the park for 19 years meeting with individuals, families, Brahmin priests, political leaders, wealthy business people and royalty.

The Buddha offered reflections on various public services ranging from administration, the application of wise assemblies, councils, guilds and the importance of sharing responsibility and being accountable for one's actions.

The texts refer to a wide variety of forms of livelihood including barbers, beggars, business people, butchers, carpenters, employers, fishermen, farmers, fortune tellers, gamblers, jewellery makers, metal-workers, potters, prostitutes, servants, soldiers, tailors and tax collectors.

I also wish to express appreciation to the Venerable Ajahn Buddhadasa (1907 – 1992), the most radical Thai teacher of the 20th century. He gave a countless number of talks in his 60 years of teaching to make the Buddha-Dharma (teachings of the Buddha) applicable to society, householders and ordained Sangha alike.

He spoke to make changes in society, to make the Dharma relevant for everybody and to generate a fundamental shift from selfishness and individualism to a society of co-operation and wisdom.

He gave teachings on Dharmic for students, Dharma Socialism, Dharma and God, Buddhism and Christianity, Dharma - the World Saviour, AgriDharma, Dharma and economics, emptiness and Nirvana.

Ajahn Buddhadasa told the people of Thailand, a deeply religious country, that the Buddha did not teach the Abhidhamma, a psychological analysis of the mind-body process. He said that monks wrote this lengthy text about 1000 years after the death of the Buddha. He also wrote that Dharma is God.

His talks and booklets provoked some dissent among orthodox Theravada monks, prime ministers, and influential lay Buddhists. After the publication of Dhammic Socialism (Dhamma is the Pali word for Dharma), a prominent Thai politician at the time described Ajahn Buddhadasa as a 'secret communist' and said that he should disrobe. The publication took place during the US war on the people of Vietnam, Cambodia and Laos. Thailand engaged in a war on communist insurgents.

A Prime Minster described Ajahn Buddhadasa as an arahant (a liberated human being, free from blemishes). Thailand's senior High Court judge had a hut (kuti) built in the forest of the Ajahn to give support to the monks and nuns there.

Despite praise and blame, Ajahn Buddhadasa kept on teaching. Just before the end of his life, he told me that he planned to arrange for the full ordination of women – a tradition that had died out in the 13th century.

I wish to acknowledge the inspiration I received from Ajahn Buddhadasa, fearless and insightful.

This book is a small contribution to keep alive the Buddha's teachings on the Dharma and social change. Every aspect of society needs to change. Our politicians, military, corporations and the wise need to work together to implement changes.

We have lost our way. The current policies lead to unhappiness, suffering and widespread depression for the young, middle-aged and elderly.

The Buddha and the Dharma depend on the Sangha of practitioners to express the teachings in daily life. The Sangha consists of men and women committed to the dissolution of suffering. We find such like-minded people within the Buddhist traditions and in countless other religious and secular organisations.

I have had daily exposure to the Dharma since first visiting Sarnath, near Varanasi, India in 1967. I endeavour to stay faithful to the depth of the Buddha's teachings and to communicate that depth to the West and elsewhere.

I am grateful to the Venerable Ajahn Dhammadharo (1914 - 2006), Abbot of Wat Sai Ngam (Monastery of Beautiful Banyan Trees), Supanburi, Thailand. I spent more than half of my six years as a Buddhist monk under his guidance in Insight (Vipassana) Meditation.

Tanja Kaller from Germany has kindly edited *The Political Buddha*, as well as *The Explicit Buddha*. She made many helpful suggestions, which I incorporated into the text. I greatly appreciate her mindful eye and great attention to detail to both of the books.

I wish to express a thank you to Jude Butler, Mark Cross, Benoit Martin, Peter McGahon, Sahar Rokah and many more for their support in a variety of ways. I also thank the Thai monasteries in Bodh Gaya and Sarnath, India, for hosting my retreats, as well as various centres on three continents.

I have drawn extensively on the translation of the Pali discourses into English of Bhikkhu Bodhi. He has engaged tirelessly in scholarship to make the texts available.

I wish to thank my daughter, Nshorna, and her four wonderful and adventurous children for their presence, quiet strength of character and confidence to speak up when necessary.

Finally, I would like to acknowledge the dedication to the Dharma of the wide network of centres, the broad spectrum of Dharma/Spiritual teachers, the retreat managers and the Sangha of practitioners. Some of these practitioners live an austere and nomadic way of life, year after year. They keep to the spirit of a very modest way of life through a basic income, humble accommodation and abide with few possessions.

Their way of life offers a greater challenge than that of most monks, who can rely upon lay people to support them in their monasteries for all their essential needs. Some Buddhist nuns, East and West, have to find ways to support themselves. There is a support structure for most ordained people, which does not yet exist for non-ordained practitioners.

The Buddha, Dharma and Sangha continue to evolve in bold and creative ways with the need to implement change to be at the forefront of a progressive vision.

Christopher Titmuss

Totnes

Devon

England

The Three Jewels

The Buddha

A fully Awakened One, of past, present or in the future, who teaches the Dharma. 'The Buddha' usually refers to Gotama the Buddha (563 BCE to 483 BCE) of the Sakyan Kingdom of north India.

The Buddha gave the name *Dharma* to his teachings.

Dharma is Sanskrit and *Dhamma* is Pali, the language of Gotama (Gautama in Sanskrit).

The Dharma

Dharma has a threefold meaning:

- *That which Supports*
- *Teachings and Practices that the Buddha taught*
- *Truth*

The Sangha

The Noble Sangha. Men and women who have realized a profound freedom and live deeply committed to ethics and wisdom.

The Sangha also includes people committed to Dharma practice.

In Buddhist countries, Sangha often refers to monks and nuns.

At the time of the Buddha, the Sangha often referred to any assembly of people co-operating together.

Contents

Introduction 1

SECTION ONE – The Buddha and… 4
   1. THE WANTING MIND 4
   2. THE MAKING OF MONEY 16
   3. GOD, PRIESTS AND CLASS 27
   4. WAR, SUFFERING AND KARMA 47
   5. THE ARMY, POWER AND PEOPLE 61

SECTION TWO – The Dharma and… 81
   6. FOUR NOBLE TRUTHS AND BIG BANKS 81
   7. ETHICS AND INSTITUTIONAL CHANGE 94
   8. GREED IS NOT GOOD 121
   9. THE PRIVATISATION OF SPIRITUALITY 136
   10. WISDOM, DEMOCRACY AND CORPORATE RULE 159

SECTION THREE – The Sangha and… 176
   11. TEACHINGS FOR ALL KINDS OF SANGHA 176
   12. THE WISDOM OF POLITICAL ACTION 192
   13. DISSENT AS A FORM OF HEALING 205
   14. THE DHARMA THAT IS DIFFICULT TO SEE 212
   15. CHARTER FOR LIFE ON EARTH 223

APPENDICES 230
   Outline of the Discourses (Suttas) of the Buddha 230
   Books by Christopher Titmuss 232
   Books to be published in 2018 and 2019 233

Introduction

I meet many people, Buddhists and non-Buddhists, on three continents every year.

I regularly ask both kinds of people what they know about the Buddha and what he taught.

The religious traditions of Buddhism and the recent spawning of secular Buddhism offer a wide range of views. People, who know nothing about Buddhism, will express a view based on what they have heard or read.

Here are some typical responses from Buddhists and non-Buddhists, East and West. They tell me that the Buddha taught:

In alphabetical order:

- *"condemned animal sacrifice"*
- *"discouraged people from getting wealthy"*
- *"gave teachings emphasising a passive way of living"*
- *"ignored political, social and religious issues"*
- *"only gave teachings to monks and nuns"*
- *"ran away from his wife and son to get enlightened"*
- *"said that householders could not get enlightened"*
- *"said that life is suffering"*
- *"said that we create our own suffering"*
- *"said that we create our own world"*
- *"said that we have no self"*
- *"said that we have to get rid of our desires"*
- *"said that we suffer because of our bad karma from the past"*
- *"taught detachment from the world"*
- *"taught meditation to get enlightened"*
- *"taught merit-making for a better rebirth"*
- *"taught people to be kind"*
- *"taught people to be mindful in the present moment"*

- *"taught that the world is an illusion"*

These responses are mostly untrue (and/or) half-true, according to the Pali Suttas (Pali is the language of the Buddha. Suttas means Discourses). The Buddhist traditions widely accept these Suttas to serve as a record of the teachings of the Buddha. These discourses offer a remarkable exploration of human existence.

The Pali texts address every aspect of human experience. There is no comparable body of teachings in human history with such an extensive exploration of the mind/body/consciousness, conditions, wisdom and liberation. We can draw upon these teachings and apply all the practical aspects to daily life. The texts can offer guidelines to address personal, social, religious, military, political and corporate issues.

Historians tell us that around 2300 years ago, people in the Buddha's nomadic Sangha got together and assembled this remarkable body of work for future generations. The majority of the content shows a remarkable degree of common sense. There is very little that falls into the esoteric, superstitious or absolutist.

One of the most discussed issues of his teachings focuses on rebirth. The term *puna jati* (literally rebirth) does not appear in the Buddha's teachings but came into use centuries later in the Buddhist traditions. The Buddha only referred to 'rebecoming' (*puna bhava*) or 'again becoming.' If the Buddha had referred to 'rebirth', he would have said *puna jati*.

The Buddha shifted from a view of the personal reincarnation of a self into another body after death to a recognition of the dynamic process of rebecoming, in which the long past influences our present condition. The argument about a single life or many lives is a straw man – a debate based on a fallacy that one view is right and the other is wrong.

Issues at the time of the Buddha and Issues in our Time

A careful read of the approximately 10,000 discourses attributed to the Buddha portray a very different picture of the Buddha. He expressed his concerns on countless issues and offered ways and means for a resolution. In the discourses of the Buddha, you will find many talks on personal, social and political issues. He spent months every year camping in the park in the capital city of Savatthi, where he offered teachings to all kinds of members of society. The King, members of the royal families, rulers, army generals, priests (Brahmins) and many citizens came to him with their concerns and questions. Most of those concerns still apply today.

These concerns include suffering, beliefs, social issues, collective action, priorities in daily life and how to make changes in society. *The Political Buddha* draws upon a range of themes found in the discourses. Readers will see the connection between"?) the social issues at the time of the Buddha and social issues in our period of history. The book divides into three sections. The first section deals with the teachings of the Buddha on some of the key issues of concern for people. I have quoted the Buddha regularly. Readers can see for themselves the relevance of his words for today.

The second section deals with the application of the teachings to various social, political and corporate issues. Again, this section also includes regular quotes of the Buddha. His voice has the potential to have a major bearing on today's society.

The third section deals with the Sangha. Sangha literally means Gathering or Assembly. The noble Sangha consists of men and women who abide with wisdom and a genuine freedom in daily life.

The Buddhist tradition has deep respect for the Buddha, Dharma and Sangha, often referred to as the Three Jewels.

In the Dharma

Christopher

Totnes

Devon, England

SECTION ONE – The Buddha and...
1. THE WANTING MIND

The Buddha's teachings on desire are radical and uncompromising. His teachings insist on a thorough and honest investigation into desire and its consequences, personal, social and political. Serious Buddhist practitioners cannot compromise in this area on the pretext of making desire more palatable for the Western mind. It is a matter of urgency that the West looks deeply into the nature of desire. This is a top priority. Why? Desire finds itself in greed, anger, fear, delusion, unhealthy mind states, addictions and compulsions. It takes a desire to hurt somebody, it takes a desire to support war or go to war.

The Buddha made it clear that the inquiry into manifestations of desire take a priority for the transformation of individuals and society. The inquiry into the nature of desire deserves widespread interest – in the personal, social and political. Transformation comes through wise application of attention to get to the root of the matter to end suffering caused by greed, corruption and grasping after power.

The Buddha said: *"As a drop of water does not stick to a lotus leaf or as a lotus leaf is untainted by the water, so the sage does not cling to anything – seen, heard or thought (Sn.812)."*

Desire (Pali: *tanha*) as well as its intensification, namely craving, brings suffering, eventually and always. The West finds it hard to understand the Buddha's teachings on desire. There is a common response. "We can't live without desire. If we have no desires, then we become a vegetable."

The world and desire mutually confirm each other. Desire makes the world or objects more real, more apparently substantial than they are. The force of desire strengthens the view of the world as objects and the world with all its objects confirms desire. The world is not the world as we know it without desire and desire is not desire without the world upon which to hook the desires. Is it surprising that the Buddha pointed to seeing the end of desire and equally to seeing the end of the "world" that desire affirms?

Through ignorance of this fundamental truth of desire, a core teaching of the Buddha, the spell of desire takes over the mind driving countless individuals towards certain habits or goals without reflecting on the consequences. Dissatisfaction, unhappiness, conflict and the whole mass of suffering derives from entrapment in desire, including the desire to have no desire.

Desire leads to distortions, prejudice and unhealthy forms of behaviour with a personal and social cost. Attempts to make desire appear socially acceptable include dividing desire up into good and bad. There is naivety claiming that the problem is not desire but attachment to results. Attachment and clinging to results depends upon desire or intensification of desire, namely craving. We need to apply mindfulness to *tanha, gross or subtle. Tanha* makes us a slave to what we want. There is no slavery in wise action.

The Buddha said: *"I describe three kinds of harmful action – bodily, verbal and mental action. Mental action is the most harmful of all. (*MN 56.4). Mental action stands as the precursor to verbal, written and bodily action – from the use of fists to going somewhere that will bring about harm. The principle of the karma of unwise and unskilful action of body, speech and mind applies to all citizens regardless of status.

Consumerism depends upon desire for its expansion, sometimes giving the impression that consumerism is the primary purpose for existence – a religious belief where the shopping malls serve as Church for the faithful with money as the form of holy communion to getting what consumers want. While certain Buddhist teachers believe there is nothing wrong with desire, nothing wrong with being open to desire, as long as the results do not affect us. Such statements ignore the Buddha's teachings that:

- *dependent on desire arises fuelling or inflaming (upadana) of situations making an impression*
- *dependent on such fuelling arises what becomes in the present and future.*

You might doubt the Buddha's teachings if you read a section on desire in the upmarket 'Tricycle Magazine', a Buddhist publication, based in New York. In large type on one page of the magazine, it quotes one Buddhist authority:

"Desires can contribute to lasting happiness, as long as they are not tainted by craving and grasping."

It is hard to know from such a statement whether the Buddhist writer wishes to make desire palatable for the Western mindset or whether he uses the word desire to mean a wish, an interest or a skilful action towards an object of interest. It may not be the intentions of the author but such views sound ominously like a watering down of the Dharma, subordinating the radical voice of the Buddha to the Western way of life. From the perspective of the Buddha, desire is a problematic movement of mind, even if it is not as intense as craving.

As well as craving, desire can also make life miserable regardless of whether it reaches the point of craving. For example, political leaders desire to go to war. Such leaders do not sound as if they crave to go to war, yet their desire for war inflicts trauma, suffering and death on civilians.

King Ajatasatthu of Magadha (includes Bodh Gaya, the place of the Buddha's awakening) launched a war on King Pasenadi of Kosala. The Magadha king defeated King Pasenadi, who returned to Savatthi, his capital. On hearing of the battle, the Buddha said:

"Victory breeds hostility

The defeated one sleeps badly

The peaceful one sleeps at ease

Having abandoned victory and defeat.

The fool thinks fortune is on his side

So long as his evil does not ripen

But when the evil ripens, the fool incurs suffering.

The killer begets a killer

The abuser begets abuse

By the unfolding of karma

The plunderer is plundered. (SN 3:14-15).

Dharma challenges the grip of desire in the mind. Without questioning desire, destruction of people and natural resources continues unabated. Those in the position of offering the Dharma to others such as teachers, editors, scholars, authors or organisers have a responsibility to show the psychological factors that contribute to suffering.

Neediness reveals another common expression of an emotional desire that produces suffering. Such desires place much pressure on others and leave despair when others do not respond. Desire lurks in every emotional problem, great or small. As an inner compulsion, it manifests in various ways through actions, speech and mind, as all kinds of issues.

The Buddha states specifically the importance of pinpointing unskilful actions rather than ignoring activities causing affliction and suffering. Ananda, the Buddha's first cousin and personal attendant, told King Pasenadi that it was appropriate to hold people accountable and offer criticism (often translated as *blameworthy*) for their behaviour.

He said: "We do not recognise anything of value in the praise and criticism of others spoken by foolish ignorant persons, who speak without having investigated and evaluated. We recognise as valuable the praise and criticism of others spoken by wise, intelligent, and sagacious persons who speak after having investigated and evaluated.

The King asked: "What kind of bodily behaviour is censured by wise recluses and brahmins?"

Ananda said that bodily action, which requires accountability, brings affliction and painful results. He said: "The wise, whether kings, brahmin priests and nomads, censure such behaviour. The same accountability action applies to speech and thought, which brings about suffering."

When Channa committed suicide, the Buddha responded: "I do not say that to this extent he should be censured. When one lays down this body and clings to (belief) in a new body, then I say one is not to be censured.There was none of that in Channa. Channa used the knife without the necessity to reproach (MN 144).

Garahati, the Pali word used for *blame* or *blameworthy*), mean censure, reproach, finding fault, disapprove and holding accountable. Having explored the behaviour of another(s), governments, corporations and organisations, we have the encouragement to speak up and name what needs censure. It is the first step towards holding people responsible for their harmful actions.

The Buddha states that there are three kinds of desire that lead to suffering. The three kinds are:

2. Desire for Sense Pleasures

If we treat desire as an innate human drive, then it means there is no possibility to live without *tanha*. Desire for sense pleasures drives consumer culture: the endless obsession to satisfy all the senses, to get what one wants and to maximise the feel-good factor. Desires for money, goods, sex, the fashionable, the new and expensive, exploit people and environments worldwide.

People experience pleasure from notions of success, getting what they want, feeling superior and putting others down.

Advertisements on our television screens, the radio, newspapers, concerts and billboards have a single unified purpose – to stimulate our desire to spend money on products. The Buddha showed the way to deeper experiences than sense gratification. He said: "How is it possible that, being bent on the search for pleasure, one could know, see and realise that which can be known through letting go? That is impossible." (MN 125). Wise action appears in the dissolution of a desire-fuelling dependency upon pleasurable sensations.

Seeing, knowing and action springs from wisdom and love.

2. Desire for Existence

Desires try to satisfy the demands of the ego in order to keep its existence:

- *desire for recognition, respect and approval from others*
- *desire for the existence of continuous health, beauty, energy and profit*
- *desire for security*
- *desire to win, to be competitive, to control and hold onto experiences, ideas, things or people.*

The desire to get and to keep and the desire to be winners, not losers makes for a small-minded way of life. Humans push themselves on to get what they want. Notions of superiority feed the desire to impose views on other nations, communities and people.

The desire to continue to exist intensifies the fear of non-existence. Consumers envy others – a world saturated with approval and disapproval, attraction and aversion. Attraction pulls consciousness towards gain and aversion feeds resistance to loss or separation. Life then spins around existence and non-existence, having and not having, presence and absence.

3. Desire for non-existence

The desire for non-existence shows itself in suicidal thoughts and, for a tiny minority, subsequent action to kill oneself. It shows itself in many other ways, too. There is desire for:

- *non-existence of debts*
- *non-existence of unhappiness and despair by escaping into alcohol, obesity, drugs and addiction to television*
- *non-existence of roles, activities and forms of behaviour*
- *non-existence of pain, trauma and abuse from the past*
- *non-existence in the future of painful results relating to the past and present*
- *non-existence of individuals, organisations and governments.*

You can drive yourself mad with the desire for something to end. The collision of two desires, namely the desire for existence, such as achieving goals, and the desire for non-existence of the task triggers fear of not getting things done, triggers the insidious building up of stress leading to burn out.

Desire to achieve along with fear of not achieving can destabilize the inner life to the point that a person barely functions; the collision of desire and fear destroys our health if not our life.

Eradication of desire also eradicates fear because desire informs fear. We need clarity around intentions, actions and results. It is not necessary to offer a defence of desire, nor enter a heady and narcissistic mix of so-called good and bad desires.

The disempowerment of these three primary kinds of desires gives access to engagement in a full participation in the world. We do no depend on desire to go to the toilet, make love, realise liberating insights or serve others. Desire constitutes a warped perception, deceptive and a corruption of the mind. A meditative inquiry points to a desire-less way of life freeing up wisdom, happiness and noble activities.

The Worldly and the Spiritual

Numerous retreat centres have opened in the West in the last generation or two. Citizens realised they need to have a break from home and work to get back in touch with themselves. While holidays give a welcome relief, the benefits often wear off after a few days back in the treadmill. A deep inner change can last not for a few days but for months, years or decades. Yet, meditators often find the transition from a retreat to home and work challenging. The wish to bridge the gap between the retreats and daily life is a common concern.

At the end of retreats, teachers offer a short talk to the participants on daily life. We usually refer to the value of a daily meditation, mindfulness, wise communication, seeing impermanence and the value of contact with like-minded people. We, the teachers, including myself, give short talks on the application of the Dharma to daily life, the benefits of a regular meditation practice, and the application of the eightfold path to every vista of existence. Retreatants often wish to bring something spiritual into daily life.

It is a commendable motivation. The interest to bring a spiritual perspective to the small tasks and major concerns contributes to the expansion of consciousness and releasing of a vision. Spiritual awareness contributes to an integrated, sustainable and caring way of life. The retreats offer an approach usually free from religious forms, such as chanting, prayer and altars.

Dharma includes the application of mindfulness to religious, spiritual and worldly experiences. Any desire to replace all worldly feelings and tasks for the spiritual will fail; it is an impossible undertaking to fulfil. Practice in daily life develops clarity and insight into both spiritual and worldly activities. It is not an easy undertaking to ensure that spiritual sensitivities form part of daily life alongside worldly responsibilities.

The Buddha addressed both worldly feelings and spiritual feelings. It is important to recognise both, worldly or secular (*lokiya*) feelings, and to recognise their place and significance in daily life from washing up onwards. It is also important to experience spiritual feelings (*lokuttara*). Spiritual feelings can arise in many situations from:

- *a deep communication with another*
- *a deep sense of mystery and wonder*

- *a deep sense of the transcendent*
- *religious service*
- *a shift in consciousness*
- *a transformative experience*
- *a way of life*
- *acts of devotion*
- *listening totally to music*
- *looking up at the night sky*
- *sitting in meditation*
- *reading a poem*
- *walking in the countryside*

Worldly and spiritual actions act as the left and right hand of our daily life without trying to impose one upon the other. The Dharma addresses both kinds of feelings to confirm a liberating wisdom around both. In pointing to such feelings, as he does in his classic discourse (MN 10) 'Four Applications of Mindfulness' the Buddha recognised the futility of trying to lead an exclusively spiritual life. Spiritual and worldly experiences arise due to specific conditions with our regular exposure to both. One hand needs to know what the other hand engages in.

The household functions as a stage for normal everyday activities. The same principle applies to daily tasks: assuming there is an ethic of non-harming in the intention, action and wisdom in response to the outcome. Dharma includes the application of wisdom to the full range of feelings and emotions.

Neither feeling experience has more reality than the other does. There is no evidence to show that worldly life is not spiritual, nor any evidence to show that life is not spiritual. The sense of the spiritual relies upon a feeling, a precious feeling, but a feeling nonetheless. The spiritual feeling is distinctly different from worldly feelings. Like worldly feelings, we can experience spiritual feelings as pleasant such as love, natural happiness and mystical changes in consciousness.

Spiritual experiences arise in unpleasant ways such as a spiritual struggle, spiritual doubts and struggles with existential issues. Spiritual feelings can arise as neither pleasant nor unpleasant – apathy, indifference, feeling of not getting anywhere, dropping of interest and vitality and dwelling in blind spots. The spiritual life can become just as big an escape from reality as the worldly life. The Buddha taught the realisation of desirelessness. He pointed to a life free from desire (SN 56.11) and its problematic consequences. He meant it. Noble action engages with life with a mind untainted with desire – a movement infected with ego.

Tanha refers to an unsatisfactory psychological movement that leads to fuelling or inflaming anything – experiences, ourselves, others, goods, views and so on. If desire inflames the worldly or the spiritual, then it will lead to disappointment and frustration. If ignored, this unsatisfactory movement will bring about suffering in some form or another. If the inner movement does not fuel or inflame anything, then it is not *tanha*. Pali scholars often translate *tanha* as desire, craving, pursuing, neediness, thirsting and longing. When a person cannot get what he or she wants or craves for, then the person ends up suffering. These painful experiences remind us of how the force of *tanha* leads to dependency on results.

Far too many human beings have become human desirers. Consumerism robs society of spiritual depth and transcendent values. Has homo sapiens become homo shoppiens? The consumer lies trapped in the construct of the desirer, the desired, and dependency on the result of the desired. Pleasure and pain are endemic in this construction. Desire holds the problematic mindset together.

We live in a world of haves and have-nots, success and failure, inwardly and outwardly. We are not gods and goddesses of the senses, as the Buddha advocated. We have become beggars at the doors of the senses.

The Language of Intention

The Buddha changed the language for a healthy inner movement from desire to wise intention, a right (or fulfilling) attitude – non-harming, non-exploitation, non-abusive and non-violent. These terms show a clear and forward-thinking intention enabling an application of skilful means. This resolve expresses itself as the application of the mind to the exploration of the nature of the sensual realm and to live in peace with the world around. The depths of meditation and the depths of experience point to the most excellent realm of liberation (AN 11.234).

The application of aspiration contributes to fresh opportunities for discovery, and creative outbursts. *Tanha* arises when the ego takes hold and becomes greedy for more. The ego wants special experiences or wants to repeat an old one. These desires override the potential in any experience for insight.

We may falsely imagine that only desire makes every action possible. Desire certainly drives some actions with unwelcome consequences, eventually. Clear intention, aspiration and resolve lead to action not tied to desire. There is also action bound to desires. Desire in Dharma language refers to a wish that has become distorted through reactions, ego or dependency on results, or all three.

Not only did the Buddha challenge the view that desire is in everything we do, but he also questioned the idea that all actions depend upon intention to stop the corrupting influences of desire (A.V.2-4). He made it clear that the process of wise involvement or exploration makes everything happen naturally if there is virtue. The Buddha said that it is then natural (*dhammata*) that we develop wisdom in accordance with dependently arising circumstances. In this process, virtue (*sila*) acts as a liberating force.

The Buddha spoke of his determination to change his worldly life as a Prince with his royal and family duties. He told the Sangha that he spent the first 29 years of his life living in an opulent palace shielded from the harsh realities of life. He had no idea that there were yogis engaged in deep spiritual inquiry to find a resolution to the cycle of pleasure and pain and the impact of circumstances on human existence for rich and poor alike.

Having turned his back on such a seductive way of life in the royal household, he optioned for a nomadic, minimalist existence for the rest of his life. The Buddha might well have reviled wealth as a great obstruction to the heart of his teachings. That, however, was not the case. He took a very pragmatic view that embraced responsibilities, action and wealth. Looking at our primary areas of focus and concentration a secular life, he considered whether our activities made us happy or unhappy. He reflected on the experience of happiness and the reasons that make us unhappy. He did not make an issue about wealth or renunciation for householders, but instead, initially, addressed the factors that contribute to happiness, contentment and well-being.

A seamless flow gives the sense of a noble path from here to there, from this shore to the other shore. The Buddha used a much-loved analogy of the near shore and the far shore, with the Dharma as a boat to cross over from suffering to the end of suffering, from sleep-walking through life to an awakened life.

Is there a significant difference between desire and right effort? To know ourselves includes knowing the difference between the two. I heard one Western *Vipassana* teacher quoted to have said: "Right effort appears on many pages of the Middle Length Discourses", a much-loved book with 152 discourses of the Buddha. Really? I checked the 1200 pages of the book. Reference to right effort appears mostly as a link in the Eightfold Path. Hardly a ringing endorsement of effort. There are a wide number of themes the Buddha encouraged us to explore. Once again, right effort need not be confused with desire and craving. Right Effort means leading onwards/fulfilling (??) and encourages creative energy.

Discourses addressed his nomadic Sangha, who prioritised their life around an austere lifestyle, a nomadic way of life, meditation, solitary practices and a communal way of living. This still leaves thousands of discourses attending to the needs of householders. In the West, we can learn extensively both from his teachings addressed to the spiritual nomads and teachings to householders. The dissolution of the grip of desire makes available inner peace and a liberated vitality for a boundless engagement with the processes of daily life. We can question the formation of desire:

- *What is the relationship of the desirer to the desired or the wanter and the wanted?*

- *Does the self, who wants something, exist before the wanting and what he or she wants?*

- *If the wanter exists before the wanted, how can he or she know what he/she wants?*

- *If the wanter and the wanted were identical, how could we tell them apart?*

- *If the wanter and the wanted were different, how could we put them together?*

Wisdom takes a deep interest in the wanter, the wanting and the wanted.

Genuine happiness emerges through seeing and knowing a way of being free from the *contraction of desire and the belief in the entanglement or separation of the desirer, the desire and the desired.*

Having crossed to the other shore, practitioners have no dependency on the boat (the Dharma).

Dharma awakens us from becoming lost in the desire-world construct, so that we 'see what has become' (*yatha bhuta dassana*) in an untroubled and unbiased way. There is freedom from imprisonment to what arises, stays and passes.

2. THE MAKING OF MONEY

Consumerism gradually undermines other social systems, communities, lives of indigenous people, and exploits natural resources, no matter what the cost to local people and their environment is. People lose their jobs, careers and livelihoods through changes in the financial markets; people lose their savings and homes which blight the lives of hard working people. Our political leaders give us the impression that there is no alternative to economic growth and corporate competition. Our prisons are full of individuals paying a heavy price for being in the grip of what they wanted regardless of the feelings of others. Yet when the corporate world robs people of their entire savings, there is very little accountability.

The Dharma would surely endorse the collapse of modern capitalism, due to the degree of greed upholding the ideology, as much as Dharma would surely have endorsed the collapse of communism due to fear upholding this ideology. Contemporary capitalism appears bound to the ideology of the consumerism making Dharma and capitalism incompatible, because consumerism operates at the expense of the deeper welfare of humanity. Franklin Roosevelt reminded us in his inauguration address in 1933 of "unscrupulous money changers (banks and big businesses) who stand indicted in the court of public opinion." Nothing much has changed.

The livelihoods of numerous employers and employees, whether large or small, have become jeopardised through the obsession with huge mergers and selfish actions of market speculators. We witness the collapse of communities worldwide who abandon their villages to find work in dirty, overcrowded cities. There is suffering and there are the causes and conditions for suffering. The modern discourse consists of naming the problem, taking bold steps and articulating a resolution.

The West feels the burden of a very heavy backlog of unresolved matters at home and abroad including waging war, domestic political unrest, a mountain of national debt, companies and families on the edge of bankruptcy and widespread unemployment. The burden of territorial and economic colonialism leaves a world of exploiters and the exploited. We witness heart-breaking poverty and devastation of nature worldwide. We can resolve this crisis through ethics, public dedication and political integrity. It will be the responsibility to co-operate, including community building, so that we embark on a spiritual undertaking for the welfare of present and future generations.

Our relationship to wealth

The Buddha explicitly stated there is the happiness born of letting go and there is the happiness through accumulation of wealth. The latter ranks second to the happiness of letting go. Rich householders would ask the Buddha for guidance as to what they need to do to be happy even while "wearing beautiful clothes, perfumes, ornaments and handling gold and silver. "The Buddha acknowledged the pleasure of prosperity while emphasising ethical values and showed respect to others produced a greater happiness.

The Buddha said that a person who "acquires wealth by energetic striving and righteously gained, experiences happiness and joy. This is called the happiness of possession. With wealth acquired and righteously gained, I enjoy my wealth and do meritorious deeds. This is called the happiness of enjoyment." (AN 4.68).

The pursuit of wealth, or name and fame, as the primary goal, diverts attention from knowing daily happiness as the norm of experience. The Buddha acknowledged the prominent place of people in society devoted to making money provided they did not exploit the welfare of others or cling to gain at the expense of generosity. He adopted a practical point of view rather than leaping on the moral high ground about money makers.

There is no direct relationship between increasing levels of wealth and increasing levels of happiness.

There is a consistency in research about the link between wealth and happiness, namely that over the long term, the sense of wellbeing in a country's citizens did not go up with income. The Proceedings of the National Academy of Sciences published the findings of their research. It left researchers with the question: "Where does this leave us? If economic growth is not the main route to greater happiness, what is?"

If the link between wealth and happiness remained a fact, then all human beings would naturally become happier and happier in direct proportion to becoming richer and richer. Then the desire to get more and success in getting more would generate more and more happiness. The super-rich would experience intense happiness, utterly blissful lives as the daily norm. There is no evidence for this. Correspondingly, human beings would become unhappier and unhappier in direct proportion to absence of wealth. There is no evidence for this either.

A very modest lifestyle or renunciation of wealth, triggered by great acts of generosity, can generate far more happiness that remains unavailable through the desire to pursue greater wealth. Those who cling to wealth live in fear of losing it. They will not know their faithful friends. They live as prisoners in opulent homes surrounded by high walls, security officers and guard dogs. The rich and famous live in fear others will cheat them, have their name trivialised or ridiculed in the media.

Capitalism depends upon keeping alive the myth that money and happiness share a real relationship. Pursuers of wealth rely on this myth. The American dream exposes the American nightmare – desperate poverty, social inequality, a crime-ridden country, and a brutal justice system. Those living with very modest means often believe it, too. The Dharma exposes repeatedly the emptiness of the myth.

I remember standing on the steps of a retreat centre in northern California. An expensive car, a Cadillac or Lincoln Continental, pulled up outside the entrance. The driver, an African-American dressed in a black uniform, promptly opened his car door, and nimbly hurried around to open the door for his passenger, a glamorously dressed woman, aged about 50 years, with a fair coating of makeup and jewellery. She had come to sit the four-day Labour Day weekend meditation retreat. She lived the sugar-coated pleasurable field of existence in an area called Beverly Hills. She had flown up to San Francisco and then booked a driver and a car to the retreat centre. I share the same point of view as the Buddha and Jesus that it is extraordinarily difficult to come to the depths of meditation, realisations and real awakening while languishing in a lifestyle brimming with comforts and the constant need to decorate the self. I could not imagine how she would find the whole experience. I appreciated her willingness to venture out of her immense comfort zone – albeit for only four days.

During the retreat, she wore a training suit, made of mohair, in turquoise blue. A woman friend whispered to me: "She wouldn't have got much change out of $3000 for that." In sitting on the meditation cushion, she said later she knew once she closed her eyes to face the condition of her inner life, her wealth and privileges meant nothing. She did not find it easy. She told me she hated the thin mattress. She hated sharing a room with somebody else. She hated the simple but more than adequate conditions. Yet she endured the long weekend - to her credit.

The wealthy woman told me afterwards that her husband had felt so lonely in his mansion without her that he had flown up to San Francisco to meet her. *I have never been to Beverly Hills and only met very few residents from that area. Does Beverly Hills house many lonely souls desiring to feel love? The rich, the poor and the middle classes are all worthy of our loving kindness and concern.*

Money has become such an emotionally charged issue that it generates immense inner stress, conflict between partners and becomes one of the biggest measurements for self-worth or lack of it. On the face of it, money functions as a useful means to purchase necessities.

There is some hesitation to discuss money issues with loved ones including spending habits, bills and debts due to feelings of guilt about the way people handle money. Millions live beyond their means through over consumption. Citizens live vulnerable to advertising and know little or nothing about spiritual happiness. You cannot buy authentic happiness which can emerge through play, meditation, to spending time with loved ones, witnessing the night sky, a poem and more.

Obsession around money has a grip over public consciousness - the number one fetish in many people's lives. Less than one per cent accumulates great wealth. There is the daily threat of a fortune diminishing on the markets, robbery and the boredom of living an extravagant lifestyle. They must cope with appeals for money from family members and acquaintances, near and far. Why would anyone want to live like that unless deep down there is an unresolved feeling of a lack of something? Money does not fill the emptiness in a person's life.

On the other hand, there is little point in taking the moral high ground by creating a virtue out of poverty, whether voluntary or involuntary. Real happiness comes from a network of loving friends and contentment with a modest lifestyle.

The forces of the market place and the values of capitalism offer the dream of wealth through challenging work and single-pointed determination. Out of the vast numbers who pursue wealth and the power and privileges that accompany it, only a few can climb the heady mountain to join the rich elite.

The rich drift increasingly apart from the poor. Most pursuers of wealth fall far short of their ambitions and continue to look up with envy at those who have achieved greater wealth. The one percent who makes €1,000,000 will envy the man or woman who has made twice as much. Those who have made €2,000,000 will feel poor compared to the person who has €4,000,000 and so on. There is no end to such desire until suffering or inquiry gets (get) underway. Desire truly seems an insatiable and addictive force. The Buddha commented: *"Those dyed in their desires, wrapped in darkness, will never discern this abstruse Dharma, which goes against the worldly stream, subtle, deep and difficult to see."* (MN 26).

An amazingly successful business woman in the USA running a capital investments company told me that in 20 years she had never had more than 10 days in a row away from her large company. She had become identified with the business making it difficult for her mind to have a break from work. One day the shares of her company totally collapsed when huge sums of money used in the market suddenly became worthless. She felt sick and in total despair. She had to endure fabulously wealthy clients screaming down her phone, issuing various law suits and various threats. Capitalism enslaves the rich as well as the poor.

It took the businesswoman all her Buddhist practices of letting go of desire and to instead cultivate equanimity, tolerance of others and wise counselling to keep her sanity.

What is the point in making wealth the primary *raison d'être* in our lives? If human beings lived for a thousand years, after retiring at the age of 65, the accumulation of a huge nest egg would make sense since it would secure comfort and peace of mind for centuries. That, however, is not the case. A heart attack, an accident, cancer, dementia, Alzheimer's disease can take away life or minimise the opportunity to enjoy. Men and women live on average for another 10 or 20 years after retirement. Time moves along much faster for senior citizens. After some years, the senses may not even have the capacity to indulge in all the pleasure available through wealth. By the age of 90 or 95 years, all interest to pursue expensive goods and indulge in excess has long since faded. Love and attention from others means a lot at the beginning years of life, final years of life and in between. If money and self-interest has taken priority, then lonely days may lay ahead.

The Buddha on Wealth

A common misperception haunts the teachings of the Buddha, namely that he demonised wealth. This view is far from the truth. He shows the way to enrich individuals and society through a wise and skilful approach to daily life. The Buddha neither supported the communist view of forced redistribution of wealth, nor a capitalist view of accumulating wealth in the hands of a few, nor a mixture of capitalism and communist thinking. The Buddha referred to three vitally important considerations in the creation of wealth:

- *wholesome action in the process of accumulating wealth,*
- *wise application of wealth,*
- *selfless acts of generosity to give support for worthy and wholesome endeavours.*

What is a Dharma perspective on obtaining wealth? According to the legend, he was born into immense wealth as Prince Gautama with access to three palaces, one for the summer season, one for the monsoon season and one for the winter season, and elevated levels of comfort, pleasure and ease helped by many servants attending to his every whim.

What is the attitude of the Buddha? "Just as the bee squeezes out the honey without harming the flower so there should be a gradual increase in wealth without harming others", said the Buddha.

In the Dharma, wealth serves to benefit everyone. The wise and loving spread their wealth "like a rainfall" rather than for the narrow confines of the self and certain family members. This attitude towards wealth firmly places personal prosperity into a much wider domain than narrow self-interest. The Dharma teachings call upon the wealthy to engage in a focused application of wealth in terms of:

- *Is there an absence of personal or family extravagance?*
- *What do you retain for use in daily life?*
- *What do you donate for the less fortunate?*
- *What is your relationship to lifestyle and the use of wealth?*
- *What do you keep in reserve?*

The same questions also apply to those on modest or low incomes or who receive support from the state in a social welfare society. Corruption of mind, greed and self-delusion easily haunt those caught up in business, engaging in speculative deals and ego driven ambition. The blind pursuers of wealth often neglect their family and friends; the fear of not achieving one's targets generates obsessive thinking.

The Abbot or a senior Buddhist monk reads out on the full moon of every month all 227 precepts, called the *Bhikkhu's Vinaya* (Monk's Discipline), to remind monks of the ethical standards required. It would be useful for a business to draw up a *Business Vinaya* of the ethics of the company for the board of directors to read monthly to remind all staff from CEO to cleaners. These ethics of the Sangha sustained the world's oldest institution for 2600 years. Most businesses will not last more than a few generations or two compared to more than 100 generations of the Sangha.

The greedy and the exploiters sow seeds of their own destruction. Those who cling to life and possessions dwell in terror of death; the Grim Reaper seals the end of all the gain. Life constitutes a very short experience. Those who spend a lifetime pursuing wealth have wasted their existence.

Knowledge and skills in any field of activity consider the human and environmental consequences. A business acts with integrity through support for the welfare and benefit of the many. In the acquisition of wealth, the individual or company cannot rest on their laurels but need to remain diligent, as the Buddha pointed out, otherwise the wealth will diminish through greedy expansionism or neglect. The obsession to be a leader in the field blocks the capacity to read the signals of danger ahead. Nothing happens by chance. Business men and women often ignore the signs that bring about the painful collapse of businesses. Accountants make huge sums of money from their audits rather than make businesses accountable for their gross errors of judgement. Bankers failed to see the economic meltdown. *Tanha* functioned as the blind spot either through ignorance or belief that greed is good.

The Buddha told King Kosala that he protected himself and his wealth through engaging in heedful and appropriate action, as well as encouraging his staff to take responsibility for their tasks. The making of money and wise sharing of it requires *upaya*, an important Buddhist concept, meaning *skilful means* that covers strategy, planning, co-operation and a systematic approach to the implementation of a wise plan. The Buddha gave the example of ants working together to build up the anthill.

Vulnerability of the Wealthy

Some wealthy people, who have exercised too much trust at the expense of wisdom, can painfully wake up to the personal cost of their wealth. When the singer Leonard Cohen left a Californian Zen Monastery, where he spent more than two years, he found that his savings of $8.4 million had dwindled to a mere $150,000, plus claims coming in for the remaining money and more. His lawyers believed that his long-standing financial manager had siphoned off the money over the two-year period. Leonard Cohen told a mutual friend he found himself "surprisingly peaceful" about this huge hole in his savings. His financial crisis forced him out of retirement to embark on an immensely successful world tour, at the age of 73, to recover his lost money. This tour made him hugely popular with young people, as well as with long-standing fans.

Leonard's humility, open-hearted testaments of his inner struggles and self-deprecating humour endeared him to money. One veteran of rock concerts in Australia told me: "Leonard's songs spoke deeply to all of us. We share together an evening of spirituality. It was a very special occasion." Leonard recovered his lost money within two years. He died aged 83 after decades of struggle with cigarettes, alcohol, and medication for a problematic emotional life.

Without the tour his popularity with a new generation would not have happened. Mindfulness, heedfulness and wise counsel with others act as an essential feature when entrusting money elsewhere.

In the early 1990's, one 24-year-old meditator on a retreat in California told me that his father called him into his office, the headquarters of a major oil company, on his 21st birthday. Sitting behind a large mahogany desk, the father said to his son. "Here is your birthday present." The father gave the young man an envelope with a cheque inside for $1,000,000. Initially excited and overwhelmed with his father's generosity, the young man told me he found it a burden to have such a responsibility for such a generous sum of money.

He mentioned his birthday present to a couple of close friends at university. The word went around. He said that his friends began to treat him differently. Some asked for loans or expected him to pay for an evening out. One friend wanted him to offer a loan of $30,000 to rent a shop and start a whole food business. Another suggested a joint business venture with a full proposal on the table. He told me he did not know whether he had friends anymore or simply hangers on who wanted something from him. He lay awake at night. He had thoughts about giving the money back to his father. The young man had not really wanted the money but now his unhappiness arose from the desire to 'do the right thing': should he keep it, share it, give it away, or return it to his father?

His anxiety showed itself in a fear of driving through tunnels in a city, so he would drive the long way around to avoid tunnels. Mindfulness, meditation, an inquiry together and a trusted friend in the passenger seat recovered his confidence.

It takes wisdom to handle wealth whether gradually accumulated or a sudden windfall. The Buddha advised the wealthy when he said *"arakka sampada"* - take steps to protect your fortune. Widespread corruption among our business and political leaders, who ignore exploitation of the system, makes it hard to know whom to trust. Some people naively believe in financial advisors from their own ethnic or religious background. They think their money will be safe with them. One Jewish investor placed all her money, around $7,000,000, in the hands of a Jewish financier. She told friends she placed her money with the Jewish financier because they both shared the same religious and ethnic history. Both families lost many close family members in the Holocaust. She lost all her money. She is now cleaning rooms in the homes of wealthy people's apartments in Florida. Corrupt financiers have no loyalty to those of the same ethnic background. Their loyalty goes to the blind pursuit of money and power regardless of the suffering of others.

Dharma Teachers and Money

The Buddha advised us to explore our relationship to incoming and outgoing expenses. If one puts weight on one of two trays hanging from a beam, then the other tray will rise. With income, the Buddha advised us to regularly examine in four ways what part of our income we use for:

- *spending*
- *wise investing in growth*
- *saving*
- *giving.*

He said that we should employ wealth to support noble ones and yogis, who dedicate their lives to realisation to a pure heart and awakening, to make families and employees happy, to honour dead relatives, to fulfil duties, conduct rituals and support the needy (DN: Nigana Sutta).

The financial circumstances of Dharma teachers in the West vary immensely. Some are monks and nuns living on the necessities, as recommended by the Buddha, while some teachers lead nomadic, homeless or virtually homeless existences, depending on acts of generosity (*dana*) and occasional other kinds of work. Some teachers own their own home or are in the process of paying off their mortgage. A few teachers are independently wealthy with a home worth €1,000,000 or more due to prior work in the business community before they started teaching, a significant inheritance, large book advances, or substantial income from teaching. It is the task of wealthy teachers to avoid opulent lifestyles, extravagant flourishes of expenditure and ensure moderation in daily life expenditures.

People who wish to explore the spiritual life may find themselves disillusioned when they hear about money making spiritual organisations and spiritual leaders charging high fees for their services. One ex-Buddhist monk charges $1000.00 per hour for a consultation.

We, Dharma teachers, need to look at our lifestyle, otherwise there is little point in giving talks on living with moderation, if we cannot walk our talk. There are Buddhist teachers who decline to go to certain centres, because the facilities are not comfortable enough for them or complain about the low attendance or low donations (*dana*). Practitioners and patrons often know a lot about the personal ethics and lifestyle of Dharma teachers to a degree rarely known in other so-called "helping professions."

Dharma teachers are expected to "practice what they preach" in matters of personal spending in a way that certain Christian evangelists, for example, seem to feel exempt from. I heard one Christian evangelist tell his congregation on his TV channel. "God said first seek the Kingdom of Heaven, then everything else will be added unto you. I found the Kingdom and God has rewarded me with wealth – various properties, personal helicopters, limousines, and the good things of life. God can do the same for you." Or, as one cynic said: "In order to be one with everything, you have to buy one of everything."

The Buddha and his Sangha of full time practising men and women benefitted enormously from wealthy patrons including royal rulers, successful business people, and numerous donations from ordinary citizens. Anathapindika, a man of immense wealth, took it upon himself to ensure that the Buddha's Sangha received ongoing support. It is this combination of spiritual practice and *dana* (donation) that supports transformation of individuals and society. The relationship of teachers, practitioners and wealthy benefactors has a long history in the Buddhist tradition. The Buddha expressed deep appreciation for the appropriate application of wealth. He never disparaged the wealthy who made wise use of their money as part of their practice.

The teachings make clear that the transience of life cannot offer fulfilment. Dharma practices invite a dedicated exploration of life for a profound awakening. A life spent in the pursuit of luxury obstructs remarkable realisations. The Buddha encouraged the rich to put their money into perspective.

We cannot buy what really matters.

3. GOD, PRIESTS AND CLASS

At the time of the Buddha, major spiritual teachers and their practitioners would debate their views in public. Yogis, mendicants, gurus, priests, brahmins and householders would attend these forums as the variety of teachers endeavoured to convey their understanding of the nature of reality and its impact on the psyche.

People filled assemblies, gatherings, festivals and Dharma halls to inquire into these significant issues: spiritual, religious and social. Religious leaders would dialogue together in front of large groups of people, including householders, Brahmins, wandering ascetics, royalty and scholars. A King (Maharaja) would take off his turban and sword in front of a religious teacher and give these two symbols to his attendant. (MN ii 119). With folded hands, people requested a religious leader to speak. The audience would not interrupt the speaker and observed a noble silence until question time.

On occasions, some people did not recognise the Buddha when he attended an assembly for debate. *"Who is this shaven headed wanderer and those with him? What can they know about the Dharma?"* (SN i 184). One respect debater, Saccaka (MN i 229) said even one who claimed to be a Buddha would *"tremble, shake violently and sweat under the armpits."* The Buddha promptly engaged in a debate with Saccaka pointing to him the suffering in claiming *"this is mine, this I am, this is my self."*

These debating halls gave the opportunity for Brahmins and other religious authorities, yogis and philosophers to debate their differences. These disputes led to hair splitting differences to understand what it means to be a human being, the relationship of human beings to each other, to nature and to a transcendent element. The Buddha warned about the feelings of elation when winning a debate and downfall at losing. (SN 825 -830).

When certain people knew that the Buddha would participate, they prepared questions beforehand to try to catch him out. If they lacked the courage to ask such questions, they would approach clever Brahmins to challenge the Buddha's understanding (MN ii 147). Some would try to anticipate what the Buddha would say, so they could follow up with another question (MN ii 122). Some spread rumours that the Buddha *"Did not have full confidence when he roared the lion's roar of the Dharma. Some did not question him, or they questioned him, and he did not answer. Or he answered but listeners experienced no conviction. (DN i 175).*

It was not unusual for a religious teacher and his followers to gain more followers if the teacher defeated another teacher in public debate. The defeated teacher and his disciples would take refuge in the superior teacher. There was a wealth of deeply experienced and articulate teachers, who spoke with much authority of their understanding, while holding onto questionable views. Regarded as the foremost of all debaters, the Buddha attracted many people from various occupations to listen to him and go for refuge in the Buddha, Dharma and Sangha.

The diversity of expressions of Indian philosophies and religions reflected the diversity of social forms. In this period, Indian civilisation included monarchies, republics, decentralised societies, tribes and indigenous communities. The Buddha introduced a democratic foundation to his Sangha, welcoming a broad range of men and women from different social and ethnic backgrounds. He knew the value of a civil society with assemblies and forums to establish rules and guidelines. The democratic processes enabled citizens to come to collective agreements on various issues. He adopted a similar approach.

This ancient influence needs to extend itself into Western society through drawing upon the wisdom of the Buddha's teaching with his emphasis on nonviolence, right livelihood, mindfulness, love, compassion, seeing into the unfolding nature of things, liberation, universal values and a fully awakened life. Tired of conventional religion and feeling disempowered through the claims that only science knows reality, more and more thoughtful and educated people today feel the inner authority to find reality for themselves. The claims of the religious and scientific authorities seem disconnected from the realities of daily life. For example, God versus the Big Bang theory has no significance for a person struggling to make sense of a crisis in his/her social life.

The Buddha made it clear that distortions of the mind have a significant impact on the perceptions of reality. Religion and science lack the expertise, methods and resources for the people to make a deep inquiry to clear away the murk of distortions affecting the capacity to see and know reality. Our capacity to know reality wakes us up and liberates the mind from the narrowness of construction, religious, scientific or otherwise. A Buddha shows the way.

The Making of a Non-Violent Revolution for an Awakening of Society

The Buddha lived and taught as a non-violent revolutionary, determined to a make a fundamental shift in society for both rulers and the ruled. He made clear that the rich and the powerful must undergo inner change and develop the ability to show a sense of real responsibility. He criticised the greedy, the violent and the deluded. He found fault with the kings, rulers, dictators, military and the religious authorities. Equally important, he offered a range of reflections, meditations and practices to change the condition of the inner life.

Those who have little knowledge of the Pali Suttas will often portray the Buddha as the founder of an organisation of monks and nun detached from the norms of daily life. The Buddhist tradition has often given the impression that householders simply serve as patrons or servants of the ordained Sangha. The tradition has promoted a message that states that if householders made sufficient merit, they would be reborn as Buddhist monks in their next life providing the best opportunity for enlightenment. Buddhists believe that making merit through wholesome actions of body, speech and mind contributes to their development as a human being. But there is little indication that the Buddha strongly promoted such a viewpoint. He addressed every aspect of personal and social life.

Punishment and Crime

The Buddha listed the cruelty inflicted on those caught up in violence and crime, including leaders and soldiers. Punishments were severe in his time. There were public executions. People were roasted alive, maimed, tortured, deprived of all possessions, speared to death, and paraded around the streets before execution with their head shaved (DN ii 321. Vin I 344. 345). Some were thrown into a pit of burning charcoal, strangled, boiled to death, and cut up from the middle (DN iii 332 – 8, AN I – 48, AN ii 122, M I 87, MN iii 164. Vin I 74). Others were left to suffer since medicine could not treat many of their wounds and traumas. In response, he taught non-violence, support for the poor and responsibilities of the rulers.

The Pali Canon offers a different picture from the Buddhist tradition and Buddhist meditation teachers. The discourses reveal the Buddha as an articulate campaigner determined to change society. He spoke to the royalty, priests and householders. He criticised the limitations of the caste system that boxed citizens into inflexible categories. He publicly made judgements on powerful figures in political and religious institutions, even at the risk of losing their support. The Buddha did not speak to please but engaged in an honest dialogue with people, rich and poor alike, to generate a deep interest in inquiry, insight and awakening.

In his only statement on the next Buddha, named Metteya (Maitreya in Sanskrit), the Buddha said that he would also *"teach the Dharma."* He said the Metteya Buddha will tell the future King Sankha *"to give up his palace, and present it to the Brahmins, ascetics, Dharma practitioners, the beggars and the destitute."*

This implied that the royalty and rulers need to show by example a modest way of life to encourage all citizens to support the poor. The Buddha urged change in the rich and powerful to recognise the needs of the poor. He, himself, had walked out of the royal palace to live a life of voluntary simplicity.

He admonished the powerful King Pasenadi of Kosala for eating too much rice and curry (SN 13.3). He told the King, who was *'huffing and puffing'* through being obese:

"When a man is always mindful,

knowing moderation in the food he eats,

his ailments then diminish.

He ages slowly guarding his life."

The King told Sudassana, a young Brahmin standing behind him, to recite the feedback of the Buddha to him before every meal and he would reward him. When the King became slim, he commented that the Buddha showed compassion for him in the present and in the future as well. Few would have dared to tell the King to lose weight. If affronted with such a statement, the King could have ordered the execution of the Buddha for his comments.

The Buddha placed the foundation of his revolution in three primary areas – ethics (virtuous intentions and actions), meditative concentration on inner/outer events, and wisdom. He advocated the questioning of authority as an important feature of the way to liberation.

The Buddha and God

The Buddha made many references to Brahma in numerous discourses. Brahman means the impersonal divine principle underlying everything while Brahma refers to this as a personal god.

There were strong claims about the status of Brahma that the Buddha dismissed. *"Brahma is the Great Brahma, the Overlord, the Untranscended, Wielder of Mastery, Lord Maker, the Creator, Most High Providence, Master and Father of those that are and can ever be."* (MN i 327). This description has strong parallels to the description of God in the faiths of Christianity, Judaism and Islam. You might have thought about that such unprovable claims of a personal God would have resulted in the Buddha ignoring totally the concept "Brahma."

He employed the concept 'Brahma' in several ways to redefine its usage. Brahma then had different meanings and different uses. This method poured scorn on a Creator God that we know in the orthodoxy of religions, reduced the authority of the Brahmins and gave people completely fresh ways of knowing God. For example, the Buddha regularly spoke about God in the following way:

- *Abiding in God or Godly abiding - Brahmavihara, divine abiding*
- *Attained God – Brahmapatta, arrived at the divine*
- *Become God – Brahmabhuta, become divine*
- *Godly conduct - Brahmacarita*
- *Palace of God or Kingdom of God - Brahmavimana*
- *Path to God - Brahmapatha, the path to the highest good*
- *Vehicle to God - Brahmayana, Dhammayana, vehicle to the divine*
- *Wheel of God – Brahmacakka, the excellent wheel, i.e. teachings of the Buddha*

The people of north India believed in God as the creator of heaven and earth. They believed that God established Brahmins to express His will on Earth. Upali, a householder, said that the Buddha had attained God (Brahmapatta) (MN i 386). Another said that the Buddha had become the "body of Dharma, become the Dharma, become the body of Brahma, become Brahma (Brahmabhuta)." (DN iii 84).

The Buddha employed language to make his teachings equally accessible to those who believed in God and those whose who did not

3. GOD, PRIESTS AND CLASS

believe in Brahma. At times, he used the word *Dharma* and the word *Brahma* in an interchangeable way, so theists, atheists and agnostics felt the Buddha understood their views. The Buddha did not stop there. He would refer to Brahma as one of the Gods, as participating in an assembly of Gods, as a Godly voice in a human being or God as pure being, pure hearted. He thus spelled out the meaning of God to people with a range of experiences in the spiritual life. People could then talk about God in a different way. He showed an imaginative way to understand God rather than simply rejecting God.

The Buddha knew that the Brahmins believed in God (Maha Brahma) as the *"Supreme One, All Seeing, the Creator, the Father of all. God exists forever while everything He made was impermanent."* (DN I 17-18). But the Buddha said he had not met a Brahmin who had seen God face to face. He dryly commented: *"People prayed and chanted prayers to God (SN i 143), but none had seen God face to face."* (DN i 244).

God ruled the lives of the people. The Suttas indicate that Brahmins worshipped Brahma. We cannot find reference in the Pali texts to the pantheon of Gods known in India today as Kali, Krishna, Parvati, Rama, Sita and Siva. If people worshipped Kali, Krishna and various other Gods, there would surely be regular references to their names in the Pali texts. The people experienced awe and fear in terms of the powerful forces of nature, earth, air, fire and water.

People were led to believe that Brahma created the Brahmins as Brahma's representatives on Earth. The Buddha said that those who believed in such views as an All-Powerful God had fallen into the hands of Mara. As an alternative to such a view of Brahma, the Buddha taught the *Brahmacariyas or Godly conduct*, (Vin. i.8. 11, 11, 16, 32, 33) having a parallel meaning to Dharma conduct, so that people would have felt they were not turning their back on Brahma.

Brahmins and people of faith could not argue with such a religious language that felt close to their hearts and minds. The Buddha spoke highly of abiding in God and Goddesses or Diving Abiding (*Brahma Viharas*) to express the depths of love, compassion, appreciative joy, and equanimity. While extolling the benefits of discovering the depths of the Divine, he made it clear in assemblies/sanghas of people, both nomadic and householders that he did not regard abiding in the Kingdom of God as the consummation of a spiritual/religious life.

The Buddha said that the *Brahmacariya* in his Sangha lived for liberation along with insight into causes and conditions for what arises and passes. It meant that belief in God or disbelief in God mattered little from his perspective. The language of Godly conduct and Godly abiding enables believers in God to feel at ease with his teachings. They knew that the Buddha's language bore no relationship to Brahma as God the creator.

Heavens (gods and angels), humans (*manussa*), ghosts (*petas*), animals and hell constituted the five primary realms of sentient existence. As realms, the Buddha considered the psychology/mentality as expressing the five realms of physicality/materiality. We use the mind to view the world. The condition of mind influences the view of reality. He mentioned gods and humans together regularly (MN i. 73-76; AN I 37-38). The Buddha said that the world was in loud agreement with gods and men and asserted they both existed. (9D I 54.69.111. MN ii 2130).

There were various teachers who taught the path to God. They found happiness of heart through abiding in God (*Brahma Vihara*) - love, compassion, appreciative joy and equanimity. The Buddha said that he accomplished) to being one with Brahman (MN i 386). The Buddha taught to know God through direct experience and knowing the depths of the heart.

A monk tried to find out where God lived. He asked humans, angels (devas, the pure hearted) gods and respected brahmins. They said that God lived where there is light and glory. The monk had a description of Great Brahma (SN I 150; AN v 172) but could not locate God. Even when seekers found God, they saw that God could only sing his own praises. Even God could not answer their prayers (DN I 220).

The Buddha said that people might find God, but his devotees were still subject to karma and under the power of karma (MN i 327 331; SN I 141). Devotees felt close to God yet still suffered from stress, unhappiness and despair. The karma of unresolved issues continues for believers in God. The Buddha made it clear that the ending of karma takes priority over an experience of God.

The Buddha further ensured that believers and disbelievers felt at home with his teachings. At times, he would drop the word *Dharma* and instead use the word *God* when he referred to setting the wheel rolling towards awakening to liberation. For example, he said *"One roars his lion's roar in the assemblies, and sets rolling the Wheel of God."* In his famous discourse on the Lion's Roar, he listed the 10 powers of *One Thus Gone* (beyond suffering). Talking to the monks, he said he set rolling the Wheel of God in 10 ways. He said he understands:

1. *What is possible and not possible*
2. *The actions, results and causes of actions*
3. *The world with its many different elements*
4. *The different inclinations*
5. *The faculties of human being*
6. *The dispositions of human beings*
7. *The defilements of mind and emergence to liberation*
8. *The recollection of the manifold becoming of the self in the past*
9. *How people, fortunate and unfortunate, arise and pass*
10. *Through direct knowledge the deliverance of the mind (MN. 12.9).*

The Buddha has used the same injunctions to develop the path of the Dharma as the Path to God. One godly man, named Baka, a Brahmin, insisted that when the Buddha had entered and experienced the world of God or the Kingdom of God *(Brahma loka)*, then the Buddha had found the eternal, the permanent. The Buddha said the *'worthy Baka had lapsed into ignorance'* with such a view while speaking kindly of Baka as a worthy man.

Owing to the temporary experience of abiding in the Kingdom of God, there could be nothing ultimately fulfilling about such a state of being. He said that the capacity to abide in God stops the capacity to abide in other realms as deep and profound. Consciousness may experience such a sense of divinity but cannot prove that the state itself is eternal and permanent. This showed the ignorance of Baka's claims.

The Buddha told Baka that he made no such claims about himself and God.

- *"I did not claim to be all*
- *I did not claim to be in all*
- *I did not claim to be apart from all*
- *I did not affirm all."*

To Baka, as a man of God, the Buddha added:

- *"I do not stand at the same level as you*
- *I know more than you*
- *I do not affirm any mode of being*
- *I do not cling to any such delight"* (MN 49; MN 50.13).

The Buddha said that he taught liberation from not taking up the experience of any state and claims about the permanence of any state.

Priests (Brahmins) and the Caste System

In India, most families were born into the caste system that fixed every family into specific duties, tasks and livelihoods. The stratification consisted of four castes, namely the priests, the military/warriors, the farmers/merchants and the workers (*Brahmins, Kshatriyas, Vaishyas* and *Sudras*) while others were labelled the untouchables (*dalits*) - an underclass of desperately poor people living on the margins of society and excluded from the caste system. The Buddha rejected the Brahmins' claim that God the Creator made the four castes with Brahmins as the head, the trunk of the body as the military/warriors, farmers and merchants as the hands and the feet as the workers. In their role as teachers/priests (*acharyas*), the Brahmins claimed that they received their authority from God. The Buddha disputed this claim also. By undermining the claim of the Brahmins, he would generate doubt about the caste system that depended on the power base of the Brahmins for its survival.

The Brahmins feeling threatened by the criticisms of the Buddha, the Buddha in turn had to deal with the Brahmins, who criticised meditation. A Brahmin householder harassed the monks for meditating. He compared them to *"a jackal waiting for fish or a cat waiting besides a dustbin or a donkey standing waiting at a door."*

He said, *"These bald recluses were swarthy menial offspring of the Kinsman's feet."* Brahmins used the word 'Kinsman' as a description of God, who they regarded as the first ancestor, the Father of all. They designated the meditators as lower than any of the castes, beneath the feet of God, since the monks and nuns of the Sangha had turned their back on the caste system.

The Buddha said caste was according to what one did – whether a king, archer, farmer or menial worker. He said that babies were not born with the identity of a caste, but believers in castes imposed a caste upon them. He told Brahmins engaged in work as priests/religious teachers that if they did other kinds of work, then they were not would not be Brahmins, but would belong to another caste. His words would have infuriated such Brahmins, who saw themselves as superior to the other castes regardless of their work. They believed that Brahma (God) had decreed their birth as Brahmins.

The Buddha referred to the injustice heaped upon the poor, especially the workers and the untouchables. Referring to the beggars, slaves and destitute, the Buddha said that the poor were treated differently from the rich. They faced greater punishment than the wealthy. He gave an example: a poor man might steal 100 times less than a rich man, such as the goat of a butcher. The poor man could be beaten or imprisoned. It would be a different matter for a rich man. The butcher would have to beg the rich man to return his goat (AN i 250-3). In that respect, nothing much has changed in the past 2600 years. The rich who exploit people and their habitats cause harm to more people, yet rarely do they face punishment.

We can find other such comparisons today. A person found guilty of robbery in a shop faces several years of imprisonment for his crime. At the same time, a nation's prosecution services worldwide fail to haul powerful bosses into court for trial for the wilful abuse of citizens' hard-earned money and their bank savings. Those who run the big banks gambled on investments which cost the homes of millions. Bankers caused suffering and stress to customers whom they had encouraged to go into debt. Banks and other corporations try to get away with immense speculative deals that inflict immense suffering on the lives of many. The law rarely sends any wealthy people to prison, except as an occasional example every few years to appease voters. The handful of wealthy people in jail receive privileges in prison, for example, staying in an open prison with their own cell. They also get an early release. People at the time of the Buddha were not equal under the law either. The same truth applies today.

The Buddha encouraged practitioners to point out behaviour that requires censure. He did not expect his Sangha of nomads and householders to remain silent in the face of behaviour that causes suffering. Ananda, the Buddha's first cousin and personal attendant, told

King Pasenadi that it was proper to state what actions deserved disapproval: "Now, Venerable Ananda, what kind of bodily behaviour is censured by wise recluses and brahmins?", "Any bodily behaviour that is unwholesome, great king."

Ananda said that bodily action which requires accountability brings affliction and painful results. "Venerable Ananda, what kind of bodily behaviour brings affliction?" The wise including kings, brahmin priests and nomads censure such behaviour. The same action applies to what is said or thought that brings about suffering. "

Orthodox Brahmins considered themselves to be the best caste, the pure class (DN iii 81). One of the foremost teachers in the Buddha's Sangha, Venerable Maha Kaccana, bemoaned that the Brahmin priests had stopped exploring ethics and simply talked about the importance of their caste. He said their practices offered only *'trifling gains.'* (SN iv 117-8). The Buddha developed a reputation for being rude to the Brahmins. *"Gautama does not offer a seat to the Brahmins or stand up to greet them though they are burdened with years"* (AN ii 22). The Buddha replied that Elders lived with *"virtue, inquired into the teachings, have access to deep meditation and realized liberation through wisdom."* He said that an elder can have black hair, be young and in the prime of life.

It is hard to imagine the furore that the comments of the Buddha and his seniors in the Sangha would have sparked among the Brahmins. The blunt criticisms of the Buddha and his senior teachers reveal a stark contrast to today when Buddhist teachers often encourage themselves and their students to stay in the present moment without making a judgement. Maha Kaccana would probably have said that such non-judging practices around the present moment only offered 'trifling gains'.

Some Brahmins received a donation (*dana*) for chanting hymns while others expected or even demanded payment (SN 979-983). The Buddha also criticised Brahmins for wanting payment for chanting or offering mantras. Religious leaders and followers chanted to invoke the gods, so the devotees could unite with God when they died.

The Buddha poured scorn on chanting and mantras for being with God. In his discourse on the way to God, the Buddha told some young Brahmins: *"It is just as if a man were to say: 'I am going to seek out and love the most beautiful girl in the country.' People might ask what caste she comes from. Whether she is tall or short, light or dark and where she comes from.*

The Brahmins said they did not know. So, you do not know the one you seek and desire. Does not the talk of such a man turn out to be stupid? The Brahmins teach a path they do not know and see." The young Brahmins had to agree (DN i 244).

Some Brahmins told devotees of God that they would curse them if did not pay for a mantra or for chanting. The Buddha only permitted donations and other acts of kindness rather than making charges for his teachings. He would not allow anybody in his Sangha to ask for payment for their teachings. The Buddha had no time for mantras, chanting and hymns. Like unhealthy views, they continue if nobody exposes their limitations (AN i 282). In the same talk to men, he also said that men have problems with the opposite sex when these problems around sexual feelings which remain hidden.

Instead of dismissing Brahmins altogether, the Buddha gave a new definition of a Brahmin that was not related to birth, religious knowledge, or priestly functions. He said: *"The true Brahmin practises austerities, experiences a Godly way of life including letting go of egotism.* "(MN 98; SN 655-656). Dismissing the significance of castes, he told his audience that if anybody realises liberation through wisdom, then that person has left behind his identity including belonging to any caste. The Sangha delighted in his words (MN 40.14).

The Buddha uttered statements to show in which way his teachings differed from the tradition of the Brahmins, the yogis, the voice of the gurus and people of faith. The Buddha summarised his teachings as *"liberation through non-clinging"* or *"liberation through wisdom"* or the *"resolution of suffering."* The Buddha pointed to a liberation from caste and a liberation from imprisonment to "I", "me" and "mine." He offered a radical message still worthy of proclaiming 2600 years later.

The Buddha engaged in a countless number of discussions with followers of other faiths, religious beliefs, practices and with spiritual philosophers. He showed the emptiness of some of their standpoints, their unprovable claims and the limitations of what they thought. The Brahmins spent many years from childhood to adulthood studying the Three Knowledges. These three areas focused around knowledge of memorising the Vedas, the ancient texts that were written in Sanskrit, knowledge of rituals and knowledge of mantras. As with other theistic religions, Brahmins believed that God revealed these texts. They claimed that humans did not conceive of them.

In an inquiry with Sandaka (MN 76), a wanderer, the Buddha said there are teachers who regard tradition as the truth. They say that the tradition has been handed down from one teacher to the next. The Buddha questioned what has been handed down as Truth. *"Some is well transmitted, and some is badly transmitted, some is true, and some is otherwise."*, *"We cannot rely upon tradition for Truth"*, he stressed. Once again, the Buddha attempted to break away from the authority of the Brahmins and their claims to Truth in their tradition. It would have been galling for them to hear such criticism. Just as the Buddha redefined Brahma, he also reinterpreted the Brahmins three areas of knowledge to offer a fresh meaning. His approach refuted the authority of the Brahmins who believed to have in their hands the most major areas of knowledge.

The Buddha said the *Three Knowledges* consisted of:

1. *Recollecting of the self in its various appearances in the past*
2. *Insight into the outcome of karma in the future if one continues in the same way.*
3. *The recognition of the arising and ending of suffering.*

The Buddha thus made it clear that it was not necessary to learn Sanskrit, memorise religious texts and engage in rituals or chant mantras. He also disputed the Brahmins' declarations of truth based on their views. Some Brahmins proclaimed the Truth as *"Everything is Unity."*, *"Everything is plurality."* (AN iv 428).

The Buddha said that the human mind lives in the belief in existence and non-existence as the true reality – like the existence of the candle flame and then its non-existence. The holding to the view of existence or being as ultimate reality depends on forgetting non-existence, dissolution. The clinging to the experience of non-existence, that nothing stays, of dissolution, of fading away avoids the arising of what exists.

'Everything' denies 'differences/plurality.' Differences deny unity. The Buddha regarded neither unity nor differences as having any ultimate truth. If Brahmins proclaimed both as absolute truth, then there would be two absolute truths. One would then deny the other.

The Buddha engaged in dialogue with the eternalists (who believed in reincarnation of a permanent self and engaged with the annihilationists (who believed that the self had no existence or a momentary one). All these religious and secular views bore no connection with the Buddha's teachings of dependent arising. He kept pointing to the absence of any substance of an independently self-existing entity. He regarded clinging onto existence and non-existence as a distorted view of reality. Those who sit on the fence on such issues and other matters also reveal a clinging to that position.

Any regular claim of a single birth or a succession of births exposes a clinging, an identity, around a view. The ongoing argument about one life or successive lives has no merit to it. This straw dog debate reveals a failure to inquire into dependent arising and non-self.

The Buddha pointed out that if existence was eternal, there would be no point in spiritual practices as they would not make any difference to eternity, which is permanent and unchanging (MN i 431). The same principle applies to non-existence. If everything ended up as non-existence/extinction, as being non-existent/extinct, there would be no point in doing anything because it could only lead to non-existence. If we declare that either existence or non-existence as true reality, then ethics, spiritual inquiry, insights and discovery become irrelevant since we have made up our mind already.

Everything matters, nothing matters, claimed some Brahmins. Some things matter. Some things do not matter. We imagine that such perceptions confirm the true reality. Some adopt the view that everything is unity or oneness. Others take up the view that there is only plurality. Those who uphold one view neglect the perception of the other view. The Buddha stated that none of these claims to reality were worth clinging onto.

Despite his concerns about the views of the Brahmins, the Buddha acknowledged that certain Brahmins achieved liberation or had the potential to achieve liberation (AN ii 210-212). Born in the military/warrior caste, the Buddha boldly described himself with immense inner confidence as *"best of the Brahmins."* When the Buddha referred to caste, he would often place the military caste first, then the Brahmins (MN i 284). The Brahmins would not have taken kindly to being treated as second class citizens. On another occasion, King Pasenadi of Kosala also placed the military/royalty caste before the Brahmins, giving the impression that the warriors and royalty were beyond the influence of the Brahmins.

King Pasenadi said that the *"first two are held to be superior and the latter two castes are held to be inferior."* The Buddha dismissed this view and said there was *"no difference"* for those who *"penetrate to noble wisdom."*

Many merchants, farmers, workers and untouchables tied to the caste system would have appreciated the dismissal of the Brahmin influence. The Brahmins considered the Buddha as belonging to the military class although the Buddha spoke as one who rejected caste/class separation. He spoke in the same way of the yogis (*samanas*) (SN verse 1082, SN verse 622, 643 646). They also could achieve complete liberation. He said the same of those people not connected with his teachings or Sangha. They also had the potential for awakening and liberation without knowing his teachings.

While criticising the Brahmins, the Buddha also offered statements to recognise the "true Brahmin." He said: "The true Brahmin loved every being." (SN iv 117). "Such Brahmins delighted in meditation." (MN ii 169). But he would still return to his concerns about the claims of the Brahmins and the power they held over everybody else, including royalty and citizens. Few dared to criticise the priestly caste, the orthodox gurus, and their religious beliefs. The Buddha dismissed prayers, mantras and chanting as being essential for liberation. The Buddha undermined their religious belief system, their power and control over society.

The Buddha was particularly critical of the Brahmins for engaging in animal sacrifices. He noted that workers who had to *"kill the animals as a sacrifice were sick with fear and tears because of the karmic consequences of their actions."* (264).

He reminded the Brahmins. *"Animal sacrifices do not seem to be popular with the people"* (AN I 272; AN ii 207-208; MN I 343-4). Brahmins claimed that they were superior to yogis, because they offered sacrifices enabling others and themselves to earn merit while yogis only thought of themselves (AN I 168). The Buddha was critical of any sacrifices that involved violence. He supported the offering of ghee, oil, butter, milk, honey and sugar only. He said that the giving of donations (*dana*) to build a dharma centre was better than violent sacrifices and cultivating virtue. He said that there were *"benefits and happiness for the devout heart that lasted for a long time."* (DN i 142).

The sense of self-importance ranked high among the Brahmins. Brahmins had a social-etiquette that they should not call on others first, and all non-Brahmins should offer any Brahmin a seat. Lohicca, a Brahmin, sent his barber to ask the Buddha to come for a meal rather than go himself. Pokkharasati sent his pupil to see the Buddha. Brahmins encouraged Canda, a fellow Brahmin, not to visit the Buddha as it would increase the Buddha's standing in society and Canda's standing would go down. Brahmins claimed they had a superior birth, learning, virtue and character, and were quick to find fault with the Buddha. The Buddha questioned such belief in hierarchy.

The Buddha did not concern himself with privileges of birth, status in society or the religious tradition in his teachings. He pointed to realisations of liberation and the contingency of whatever arises (DN ii 244). He campaigned to dissolve the caste system and the slavery of the untouchables and replace it with a system in which people were judged according to their actions, not according to their birth. He criticised the Brahmins for supporting crude prejudice, active discrimination and racism due to a person's birth.

Brahmins claimed that the qualifications to be a Brahmin came from their parents; the family tree of Brahmins going back seven generations, being learned in the Vedas, good looking, inspiring trust and with a beautiful complexion and colour. Brahmins looked upon skin closest to white as the most beautiful since it signified they never toiled in the sun as the other castes did. The Buddha dismissed such qualifications and said ethics and wisdom were the only qualifications, not the colour of the skin. The same view of light coloured skin as a sign of superiority continues in India and elsewhere in the world. Racism has roots in the wealthy discriminating against the poor, the powerful against the powerless.

King Avantiputta of Madhura visited Kaccana, one of the wisest in the Buddha's Sangha to speak to him about the views of the Brahmins (MN ii 83 – 90). The King said: *"The Brahmins say they are the highest caste. They are superior. Other castes are inferior. Brahmins are the fairest caste. Other castes are dark. Only Brahmins are pure. Only Brahmins are the sons of God and heirs of God. What do you say about that?"*

Kaccana gave the King three examples of what all four castes have in common.

1. *If a person in any caste becomes incredibly rich, all four castes will seek to please that rich man regardless of his caste. In that way, all these four castes are the same.*

2. *If anybody violated morality such as killing and stealing then that person would end up in a miserable destination, a hellish place. In that way, all four castes are the same. Kaccana asked the King what punishment he would give for a crime. The King said he would have the person executed, fined or exiled regardless of his caste.*

3. *If a person became a recluse and lived a virtuous life, you would treat him with respect regardless of his caste.*

King Avantiputta agreed and responded: *"Then all these four castes are the same. There is no difference at all that I can see."*

The King then thanked Kaccana. *"You have made clear the Dharma in many ways. You have revealed what was hidden. I go for refuge in Kaccana, the Dharma and the Sangha."*

Kaccana told the King to go to his teacher, the Buddha, for refuge.

On an earlier occasion, the Buddha made much the same point as Kaccana when he famously said:

"By birth one is not an outcaste,

By birth one is not a Brahmin;

By deeds alone one is an outcaste,

By deeds alone one is a Brahmin." (Sn 1.7).

With their notions of superiority and purity through their lineage, knowledge and animal sacrifice, Brahmins believed they descended directly from God, as God's representatives. Brahmins referred to God as the Supreme One, the Mighty One, All Seeing one, the Ruler, the Lord of All. God existed forever, but his creation was impermanent. People prayed to be united with God after their death. The Buddha dismissed this view.

The Buddha responded to the belief in God with a powerful simile. He said Brahmins were like blind men walking in a single line trying to see and know something they did not see. They were all blind whether at the beginning, middle or end of the file of men (MN 95.13). He said that faith, tradition and acceptance of a view may be *"empty, hollow and false."* He added: *"It is not proper for a wise man who preserves truth to come to the definite conclusion: only this is true. Anything else is wrong."*

He gave the Brahmins a tough time for clinging to the past, for their pride and their desire to preserve the caste system with themselves as the foremost caste. It is no wonder that the Buddha said that those who engage in Dharma practice/Brahma practice had turned their back on the caste system and the orthodox religious beliefs of the Brahmins. The same principle applies today. Those who engage in Dharma practice/God practice let go of their identification with powerful religious leaders/royalty/the wealthy/military/the middle classes/working classes and the homeless. They have stepped out of the class system.

In his talk on inquiry, the Buddha said that: *"Trust in awakening, supported by reason, rooted in vision, is invincible. God, priests or yogis or anyone else in the world do not have the power to weaken profound realisation."* This is the benefit of deep investigation into the Dharma, free from dependency on tradition, various institutions, religious, political or scientific.

In the famous Net of God discourse (Brahma Jala, DN 1), the Buddha listed 62 different views which various people, religious and materialist, may subscribe to:

- *One group believed in the eternal unchanging self.*
- *One group believed one part of us was eternal and one part not.*
- *One group believed the world was finite, or not, both or neither.*
- *44 thinkers emphasised the future of the self and the world.*
- *Some were afraid to form a view*
- *Some expressed views about how the world began.*
- *Some expressed the view that the self ended at death.*
- *Some believed in a subtle continuity of patterns of the mind.*
- *Some believed in karma and the results of karma and some did not.*

More Religious Views

Some teachers at the time of the Buddha taught that no matter what actions one engaged in, it would not make any difference because the self (soul) was permanent and unchanging. These teachers taught a way of life of non-doing, non-action. Since the self was permanent there was nothing to be done (DN i 56; SN iii 210). They had the view that only names and forms were subject to change and the self was one with God, one with Being, the Ultimate Reality. Everything arose through concurrence of circumstances or fate. (DN i I13.45). Certain spiritual teachers/gurus subscribe to such. They give the impression that they have permanently achieved an ultimate state. They regard themselves as enlightened.

Pakudha, a teacher, went as far as to claim that a sword that cuts off another person's head does not deprive another of their life but only cuts through the elements. The Buddha certainly referred to karma including intentions, desires and actions. *"One experiences the results of what one does. It becomes a life of hell for the wicked."* (AN v 300). He said: *"People who are generous, kind in heart were truly rich"* (AN ii 203-204). He pointed out that Brahmins taught that union with God was the highest truth. (AN iv 103-104, 135; AN iv 371; Iv 135).

The Buddha repeated that Brahmins were like blind men trying to see something they did not know and could not think of. The most damaging statement came from teachers like Purana, who promoted the view of non-action and Gosala, who believed in fate, destiny and no human effort could bring a person to any purification (MN i 407. 516), (SN iii 210). Referring to Purana, the Buddha commented. *"I know of no other teacher who brings so much discomfort (due to his views of no deeds, no doing and no energy)"* (AN I 286; AN I 33).

The Buddha's spoke up to break the stranglehold of the religious beliefs and caste system over people. *"If any Brahmin, military, merchants or workers leaves their caste to encounter the Dharma and the discipline for love, compassion, appreciative joy and equanimity, then he practices in a proper way."* His words would have sent shock waves through the religious authorities. He applied the same message to the identification with the nation state. One turns ones back on being identified with the Sakyan nation to realise liberation through direct knowing of it.

Sariputta gave some advice to Anuruddha who was not liberated from confusion and felt remorse. He advised him to stop attending to problematic states of mind. *"Instead direct your mind to the Deathless (liberation)."* Having taken the advice, sometime later Anuruddha realised the *"consummation of the spiritual life."* The text said that he *"had done what had to be done."* (AN i. 283).

One godly man, Brahma Sanankumara, sang a song saying that the Noble Ones, the ones who know liberation and love, form the best clan. *"They are the best of the gods and humans who know liberation and wise conduct."* The Buddha agreed. He said that the song was *"well said with meaning and not ill spoken."* (MN 53. Sekha Sutta).

While the Buddha remained polite to the Brahmins, he had no regard for the view that emphasised the privileges of birth through wealth, the priestly class or birth into royalty. The Buddha questioned the privileges and the power of groups of people and the views that supported such positions. We need to question the modern Brahmins of contemporary society whether religious, political or corporate. Real change takes place through questioning the powers-to-be. The Buddha made this clear and we should not forget.

The Dharma points the way to the exploration of the inner and outer life and the impact the inner-outer have on each other. Those who treat the Dharma as a self-improvement programme have failed to understand the penetrative depth of the teachings into the core of society.

4. WAR, SUFFERING AND KARMA

The Buddha expressed unwavering views about his opposition to war leaving no room for any ambivalence. In the approximately 10,000 discourses of the Pali Canon, he did not offer a single word of support for war, including the so-called 'just war' of secularists or 'holy war' of religionists. His teachings concentrated directly on suffering and the causes and conditions for suffering. He showed no interest in supporting the policies of the nation state, especially if the policies led to war.

The Buddha actively pursued alternative means to resolve human conflict rather than relying upon military assaults and the suffering of people to change realities. He advocated a strong moral imperative of wise action to end the suffering. He campaigned to change the conditions that start and perpetuate war.

In the various Buddhist traditions, certain senior Buddhists have given support to the waging of war; some of these voices view war as unavoidable or as a means to create good karma through supporting a so-called noble cause. Buddhist monks would bless soldiers. The Buddha's discourses offered no such justification for such views of people, who ignore a core teaching of the Buddha: namely to end the desire to cause suffering to others, as well as to oneself.

The Buddha emphasised the profound importance of non-harming/non-aggression/non-hatred/non-violence in every area of life. This principle is a core theme of the Dharma. He pointed out that the root (Pali: *mula*) of suffering shows itself in greed (such as lust for power and lust for control), aggression (whether by the State, organisation or individual) and delusion, such as fear, narcissism harmful views.

The violence of the democratic State, and the support for it, comes from enough influential politicians, oligarchs who own the media and voters. The Dharma disciplines and training include an unshakeable commitment to treat people the way we wish others to treat us. Practitioners of the Dharma stay true to such principles, regardless of the demands of the nation state.

Today, people in cities, towns and villages find that they have to endure suffering and pain, sometimes for weeks, years or for the rest of their lives, due to weapons of war such as bombs, drone attacks, shells, tanks landmines and assault weapons. Living in remote areas, towns or cities, these victims of war find themselves left with little or no medical help, without safe water, food or access to doctors and medicine. Contemporary warfare destroys hospitals, clinics, hotels, schools, mosques, churches, government buildings and locations, where people gather on the ground and under the ground for safety.

Has there been any real evolution of human behaviour in the past 2600 years? As a species, we had sunk to the lowest levels before the time of the Buddha and our current leaders, the military and the armed militia, continue in a similar fashion as many earlier generations did. War confirms barbarism. Greed, violence and fear still haunt humanity today. We still resort to wars to resolve deep conflict between societies. The Buddha knew this and refused to sanction any violence.

The Dharma goes further than simply endorsing non-violence through a moral conviction. The teachings encourage:

- *reflection and inquiry into causes and conditions for war,*
- *the willingness to speak up,*
- *the application of compassion,*
- *the development of communication skills*
- *wise action to resolve conflicts, no matter how intense.*

Such conviction and practices have the power to enable the heart to stay steady, even when those around clamour for war with their host of rationalisations. It takes strength to stay true to the moral imperative to refuse to endorse the slaughter of others. The violent demands of the nation state or political organisations have no place in the practice and application of the Buddha-Dharma.

The heart of the Buddha's message on war and violence shows itself in a verse in the Dhammapada, a small book of 426 verses chapters in 23 chapters:

> *All tremble at violence,*
>
> *All fear death;*
>
> *Comparing oneself with others*
>
> *One should neither kill nor cause others to kill.* (Dhp 129)

The Madness of War

Far too many human beings share this propensity to kill or support such actions, wilfully and mercilessly compared to others who think and act in a different way. The killing, maiming and traumatising of soldiers and citizens takes place not only between the sworn enemies of the military class, but the same armies will unleash their violence upon ordinary citizens, men, women and children. No other species engages in such destructive behaviour, with the intention to make the other side suffer as much as possible, until they eventually admit defeat.

Science and industry co-operate to produce increasingly sophisticated weapons to kill people from the skies, sea and land, destroy entire cities, communities, institutions and demolish infrastructure through a range of bombs, shells, explosive devices and rapid-fire artillery. They use weapons and explosives to make farmland unusable for crops.

Political leaders of the nation state, whether from a democracy or from a single party state, often share the same lust for power and desire for a place in history. They show a brutal determination to control the lives of others, which often acts as one of the fuses that lead to persistent war that fades and then reignites.

One respected Dharma practitioner in Israel emailed me: "If we want to really influence the external reality we live in, we need to get closer to it, open to it and get to know it from all aspects:

That means making room for the Palestinian narrative, the Palestinian point of view, and stop trying to erase, ignore and manoeuvre. To do that, we need to be able to listen to the Palestinian story and pain.

Governments spend vast sums of money on armaments, mostly for the young, poor and powerless, to go and kill others in the name of protecting the belief system of the old, rich and powerful. In the U.K., the military will often refer to serving 'Queen and Country,' rather than admitting to follow the demands of ambitious politicians waving the Union Jack from the safety of their office.

A momentous day took place in British history in August 2013, when Parliament refused to endorse military action against Syria. The defeat of the government by 13 votes guaranteed that Britain would not play a part in a war on the Syrian government and huge sections of the Syrian people. A Conservative MP said that he hoped the vote would "relieve ourselves of some of this imperial pretension of a country of our size."

Historians believe that it was the first time in more than 200 years that the Parliament had resisted going to war. Yet, there is still no legal requirement for the British Parliament to ratify a government's decision to launch a war.

Modern warfare, whether within a nation or between nations or between nations and organisations, encapsulates a detachment from reality. The army, navy and air force press buttons on a computer screen in an office to bomb citizens, crouched in fear in homes and public buildings. The military that drops bombs, fires rockets or blows up properties must justify within themselves the terrible suffering their weapons inflict on the population. They obliterate the formations of people and buildings appearing as shapes on the computer screen. Human beings endowed with consciousness and feelings become shadows on the screen that the military strategists can decimate in a split moment. There is a disconnection from people as much as in assassinations, death camps and ground wars.

Obsessed with staring at the screen, they appear in a trance that reveals a denial of the consequences of their actions. This denial enables military operators working on computer screen to survive emotionally and psychologically the launching of warheads onto people. It is as if they are playing a computer war game. They repress empathy and compassion for those they annihilate. These formations on the screen represent people, young and old, whom the military have decided to obliterate as being unworthy of any present or future existence.

War produces an unholy alliance of the conflict of views and the production of arm sales. These alliances mutually support each other through civil wars, wars between neighbours and wars between ideological adversaries from one side of the world to each other. This alliance works to harm people and their way of life. Many citizens, who regard these battle zones as abhorrent, find themselves equally marginalised in democratic and undemocratic states, as the ferocious proponents and the harbingers of war ensure their destructive views take predominance. They repeat a handful of endlessly repeated rationalisations to kill and maim people, in and out of uniform.

The army constituted a major institution in ancient India. The army consisted of generals, officers and soldiers. In going into battle, the army employed elephants, horses, chariots, archers, swordsman, flags, daggers, shields, javelins. A shield would be tied to the trunk of the elephant. Trainers would teach the elephants to stay steady in the heat of battle. Soldiers would smear their weapons with poison. Young men received a thorough training in the art of war while slaves were also taken to the battlefield to support the military. A warrior carried with him a sword, a shield, a bow and arrows. Some men ran away at the sight of the dusty created by other army coming towards them. (Vin ii 86; DN ii 321; MN ii 165; SN ii 100; MN I 244; DN iii 328). The army used drums and conch shells to make as much noise as possible.

The King inflicted a heavy punishment on those who fled the battlefield and sought refuge in ordination in the Buddha's sangha. He ordered the beheading of the monk (upajjhaya) of the monk who ordained the soldier. The monk who announced the day of ordination would have his tongue cut out and those monks who attend the ordination would have half of their ribs broken. The Buddha promptly banned ordination for soldiers or deserters (Vin. I 74).

The Discourse on the Greater Mass of Suffering

In the Discourse on the Greater Mass of Suffering, the Buddha explained that war arise due to unexamined desires and views about the lives of others. The lives of those people matter less, or not all, compared to the lives of those in the same group as ourselves. Political leaders, who launch wars, blame their enemies for ordering their army to bomb and decimate their enemies. They tell TV audiences worldwide that these countries brought the war upon themselves. Political leaders order the army to attack other nations or organisations; they humiliate, punish, harm, burn, maim and kill people. They refuse to take responsibility.

Armies, militias and armed units threaten each other, as well as rural and urban populations, with the varying prejudices taking sides that decimate entire communities. The coercion of politicians, religious leaders and armed units engage in routine slaughter to serve their own vested interests.

We see through our news broadcasters the terror of events from one day to the next, along with distortions by the media, and its submissive obedience to disinformation. Programmes blindly report the lies and manipulations of spokespersons for the government, as well political leaders. We cannot trust the media to inform society of truth, of the reality of what politicians and generals have set in motion. Politicians on both sides of the divide cannot take responsibility for their determination to decimate their enemies.

In these regional wars, whether in the Middle East, Africa or elsewhere, there is no morality, whether the rich Western block supports or ignores these conflicts. Politicians on both sides sell arms to the side that seems aligned to Western demands. The defenceless serve as the most common target of soldiers. Fuelled with aversion, the leaders of democratic and authoritarian regimes intensify social/ethnic/religious differences through blindly taking sides, until the accumulated pressure spills over into violent conflict.

The King sent his chief minister Vassakara to find out about the Buddha's views on his decision to invade the Vajjis and whether the Buddha could predict a victory. King Ajatasattu said: "As powerful and mighty as these Vajjis are, I will annihilate them, destroy them, bring calamity and disaster upon them." The Buddha disregarded the determination of the King to annihilate the Vajjis and praised the Vajjis for upholding democracy and a healthy republic. He said the people would continue to stay strong.

The Buddha said the King would not defeat the republican institutions of the Vajjis and get them to accept a monarchy. King Ajatasattu postponed the declaration of war when Vassakara told the King he could only bring about collapse of democracy of the Vajjis through treachery and dissension. Not long after the death of the Buddha, King Ajatasattu engineered dissent and conflict leading to the breakdown of democracy for the Vajjian people. The King then ordered his army into the country to impose a monarchy on the people of the republic.

In September 2014, and less than four weeks after a war on Gaza, 43 reservists in Israel's elite military corps called Unit 8200, took the ethical step to refuse to engage in further intelligence gatherings on Palestinians to "deepen military rule" of the occupation of Palestinian territories since 1967.

The signatories sent the letter to Prime Minister Netanyahu and the Chiefs of Staff of the Israeli Army. Unit 8200, the largest unit in the IDF, expressed a convergence of ethics. Their letter provoked a public debate and discussion on ethics within Unit 8200. The signatories said that the intelligence gathering "harms the innocent and serves for political persecution and sowing discord in the Palestinian society." King

Ajatasattu, the Israeli Prime Minister and other leaders have much in common in the widespread use of the British former colonial maxim "divide and rule". The Buddha, however, gave teachings to bridge the divide.

The Dahiya Doctrine of Israel and an Armchair Existence

Wars continue with a desire held by both sides for the destruction of the other. The military launches its bombs and shells on civilian populations where armed groups live. Such armies adopt the principle of the Dahiya doctrine, a concept developed by the Israeli government and army. The Dahiya Doctrine refers to the application of widespread destruction as a means of deterrence. Consciously or unconsciously, armies have adopted the Dahiya Doctrine of pervasive destruction as a deterrent.

The invading army knows that the armed bases of their enemies have bases in the centres of population, cities, towns and villages. The government claims that their enemies use the population as a shield to stop bombing and shelling. Army headquarters, bases and garrisons found in areas of crowded population might simply enable the military to work near their homes. We must not assume that the army of any nation deliberately locates its bases in populated areas, so they can use civilians as shields against attack.

Governments will sanction attacks on civilians. The Dahiya Doctrine refers to the Israeli Defence Force attack on a southern suburb in Beirut with large apartment buildings that the IDF flattened during the 2006 war on Lebanon. The UN accused Israel of applying the doctrine to the Palestinians in Gaza during the invasions in recent years. The Doctrine seeks to bring as much suffering as possible to citizens trapped in a war zone.

This Doctrine has now come to legitimise the destruction of homes, schools, offices, hospitals, public buildings, shopping malls, factories, depots, industrial estates, public utilities, such as electricity, as a form of collective punishment. The application of the Doctrine generates immense hardship upon families, as well as entailing their subjugation and humiliation. This widely used doctrine fuels immense rage among some young men, who take up arms to try to get revenge on attacking armies. Traumatised citizens, who endure daily attacks, rarely turn on their own leaders but look to them for support.

Governments believe that they have the power to limit their wars to a specific time and place. This shows a depth of naivety and irresponsibility for the growing number of people dragged into the killing fields in neighbouring countries. The Buddha's teachings on karma consistently examine intention, action and their consequences.

The invasion of many Muslim countries and the ongoing Israeli occupation of Palestine, have brought about immense hostility from the Arab countries to Western policies. The West has spent billions of dollars sending in the troops and armaments in trying to control the wars they helped create in the Middle East. These military excursions to bring 'order and democracy' to the Arab world disguise irrational and compulsive behaviour by our Western leaders.

Apart from the small numbers of people campaigning to end war, or engaging in humanitarian actions, citizens find it hard to cope with the information overload on death and destruction, and rarely act. To their immense credit, compassionate citizens do dip into their pockets to contribute to relief work for those who suffer. Although deeply welcomed by all charities working to relieve suffering, the donations cannot empower the donors to take actions themselves to stop the wars.

News readers on Western television tell their TV audiences that a news clip may be "disturbing." With few exceptions, the short clips fail to disturb. The news clip might show a large cloud of smoke from a bombing, the aftermath of a suburb reduced to rubble or a crying mother in a hospital. This is the sanitisation of war in which the real horror of war on men, women and children still remains hidden.

TV clips could show people screaming through loss of limbs or terrible burns or a beheading. Even if television studios permitted such horror on the screen, it is still unlikely that it would galvanize viewers into action to force their government to stop the perpetuation of suffering. We do not witness the consequences of the atrocities committed by our armies, whether launched from the air, sea or land. The military launches highly destructive weapons decimating entire groups of people. Hard-core clips would shock initially but audiences become inured. Scenes that shock do not produce compassionate action to force governments to change their policies. Instead, we give money for the refugees – an important but small step.

You might imagine that news on television, night after night, would galvanise the public into widespread dissent at the promulgation of wars in our name. We become numb to any horrific scenes that appear on the screen. The government and military control journalists on the ground to ensure that they only see a selective representation of military action. Israel refuses to allow Israeli journalists to travel with the Israeli army (IDF) when the country engages in its periodic invasion of Palestine or Lebanon.

Television renders viewers as armchair spectators to reports of the daily killings and violence at home and abroad. The news item and the follow up documentaries intended to wake us up to terrible events, puts us to sleep. Movies generate more excitement than the reality. While a minority of viewers feel indignation at what they watch on the news. Only a few of those take initiatives to stop the carnage. The heavy hand of punishment and revenge feeds the very situation that the leaders want to stop.

Sacrifice and Suffering

The Buddha pointed out that advocates of war, and those who engage in war, get a certain heightened pleasure from their desire (*kama tanha*) to engage in military conflict. Armed organisations and soldiers, as well as their leaders, experience a heightened sense of self, in declaring and making war on their enemies. They feel excitement in their willingness to make the ultimate sacrifice on behalf of their cause. The Buddha had no regard for such sacrifice since it involved so much pain on both sides, as well as for their families filled with anxiety for their loved ones in the war zone.

The Buddha gave a clear illustration of the power of belief in the views and behaviour of so-called on 'heroes' and 'terrorists.' One man in one country assassinated a king. One group of people, who hated the king, saw him as a hero. The police caught the other man trying to assassinate a king. So, the king ordered him beheaded. One received the adulation of the people for killing the king while the other group, who supported the king, cheered the man's execution (SN IV 343). One group considered the man a 'hero'. The other group labelled the man a 'terrorist'.

Instead of heavy punishment, the Buddha took an opposite view telling people in power to give support to the poor, deprived and marginalised (DN 5/1 135). He proclaimed that acts of compassion, provision of homes, work and community reduce violence, use of weapons and acts of terror.

In praise and blame, the view of the people depends upon who and what they identify with. Sadly, it does not occur to citizens that non-identification with one side or the other can lead to a clear response to the situation. This is a core maxim in the Buddha's teachings. The wisdom of equanimity and impartiality enables the possibility to explore and understand the conditions for conflict. The taking of sides leads to views of good and bad, right and wrong. Such views block the capacity to look at a deeper level.

The issue of sacrifice plays a key role in matters of war when soldiers and militants can receive immense rewards and prestige for making great sacrifice. They can return home as heroes, receive medals, get a promotion in military service and receive media attention. Some believe that if they die they will go straight to heaven, since they gave their life in a just or holy war – two terms widely used by those of a secular or religious persuasion. For the Buddha, these views of personal sacrifice and subsequent rewards in the military have no merit.

Yodhjiva, a senior in the army, said to the Buddha that if a soldier dies in battle, he would go to heaven. "What do you say about that?" he asked the Buddha. Three times the Buddha refused to reply and then he responded bluntly.

"One who exerts himself in battle, his mind is already low, depraved, misdirected by the thought 'Let these people be slaughtered, annihilated and exterminated.'" The Buddha said such soldiers go to hell, not heaven.

Then the Buddha added another blunt point. He said that those who promote the view that soldiers killed in battle go to heaven will also go to hell for holding to such a view.

Yodhijiva starting to cry and said: "I am not crying because of what you said. I am crying because I have been tricked, cheated and deceived for a long time by religious leaders."

Such views from Yodhijiva and religious authorities confirm his unexamined mind-states and the delusion in believing in the inherent reality of 'us' above 'them'. The greater the identification with the notion of 'us', the greater the transference onto 'them'. This duality of us and them feeds fear, blame and ongoing dehumanisation.

The Buddha said: *"I do not praise every sacrifice. I do not withhold praise from every sacrifice."* (MN 96, 11, 177). He praised those who made sacrifices to support non-violence and protect life. He admonished those soldiers willing to sacrifice their lives in the pursuit of killing others. He also criticised those who blindly followed their leaders, pursued excitement through acts of war or engaged in animal sacrifice, as the priests advocated.

The state and religious justification for war dates back thousands of years to mobilise, into a unifying thought, the fears and aggression of a group of people to inflict suffering and death on another group of people. Citizens, who swallow the bait of the views of their leaders, remain obedient to the institutional violence of their political/religious/military masters. It is important to raise questions about our relationship to authority. This requires an honest examination of our perceptions of authority:

- *Where is the moral integrity?*
- *Have we submitted to the will of the dark figures of authority?*
- *Have we given up our capacity to think for ourselves?*
- *Can we develop a foundation of empathy and wisdom?*
- *Are we willing to sacrifice the military objectives of the nation state?*
- *Can we find imaginative ways to resolve conflict and suffering?*

War confirms the death of creative imagination.

In the Greater Discourse on the Mass of Suffering (MN 13), the Buddha also referred to social and economic causes for suffering as well as the psychological factors. The inner world of fear and blame often shapes our political views. We need to address the grasping onto beliefs that creates so much horror. Violence follows on from a belief in greed, aggression and delusion, by one nation or organisation, grasping onto political/religious ideology or exploitation of people and resources. Such actions breed resentment in citizens that eventually lead to an uprising and more retaliation. Freeing ourselves from the poisonous mind benefits society. Authentic sacrifice includes letting go of harmful actions and supporting healing actions.

Those who actively engage in war do to themselves what their enemy would wish for. The other side wants their enemies to suffer as they, themselves, suffer. The suffering of our soldiers may arise through suicide, self-harm, domestic violence, clinical depression, post-traumatic stress disorder, and addictive behaviour. Our men and women may return home from war zones and inflict violence, suffering and death on their loves ones or strangers after a mild dispute owing to the damage to their psyche. This is an expression of karma.

The violence of self-other flows backwards and forwards. Men in military uniform find themselves rejected and forgotten. Their lives may fall apart knowing the terror of what they have done to others or what they have witnessed or imagined. All of this contributes to the whole mass of suffering.

Television news and reports of blood swept streets, wounded children in hospitals and horrifying stories from families and Non-Governmental Organisations (NGOs) occupy our consciousness for a brief interlude. We hear politicians condemn nations and political organisations that wish to establish the Sharia law in Islam, because of its brutal treatment of criminals and subjugation of women. Yet we ignore the brutality of carpet bombing of Muslim cities and our invasions of some of the world's poorest countries. Such condemnation of others stinks of hypocrisy.

Karma and Conflict

With the refusal of the leaders to support the needy, the Buddha said that, as a consequence, poverty would become rife. From the growth of poverty, the taking of what was not given would increase. From the increase in theft comes the increase in weapons; with increase in weapons, so the taking of life increased would increase. Enmity would prevail for one another. He said: *"Fierce hatred, fierce anger and thoughts act like the hunter who stalks the animal."* We become addicted to harmful ways.

The Buddha added: *"The people of your kingdom come to you and consult you as to what is to be followed and what is not to be followed and what action will eventually lead to harm and what will lead to happiness. You should listen and advise."* At the end of the Buddha's discourse, the Sangha rejoiced at his words with his uncompromising support for social change.

In another discourse, the Buddha engaged in a conversation (AN iii 38, iv 79) with General Siha, an army commander, who sought advice from the Buddha. The Buddha instructed the army general on his responsibilities through the practice of the profound importance of:

- *ethics*
- *generosity*
- *happiness*
- *the benefits of letting go*
- *the corruption of vanity*
- *the dangers of desire*

At the end of the exchange, the general experienced the "*pure stainless eye of the teaching.*" It meant he had undergone a profound realisation. The commander wanted to join the Buddha's army of the wandering community, but the Buddha discouraged him from resigning his commission. Not bothering with the general's title, he told him with what sounded like a little flattery:

"*Siha, it is proper for a popular person of your status to always reflect and examine when attending to affairs and making decisions.*"

The Buddha insisted on the importance of examining karma, namely any questionable volitions that determine actions of body, speech and mind. With aggressive actions, he explained that there are consequences that we can neither ignore nor postpone. He asked:

- "*Can you postpone the fruit of your harmful actions (karma), which ripen here and now?*
- *Can you change a painful consequence of your harmful action into a pleasant result?*
- *Can you make what ripens in the present not ripen in the present?*
- *Can you cancel the fruit of your harmful actions?*" (MN ii 220)

The teachings make us realise how little real control we have of actions and the consequences of our actions:

- *We never know the hour and the day when we start to bear the consequences of the past*
- *We never know the experience of the present harm we have caused others*

- *We may have no idea of the impact our violent actions cause us, our family, friends and community*
- *We cannot postpone the fruits of the suffering we caused until a later date when we feel ready We cannot choose to make our grief and lamentation into happiness and joy*
- *We cannot choose to stop immediately the experience of our guilt and anguish*
- *We cannot choose to wipe out what we did in the past and ignore the present impact upon ourselves and others.*

In another discourse, the Buddha said that our time on Earth gets less through killing, stealing, our refusal to share goods, along with violence and destruction (AN iii 369; AN iii 372).

5. THE ARMY, POWER AND PEOPLE

The Buddha compared the grip of painful situations, like war, to a creeper strangling a tree. The war zone leaves such dark impressions and traumatises men, women and children. The violence from land, sea and air act like a deadly creeper strangling the life of the community. As a loving father, the Buddha strongly encouraged his young son, Rahula, to reflect frequently on his actions of body, speech and mind, otherwise he might harm himself and harm others resulting in anguish.

Many soldiers sent to war must wish they had received such basic teachings in ethics as they live through one horrible nightmare after another. Some countries enforce military conscription on young men and women robbing them of their choice to follow another way of life. Those who refuse conscription may face imprisonment, alienation and suffer loss of career opportunities, as employers perceive the 'refuseniks' as disloyal to the aims of the nation state. The military officers never encouraged young people to reflect on the possible personal consequences of their violent acts in warfare, nor the consequences of their actions upon others. They may well have to live with this guilt for the rest of their lives. There frequently is a painful karma to face in the future for those who make others suffer.

Like fish to the bait, young men and women who volunteer, find themselves sucked into the desire to taste the so-called glamour and adventure of war, only to find it is the most depraved and corrupt form of human behaviour. Hollywood movies, computer war games and commercials seduce viewers, especially young men and women, to join the army and thereby incite their desire for adventure. We watch on our television screen endless documentaries telling us of the great sacrifices our soldiers made for the people.

The strict hierarchy of the military demands obedience and a complete submission to authority. Society condones such blind obedience instead of applying intelligence. This submissive behaviour leads to an unquestioning grasping of standpoints. The Buddha expressed his concerns about surrendering to the voice of another. Our leaders have misled our dedicated men and women in military service who could make precious contributions in military service to the rebuilding of countries and the improvement of the lives of citizens in far-away countries.

The Buddha commented:

"The young people, who make an onslaught on people, are cruel, bloody-handed, intent on injuring and killing, and without mercy. Because of that deed, they experience a downfall, a hell." (MN 135/III 303).

A man may harm another
As it may serve his ends, but when he is harmed
By others he, despoiled, harms yet again.
So long as evil's fruit is not matured
The fool does fancy: "Now's the hour, the chance!"
But when the deed bears fruit, he suffers.

The slayer gets a slayer in his turn,
The conqueror gets one who conquers him,
The abuser wins abuse, the annoyer worries
Thus, by the evolution of the deed
A man who harms is harmed in his turn.

The harm we inflict upon others, we often find one way or the other, harm inflicts itself upon ourselves. In his resolute teaching of moral integrity, the Buddha sees nothing worthy of support, approval or praise in war and violence. The Buddha never named military units as praiseworthy or fighting soldiers as heroes. He completely dismissed the idea found in religion, especially the Abrahamic religions, that a soldier who dies in battle goes to heaven. The Buddha treated such a view with utter disdain.

The Buddha said that the army carried the corrupted idea: *"Let them be exterminated so they have no existence."* He said that the mind set on the killing of others can only *"lead downwards to a hell."* He did not mince his words. He had no interest in offering consolation to soldiers, uniformed or not, who risked their lives for their cause. He made clear that aversion and the desire for the death of others corrupted the mind of political leaders and generals as they waged war. War serves no purpose in the Dharma way of life.

Dharma teachings reveal some of the conditions for war including fear, blame, humiliation, poverty, deprivation, political systems, colonisation, occupation, as well as the condition of the inner life. All the conditions belong to states of mind. Fear, violence and war remain inseparably related intensely as the connection between crippling creepers and trees. Prior to his awakening, the Buddha said:

"Fear results from resorting to violence – just look at how people quarrel and fight. But let me tell you now of the kind of dismay and terror that I have felt. Seeing people struggling like fish, writhing in shallow water, with enmity against one another, I became afraid. At one time, I had wanted to find some place where I could take shelter, but I never saw such a place.

I had seen them all trapped in mutual conflict and that is why I had felt so repelled. But then I noticed something buried deep in their hearts. It was – I could just make it out – a dart. It was a dart that makes all its victims run all over the place. Once the dart is pulled out, the running stops. We can learn from this. We do not pursue bondage to the world (of unhealthy and violent actions)" (Sn 935-40).

Weapons serve as the outcome for the poisonous dart in the mind. Poisoned inwardly, a person becomes determined to inflict pain on others, to punish those who go against their view of reality. The Buddha reported an account of such circumstances. A king felt determined to punish harshly those who went against him, but a wise sage told him that inflicting fines, incarceration and death would not resolve the conflict. Such ongoing punishment sustained hardship and injustice for the people, which will bring about further violent uprisings.

The sage said that the agitators and militants will live in peace when the king and government feed the people, pay the people wages for work, give them the opportunity to develop themselves and society, and encourage business and prosperity. *"Families will be happy; the people will dance and live with open doors."* (DN 5/1 135).

The Buddha offered here a social agenda to bring about an end to unrest and war. The texts show that the more brutal the punishment, then the people will show a more extreme violent reaction. Corrupt and violent governments generate punitive behaviours among its own people.

In its war on crime and drugs, the USA has jailed 2.4 million of its citizens, more than any other country on Earth. The US courts have given more than 45,000 prisoners lifelong sentences without parole. The

US judiciary firmly rejects the possibility of redemption as advocated in the Christian tradition, the main religion followed in the USA. Most states in the USA continue their policy of executions for certain crimes.

The Army inspired the Buddha

The Buddha never opposed the formation of an army, but reinterpreted its function. He accepted the presence of an army in its peace keeping responsibilities. He encouraged a wholesome relationship with the kings, leaders and tribal chiefs of neighbouring kingdoms and advised them on ways to develop a healthy and peaceful society. King Bimbisara of Magadhi told the Buddha not to ordain soldiers who refused to go to war or he would behead the monks, have their tongues cut out or break the ribs of the soldiers who ordained (MN 1.40).

While agreeing with the King not to accept deserters into the Sangha, the Buddha continued to speak on non-violence and right livelihood. He knew that the Kings would not tolerate any undermining of the army as it could affect the affairs of the State. King Pasenadi told the Buddha about his intelligence network that he used for spying on people, including the Sangha (SN 3.2.1.).

We could assume that the Buddha would have welcomed into his Sangha of Dharma practitioners those men and women fleeing the army, the law, the debtors, jails or slave owners. However, the Buddha only allowed those men and women into his Sangha whom he knew to be fully committed to the exploration of an awakened life. He only allowed those with a strong motivation for awakening to join the Sangha. The Buddha did not accept into his Sangha those wanting to avoid responsibilities.

There is every indication that the Buddha drew upon the disciplines for people in uniform of the king's army in order to establish his non-violent 'army' of the Sangha. The Buddha enunciated 227 rules ranging in gravity from serious offences to minor offences. Severe offences included killing and theft which could result in expulsion. He thus adopted a similar view as the army with a court martial on soldiers, who violated the army's code of conduct. The rules of discipline of the Sangha taught monks and nuns to behave mindfully and respectfully to each other and to citizens. Devotees of the Sangha, citizens, armies and political leaders respected the disciplined way of life of the Sangha. People everywhere acknowledged the Sangha's integrity and deep sense of community.

Members of the Sangha shared a lifestyle and values. The assembly of seniors in the Dharma could suspend a monk or nun for a brief period of days, weeks or months. This usually meant confinement to a marked off area in a monastery (a kind of monk's prison without walls). For disregarding and disrespecting lesser rules, monks and nuns would confess to the assembly, which would decide the course of action. The Buddha knew that the army adopted similar procedures when officers and soldiers ignored the rules of army behaviour. Officers and soldiers also had to pay a penalty for any disrespect shown to army discipline.

Both Sangha and the Military employed the practice of daily disciplines, the application of rules and regulations, to ensure mindfulness of body, speech and mind for social harmony.

The king's army wore a uniform and carried a weapon, the Buddha's army wore ochre coloured cloth wrapped around the body and carried a begging bowl. Just as soldiers marched in silence in a single file with the General at the head, so the Sangha walked in silence in single file on their Yatras (pilgrimages) with the Buddha (or senior) at the head. People knew that the Buddha was from the warrior/military caste, who applied his military training and discipline to the Sangha, but with a different strategy. He trained the Sangha to live in peace and express wisdom and compassion in their lives. He made it clear that his non-violent Sangha would give security within a country and between countries through the practices of mutual respect and support of citizens either side of the border.

The King's army expected soldiers to obey orders or face disciplinary action. The army consisted of a tightly controlled hierarchy through which soldiers deferred to their commanding officer, who, in turn, showed the same deference to his senior officers and up and through the ranks to the General-in-Chief. He showed the same deference to the King or President of a republic whose orders he carried out. The Buddha provided a democratic institution for inquiry into the values and development of the Sangha with a minimal of hierarchical structure.

The Buddha would compare the military with the Sangha and point out the significant differences (AN IV 133). He said a worthy soldier/warrior in the king's army possessed three factors:

- *the capacity to fire an arrow a long distance*

- *a sharp shooter to hit the target*
- *the capacity to split the human form.*

He said the warrior in the Sangha also possessed three qualities:

- *the capacity to go a long way into seeing the human condition with wisdom*
- *the capacity to be a sharpshooter in seeing into causes for suffering*
- *the capacity to split up the great mass of ignorance to reveal wisdom.*

He said that such a warrior in the Sangha is worthy of gifts, hospitality and of reverential salute. People agreed. They bowed to the Sangha in respect of their way of life.

The Buddha referred to five qualities of young men in the warrior caste who yearned to be a ruler or head of the army:

1. *"I am impeccable with respect to birth in the warrior/military caste*
2. *I am handsome with a beautiful complexion*
3. *I am pleasing to my parents and intelligent*
4. *I am pleasing to the people*
5. *I am trained in the military including elephant riding, driving a chariot, archery and swordsmanship. So why shouldn't I yearn to become king?"*

The Buddha said the dedicated practitioner in the Sangha had five qualities. Why shouldn't he yearn for liberation?

1. *"He has truth in the Buddha-Dharma*
2. *He has good health and suitable for striving*
3. *He is open and honest and willing to reveal things about himself to his teacher and the Sangha*
4. *He has the energy to overcome the unwholesome and develop the wholesome*
5. *He has wisdom that is noble and penetrative that leads to the destruction of suffering."* (AN 5 135 (5))

In another comparison between soldiers and monks, he spoke of five kinds of soldiers in the world: (AN v 76 (6))

1. *A soldier dies in battle*
2. *A soldier gets wounded and his comrades carry him away from the battle. They try to bring him back to his relatives, but he dies on the way.*
3. *A soldier gets wounded, soldiers carry him back home where he is nursed but he still dies.*
4. *A wounded soldier is nursed at home and recovers.*
5. *A soldier enters battle and is victorious.*

He then made an analogy of a Dharma practitioner going into a village and referred to five kinds of practitioners in the world.

1. *A practitioner goes into a village where he sees a woman's dress in disarray and loosely attired. With his mind invaded with lust, he has sex with her. The Buddha said it (is) like going into battle and suffering a spiritual death by giving up the training.*
2. *A practitioner has sex in the village and wishes to confess to fellow practitioners but cannot, so he gives up the training.*
3. *He returns to the monastery and confesses but still leaves the Sangha.*
4. *The Sangha gives him teachings and practices, so he can carry on.*
5. *The practitioner enters the village with mindfulness established, so he does not grasp onto the marks and features of the women he sees. He guards his eyes, ears, nose, tongue and touch. He meditates afterwards to clear his mind of any doubt.*

In the same discourse, the Buddha commented that there is "little gratification" in having sex.

Responsibility of Royalty and Leaders

In the Lion's Roar on the Turning of Wheel (DN 26), the Buddha related a story of a certain King Dalhanemi, who renounced the throne to live a nomadic life to inquire into truth. In his talk, the Buddha gave support to the King's former need for an army to offer security to the citizens of his kingdom. The Buddha also made clear that the King should offer the Dharma of ethics, meditation and wisdom to all citizens to protect them from suffering.

The King told his son to *"revere, cherish and venerate the Dharma as your badge and banner and as your guard and protection for your nobles, your army, Brahmins (priests), householders, spiritual seekers, animals and birds, then no crime prevails in your kingdom."* Gurus held a similar position as Kings and Army Chiefs in terms of the power their wielded, but the Buddha rejected this model of centralised authority and instead took inspiration from the republicans in the small countries, north of the Ganges.

These republican countries had frequent debates to establish legislation, rules and social development. The voices of wisdom of the elders (in wisdom, not age) in the Sangha had a valuable role to ensure concord amidst differences. Like the republics, the Buddha empowered the Sangha to make decisions through assemblies that he said should be *"held frequently and be well attended."* He said if these meetings took place with wisdom and free from "falling prey to craving," the Sangha would *"prosper and not decline"* (DN 16.1.6). He encouraged the Kings and leaders of republican countries to adopt a similar model of assemblies with wise action so that countries could live in peace with each other.

Citizens in ancient India used the word 'Sangha' for committees, groups and organisations. The Buddha adopted the same term. This helped to bridge the gap between householders and his Sangha of mendicants.

The Political Ego

Western democracies, especially the six nations of the Security Council at the United Nations, along with NATO, display a cynical regard for human life through their production, buying and selling of weapons. They promote their arms productions in arms sales around the world. They tell arms buyers that weapons used in the 'theatre of war' have proved their worth. Arms dealers will sell dated weapons to the poorer countries.

The Buddha referred to people whose behaviour is worthy of censure Everywhere we turn we can offer criticism of power-hungry leaders of nations, who engage in civil war or neighbour wars, as well as Western political leaders, who launch war after war. We have to look deeper than that. The Buddha frequently encouraged the seeing into the cause and effects of actions and to find ways to change the conditions for suffering. Based on wisdom, he encouraged the naming of that which requires censure and to hold accountable those who deliberately inflict suffering on others. We can offer critiques on:

- *global corporations and banks who mistreat workers and exploit customers*
- *exploitation of resources*
- *religious convictions, which harm others*
- *the justifications for war*
- *evolutionary theories to support massive reduction of populations*
- *fatalistic views on the violence of our species*
- *collective passivity and despair of a so-called informed public.*

In the West, we rush to interpret religious fanaticism as signals of inferiority, of mediaeval thinking and expressions of unresolved tensions running back centuries between tribes, religious sects and regional differences. None of these views shed any light or wisdom on the current psychological/social dynamics.

Western leaders/analysts/academics display their own notions of superiority, whether in the guise of a conservative or liberal appearance. The Western policy towards the Arab nations is part of the problem, not the cure, as much as anywhere else. Obsessed with notions of progress and evolution, we confirm our collective lack of inner progress, inner development and inner evolution while treating other societies as inferior.

Saudi courts can impose capital punishment, such as beheading, stoning to death and amputations of limbs for theft and other crimes. The courts execute their citizens for various offences including murder, rape, armed robbery, drug imports, apostasy, adultery, witchcraft and sorcery. Public beheading is a common form of execution. The courts treat homosexuality as a crime punishable by flogging or death.

Western governments buy oil from Saudi Arabia, sells billions of $$$ of arms to Saudi Arabia and treat the monarchy with a level of shameful deference. The West stays mute when it comes to criticism of the Sharia law in Saudi Arabia but condemns Sharia law elsewhere. In

1948, Saudi Arabia refused to sign the Universal Declaration of Human Rights that other member nations of the UN had agreed upon.

The Buddha also related a historical situation where the authorities arrested a thief and brought him to the King. The King asked him why he stole. The thief replied: "I have nothing to live on." The King forgave him and gave him his basic needs. The same situation happened again. The thief told the king he had nothing to live on. Having absolved the first thief of a similar crime, the King felt the second thief had taken advantage of his earlier generosity, so he ordered the execution of this thief through beheading.

The Buddha said that other thieves would follow the example of the king. The thieves would rob and take to arms, including beheading their victims. The Buddha said that thieves would carry arms to kill their victims owing to the behaviour of the king, who inflicts the death sentence on those whom he found guilty of crimes. Criminals kill their victims to stop them speaking up against them.

We see examples of this today. The USA inflicts the death sentence, lifelong imprisonments and the 'three strikes and you're out' punishments. The same country has the greatest number of prisons per population in the world. Violence begets violence. Capital punishment and long prison sentences increases crime, violence and murder, as criminals take steps to avoid arrest.

Human Rights. For Whom?

The UN Declaration guaranteed the right to life, to expression, thought, religion, work and health. These declarations have limited merit to them since they promote an ideology from a Western viewpoint. The poor and homeless might write a distinct set of human rights, such as the right to travel anywhere for work or the right to live in another country to escape hardship, hunger, environmental destruction and war. We are all sons and daughters of the Earth. These Declarations have little relevance for the suffering poor worldwide.

The rich nations show no qualms in ignoring the UN Declaration, if it is in their interest in matters of war, abuse of labour and exploitation of resources. For example, the US government has ordered the invasion, occupation, downfall of governments or rigging of elections in 60 countries in the past 100 years including 14 Muslim countries in the last generation.

Countries in Africa and Asia have permitted more refugees from war and famine into their countries than any Western nations. As with human rights, the West regards hospitality and compassion in very selective ways. The US government has ordered military invasions, aerial bombing or drone attacks upon around 25 countries or more in the past 30 years. The death toll runs into millions.

Supported by other Western nations, the USA acts like a mediaeval superpower unwilling to take responsibility for more deaths and decimation of societies since World War 2 than any other country on Earth. Has the world's largest superpower a superego? Do the EU and other Western societies acquiesce to the USA rather than question the pernicious immorality of any war? Where is the morality of the subjugation of citizens in war zones? In religious terms, we have much soul-searching to do. The Buddha's response to war and crime can shed light on contemporary situations.

Various governments exploit the world's poor, disparage the traditions of other cultures, religions and lifestyle until their resentment grows and explodes. The gap between the haves and have-nots increases decade by decade within Western countries and between the West and the rest. We engage in international economic colonialism hidden in the name of globalisation. This confirms the political superego, namely the desire to pursue, control and exploit regardless of the impact on poor nations.

Victory Breeds hatred for the Victims

The brutalised will also turn on each other as their rage explodes. The Buddha commented:

> *"Victory breeds hatred,*
>
> *The defeated live in pain.*
>
> *Happily, the peaceful live,*
>
> *Giving up victory and defeat." (Dhp 201)*

This verse serves as resource for reflection, a point for inquiry. Rather than regarding it as a simple aphorism to gloss over momentarily, we can ask ourselves, and each other, questions based on those four lines:

- *Why does victory breed hatred?*
- *Why do the defeated live in pain?*

- *Can we dig deep into ourselves?*
- *Can we uncover a deep empathy for others?*
- *Can we see human beings not as labels to identify?*

We know that we share common fears about the impact of violence and death upon us. We reflect on these fears, so they can serve to develop a moral basis to stay true to ethics that outweigh social and political pressures. We might foolishly imagine that the evolution of human behaviour makes it a historical necessity for certain numbers of our species to go to war with other members of our species to reduce the global population. These violent views justify war as an evolutionary means to reduce the explosion of population, to ensure the continuity of the species.

If that were the case, then there is little point in these wars taking place in some of the poorest regions of Africa and Asia, since their modest use of raw materials and depleted resources matters little compared to the wealthy nations totally in the grip of corporate consumerism. Theories of evolution, biological determination and instinctive impulses have nothing to offer in terms of understanding the suffering of war. There is a common fallacy to regard war as part of the evolutionary process; thus, making war morally acceptable and justifiable.

The Buddha refuted the view that we live under the spell of evolutionary forces of nature removing all our potential to develop an ethical way of life. The Buddha reminded us of our capacity to reflect, to meditate and transcend our identity with any group, tribe or nation. This provides the opportunity to find enough to space to look at the so-called division between self and other, us and them.

The Buddha said that when governments do not support people, whether at home or in neighbouring countries, then evil actions, such as violence and killing, grow rife. They will dehumanise the people who take to weapons by referring to them as "*wild beasts*" and "*deprive them of life*" (DN 111 73). The Cakkavatti Sutta says that poverty, hardship, social and economic injustice feeds violence.

The Buddha reminded the rulers of the inner and outer conditions for war with his core insight that everything, without exception, including war, dependently arises owing to conditions. If leaders co-operate to end the conditions for war, then war cannot arise.

The Buddha uttered his famous statement; words well-worth remembering. It is the founding principle to initiate meaningful change:

"When this is, that is; this arising, that arises."

"When this is not, that is not; this ceasing, that ceases."

In Pali, this profound insight reads:

"Masmiṃ sati idaṃ hoti; imass' uppādā idaṃ uppajjati.

Imasmiṃ asati idaṃ na hoti; imassa nirodhā idaṃ nirujjhati." (DN 15).

The Buddha interpreted all events and tendencies, without exception, from the standpoint of such causality.

The Buddha and the Nazis

Political leaders and monarchs for centuries have employed the language of "We have to defend ourselves", even as they sent their army into another country. Rulers perceive the language of defence as palatable to their citizens, even while engaging in an attack on other countries. Even the Nazis, with their obscene ideology, as they invaded some 13 countries between 1939 and 1945, used the language of self-defence.

The Nazis reminded German citizens that Germany was squeezed between two ideologies determined to destroy the national socialism of Germany. To the West of Germany, Britain had a capitalist and imperialist empire that exploited a quarter of the world's population, plus the support of the might of capitalist America. Millions lived in desperate poverty in the United Kingdom. To the east of Germany, the Russian empire had developed communism for 20 years that robbed citizens of their rights to personal ownership of property and private land. The Russian government also denied its citizens the right to self-employment or to form private businesses.

The Nazis incessantly told the German population that they went to war to defend German values and German culture while preserving European civilisation from capitalism and communism. Most German citizens gradually absorbed the propaganda. They got used to the megalomania of Hitler and his desire to establish the Third Reich. Most ignored his determination to exterminate Jews, Communists, gypsies and the mentally/physically disabled.

The German media in Germany regularly showed pictures of mass unemployment and miserable living conditions in Britain, the USA and Russia. The Nazis claimed that National Socialism had eliminated such poverty. The Nazis exterminated the intellectuals, the non-violent activists, the liberals and dissidents, as Hitler mercilessly pursued his political/military agenda. They used the language of defending European civilisation yet did more to destroy it than any nation in history. The relentless propaganda seeped into the DNA of a civilised people with the deaths of some 50 million people worldwide in the space of six years.

Joseph Goebbels, the Nazi Minister for Propaganda, stated: *"The most brilliant propagandist technique will yield no success unless one fundamental principle is borne in mind constantly - it must confine itself to a few points and repeat them over and over."*

He also said: *"If you tell a lie big enough and keep repeating it, people will eventually come to believe it. The lie can be maintained only for such time as the State can shield the people from the political, economic and/or military consequences of the lie. It thus becomes vitally important for the State to use all of its powers to repress dissent, for the truth is the mortal enemy of the lie, and thus by extension, the truth is the greatest enemy of the State."*

Our politicians incessantly lied to us when they stated repeatedly that the people of Afghanistan were responsible for the attacks on 9/11. No Afghani citizen took part in the vile attack on 9/11. Citizens from Saudi Arabia were primarily responsible. Our politicians incessantly lied to us when they stated repeatedly that Iraq kept weapons of mass destruction to launch on the West. The lies cost the lives of hundreds of thousands of Afghani and Iraqi citizens, as well as the deaths, including suicide, of thousands of US and NATO troops.

Our leaders betrayed democracy and the people. They authorised war crimes. Our leaders ignored truth due to a preconceived determination to go to war.

The Buddha demanded from thoughtful human beings to:

- *communicate free from aversion*
- *end speculative views*
- *find intelligent solutions to conflict*
- *refuse to engage in manipulation of the minds of others*

- *speak the facts*
- *speak the truth.*

The Buddha showed his abhorrence of those who have little regard for the preciousness of life. Of such a person, the Buddha said he *"is malevolent in mind, corrupt in thought and purpose, and thinks: "Let these people be killed or slaughtered or annihilated or destroyed so they may they not exist at all."* (MN 41/I 287).

At the end of World War One, the victorious Allies' hatred of Germany led to the collective punishment of Germans with subsequent poverty and hardship. Supported by the pernicious Versailles Treaty, such terrible deprivation exacted further punishment of German citizens leading to the conditions for World War Two. The punishment of Germany at the end of the First World War contributed to planting the seeds for Fascism, the Blitzkrieg and the Holocaust.

France, the U.K., the USA and other countries forced Germany to accept full responsibility for causing all the loss and damage of World War One between 1914 - 1918. The people of Germany saw this as a national humiliation. They developed a growing resentment towards other European nations and became determined to assert their superiority in Europe through forming extreme nationalistic parties with a fascist ideology. The Nazis exploited the political rage in Munich and elsewhere with terrifying consequences.

In power, the Nazi government drew upon the concept 'Aryan' (meaning Noble) used in ancient Indian culture, especially by the Buddha, to indicate a 'noble' human being grounded in ethics and wisdom. The Nazis redefined the concept to indicate a pure and superior race. It is hard to imagine a greater perversion of the Buddha's teachings. The Nazis also adopted the Hindu swastika that showed paths that lead to the centre. In Sanskrit, the symbol meant to *be making good* - to reach the Centre (*su* – good/beautiful, *asti* - to be, *ka* – making). The Nazis used the Swastika as the emblem of themselves as the superior race.

During the 1920s, Berlin established the first Buddhist centre in Europe that continued throughout the war, with the support of Magda Goebbels, the wife of Joseph Goebbels. Magda Goebbels had years of interest in Indian philosophy, especially Buddhism, which she learnt from her father's interest in the religion. Because her children were still innocent, she believed they were guaranteed rebirth in more favourable conditions than in the present life. Magda once remarked that she *"wished to offer the children a new and better chance in life and for this they would first have to die."*

With the defeat of Nazism, Magda Goebbels said that she and her family had no right to go on living. She continued to take comfort in her belief in rebirth that emerged from her warped reading of Buddhist books. She then poisoned her six children the day after Hitler committed suicide, then she and her husband took their own lives. The dust from the wind blew back in the face of the Nazis.

While holding certain political and military leaders and individuals accountable for their war crimes at the Nuremburg trials, the Allies began a massive programme of rebuilding Germany, rather than applying collective punishment, as had happened after World War One. The Allies flew in thousands of planes into Berlin to feed the population during the time of the Russian blockade. The Buddha would have fully supported such an approach since these acts of kindness to end poverty and injustice ensured the welfare of the people and the reintegration of Germany into European society.

The Nazis lived a vile conceit of themselves as superior to everybody else. Notions of superiority of the State feed into the dogma of views manifesting as *"this is the truth, all else is false."* The adherence to such a view comes through its repetition and often the slow, insidious identification with the view as the truth that a large section of society blindly follows. The dark shadows of North American and European superiority continue to cast itself on Muslims and the rest of the world. The Buddha said that conceit consists of the measurement of oneself with others.

Corrupt in Thought and Purpose

A Brahmin of the Bharadvaja sect asked the Buddha if there was any killing that the Buddha would approve. The Buddha replied:

"The killing of anger with its poisoned root and honey tip is the killing the noble ones' praise. For having killed anger/violence, one does not sorrow. He added that the one who *"abuses the abuser partakes of the same meal."* Both enter an exchange. *"One who repays violence with violence makes things worse for himself. Not repaying violence with violence, one wins a battle hard to win."*

"The fool thinks victory is won. When by speech, he bellows harshly. Patient endurance is the true victory. He added that when one wrongs or harms an innocent person, the evil falls back on the person like fine dust blow against the wind." (SN V11. 7).

The Aganna Sutta shows how an entangling of conflicting desires brings about downfall and ruin. Desire, conceit and views form together through the proliferation of negative thought that leads to the taking up of weapons. The self of the individual and the collective claim the right to be angry, to get revenge and to punish. Leaders and citizens regard the 'other' worthy of punishment so they take to arms to deprive them of life (DN 111 73). Much preparatory thought arises beforehand. Conflict and war depend on the proliferation of negative thought (*papanca*), words and actions. The ending of the proliferation of negative thoughts ends the quarrels and the violence.

The ending of such *papanca* makes discernment clear in terms of criticism and appreciation. The Buddha did not ignore the violence of humanity or treat it as some inevitable outcome of human behaviour. His discourses offered the Sangha of householders and mendicants the tools to go deep into themselves, and into social institutions which provided the Sangha with tools to give deep into themselves, and into social institutions. He certainly did not confine himself exclusively to teach mindfulness and meditation to a Sangha of men and women detached from worldly life and worldly issues.

Having been born into the warrior/military caste, the royal family and society would have expected him to lead his army into war. The finest military figures trained him in the art of war. He knew the madness of such actions. Instead he addressed the psychological, social, religious and national conditions that lead to war (MN 21/1 129).

In the Pasura Sutta of Sutta Nipata, the Buddha said he saw only misery in holding onto harmful views. He concluded that peace gets established through a mutual understanding of a situation. He explained that the origins of violent disputes leading to war require slander of the other and arrogance.

The Buddha made clear: 'Holding onto things" (views, religious beliefs, land and coveting what others have), brings about painful consequences. The constant putting down of others brings strife, so the wise refuse to enter dogmatism, which perpetuates conflict.

The Buddha showed a determination to speak out on social and political issues rather than avoid these issues of national and international interest. His fearless communication revealed a departure from meditation teachers, yoga teachers, abbots, monks and nuns, who had withdrawn into a spiritual consciousness. They rarely expressed concern or acted regarding such depths of suffering in the world. Few spiritual teachers, gurus, psychologists and mindfulness leaders today address global issues, such as war, crime, poverty or offer for ways for ennobling action.

The Buddha criticised those who engaged in harmful actions, rather than adopting a passive approach to the plight of people living under corrupt leadership. He discouraged young men from engaging in the killing of others and undermined the caste system with its warrior/military caste.

"Service should only be engaged in if it is wholesome, not harmful. I do not say everything should be followed, nor do I say everything should not be followed. When following something, if trust, virtues, learnedness, benevolence and wisdom increases, I say that should be followed."

Reconstruction

We must find the individual and collective skills to stop war, to stop the bloodshed and the production of weaponry. We must discredit the puerile symbols of the national flag and the national anthem. We must be willing to challenge the significance of the nation state, the leaders and their demagogues, who revert to history. They propagate war stories from the nation's past to show the special status of the nation in the world.

Resentment over conquest lasts not years or decades, but centuries as a minority endeavours to free itself from the governance or occupation of the powerful. For example, the English occupation of Ireland triggered a max exodus of Irish citizens to North America and elsewhere with a 50% fall in their population during the 19th century and into the 20th century. The numbers of citizens in Ireland during this period of occupation slumped from eight million to less than four million with 1.5 million deaths due to the famine. When people live in desperate circumstances, they will do everything possible to make a new life at home or move themselves and their families to other parts of the world, whether welcome or not.

Family after family today find themselves camped out in appalling conditions in the aftermath of war as well as during it. These refugees living in a state of utter destitution have little in the way of survival, whether food or water or a change of clothes. They experience the absence of necessities to keep clean, to go the toilet, let alone having medicine. Yet, war refugees show a determined resilience to carry on as well they can, even as their loved ones lie dead under the rubble or trapped helpless waiting to die, due to lack of rubble shifting equipment.

Out of the rubble, the work of reconstruction begins – providing the victorious warmongers allow it. Instead of waging war, armies could devote their considerable expertise to the work of construction rather than destruction. We need to start transforming our weapons factories into wholesome factories for the improvement of conditions of people. The reconstruction of the inner life can take much longer. We need teams of people to show the power of the teachings and the practices to develop ethics, action and wisdom. We need to engage with those who suffer from armies, so they feel supported in practical terms. The teachings also examine all forms of grasping including any identification with any nation that places one country above others. We have to learn to relate to each other.

We live in a world with a desperate shortage of wise leadership. We cannot expect change from the top down. Our political leaders promote themselves through publicists, financial advisors and powerful military/businesses agendas. We see widespread corruption in democracy while small networks of thoughtful people have the unenviable task of keeping alive the flame of spirituality, justice and sustainable living.

We need to:

- *convert our factories to factories of constructive materials not destructive weapons*
- *employ our scientists to develop tools for mass construction not weapons of mass destruction*
- *employ words not weapons with our so-called enemies*
- *establish Ministers for Peace in our government, not Ministers for (so-called) Defence*
- *explore causes and conditions for war*

- *establish intelligence gathering to develop ethics and social responsibility*
- *make a fundamental change in the relationship between nations, organisations, religions and politics*
- *start to listen, learn and offer badly needed resources*
- *stop trying to impose our will on the rest of the world*
- *train our armies to offer constructive resolution to conflict not destructive*
- *work on our inner life and develop our humanity.*

Without exception, wars are crude, brutal and utterly irrational. Mostly old men develop conflict and send other men to engage in the brutality of the killing fields. The formation of a state often gives priority to the dominant ethnic group at the expense of minorities, who receive far less favourable support from the state. The State often treats refugees, asylum seekers and immigrants as the lowest 'caste'.

The Buddha's teachings address suffering and its total transformation. Transformation means consciousness of men and women engaging with major issues and finding the skilful means to end the suffering.

Wisdom reveals a profound liberation from the narrowness of harmful views. Wisdom then engages with life. The notion of 'us and them' is a false mental construct.

SECTION TWO – The Dharma and…
6. FOUR NOBLE TRUTHS AND BIG BANKS

The First Noble Truth of Suffering Applied to the Credit Crisis

The Buddha made it abundantly clear that trust, a power of mind, gives support to peace of mind when supported with wisdom and reciprocated in the object of trust. We often take our trust for granted. The recipients of trust include our banks with whom we deposit our money based on the assumption that our bank will act in a responsible and caring way to our trust. The abuse of our trust brings a rightful indignation often severing a bond between the customer and the bank. The Buddha commented that trust can make wisdom shine and wisdom can make trust shine. This assumes the application of trust lands in a rightful place. It is easy to assume that the wise application of trust in the past will continue into the present and future. We cannot trust big banks.

The principle of a bank is very simple. The bank is a point of contact between three kinds of people. One group has extra money which they deposit in the bank. Another group needs to borrow money for certain purposes. The third group simply keeps their sums in the bank and draws upon it regularly.

The bank acts as the intermediary and the collection point for money. There are those with surplus money. The bank gives the large depositors extra interest on that surplus money called savings. There are those who need to borrow money. The bank lends them money and charges interest on the loan. There is a difference between the interest given for placing money in the bank and interest charged for borrowing from the bank. The bank makes money from that difference.

The profit pays the salary of directors, management and staff. People who wish to buy their own home form an important constituent of those who wish to borrow money from the banks to pay their mortgage.

This principle requires the major depositors, the borrowers, the users and the bank to act with principles to ensure there is no abuse of the collective agreement between the three kinds of customers and the bank.

There is increasing evidence to show that banks, investors and borrowers took advantage of the three kinds of bank customers by seizing on the opportunity to create a culture of easy credit that eventually led to a massive credit crisis. Banks must take a major responsibility for this crisis and customers must bear a portion of the responsibility as well. Banks have lost their direction. Instead of being pillars of support for the local community and acting as guardian angels for our money, they have betrayed this trust through their reckless ambition that helped produce the credit crisis.

The credit crisis inflicted hardship and anxiety on countless numbers of householders. The crisis arose through the banks' intensity of desire to make more money from their interest charges of bank loans, including mortgages, usually the biggest household debt. The banks took advantage of the trust of their customers and used our money to go on a massive buying and spending spree of assets that caused the credit crisis.

Big banks and brokers dominated the housing market making large sums of money from the substantial home owner population. Interest charges on mortgage repayments amounted to more money than the actual repayment. Investment banks and investors, namely those with large sums of surplus money, saw an opportunity to increase their wealth even more through the housing market. The greed developed through the collusion of the high street banks, investment banks and investors to maximise profit regardless of the risk to customers, rich and poor alike.

Banks held a widespread belief that the value of property could only rise and rise. Insurance companies, pension funds, mutual funds also supported the expanding numbers of singles, couples and families entering home ownership. They knew householders preferred to pay for their own mortgage rather than paying rent. Renters did not like paying off what often was someone else's mortgage on their second or third home or paying rent for social housing.

Investment bankers and their clients wanted a big slice of the cake. They offered to buy the mortgages, so the banks sold the mortgages for a significant fee. The same investment bankers borrowed even more money to buy even more mortgages and collected monthly the mortgage payment from the home owners and sell them on for a profit. Mortgages were classified as safe, minimal risk or high risk with interest payments according to the degree of risk. Other banks would buy the safe mortgages while hedge fund operators and other investors were willing to buy the risky mortgages.

Bankers used leverage, namely borrowing large sums of money and then selling the purchase such as houses, land, businesses for a profit, and then again, and again. This triggered the huge financial crisis. Accompanied with surplus money from China, Japan and oil rich Arab nations, the Stock Exchange, Wall Street and their European counterparts took out a massive amount of credit to loan money to homeowners. The middle people, namely the estate agents and brokers, also made their commission. High street banks and investment banks, and their investors, decided to make it easier for people to take out a mortgage so banks and investors could make even more money on the interest they charged.

To give a personal example. In 1982, I bought a terraced house for £24,000 in Totnes, Devon, England. Government regulations then only allowed a prospective home owner to borrow two and a half times their annual income. The buyer had to put down a 20% deposit and complete payment by retirement age of 65 years. Regulations did not permit addition of part time earning as income.

I paid the Nat West bank a deposit of £4000 and stated my income was £8000 per year. My bank statements confirmed that I received that amount of money on an annual basis in my current account. At that time, I had a significant cash flow due to travel expenses coming from flights to four continents per year to serve the Dharma. The bank counted this as a form of income, so I qualified for the mortgage.

These government regulations protected customers from getting into an unmanageable debt. With deregulation, far too many homeowners bought a dream and lived a nightmare.

The Second Noble Truth of the Causes for Suffering Applied to the Credit Crisis

With the relaxation of regulations, a prospective home owner could take out a mortgage without any deposit and borrow four to six times their income. Banks even encouraged new homeowners to borrow more money simultaneously to buy a new car and furniture for the house. They told first time home buyers that they could borrow money based on their projected income in two years. They permitted part time work to be included as salary, no matter how temporary such work was. Customers could take out a mortgage that would finish years or decades after retirement.

Banks would charge very little interest for the two years of the mortgage and then dramatically increase the interest charges. Credit was never so easy to obtain. Brokers and real estate agents were happy to bring people into the housing market since they made more and more commission. These subprime mortgages generated the risk that individuals and families would not be able to repay their mortgages, even on their present income. Mountains of debts, loss of employment, sickness, divorce and birth of children had a devastating impact on new home owners, sometimes within weeks, months or two or three years of signing the agreement with the bank. Such home owners had to default on their monthly mortgage payment.

The banks did not try to minimise the risk, because house prices were always increasing so they could take back the house, if the mortgage owner defaulted. In any case, the mortgages were sold on to banks in their thousands who could package them into Mortgage Backed Securities. Hundreds of these could be turned into a billion-dollar Collateralised Debt Obligation. Derivatives like CDOs and Credit Default Swaps eventually sunk the big banks when banks ran out of money. In a Credit Default Swap, the seller of the CDS will compensate the buyer if there is a loan default. Banks and investment banks were living on credit.

Banks were offering credit to anybody who needed to borrow money for their home, car, business, weddings, consumer goods and holidays. Poor families got into debt one Christmas and by the following Christmas still had not paid off the debt from the previous year. Finance companies were lending money to those in debt to pay off other debts while charging sometimes up to 4000% interest. Banks imposed higher and higher charges for customers even if they went into the red for only a day. The banks' desire for the maximisation of profit also generated the greed, the deceit and the ruthless ambition to take over other banks at home and abroad regardless of the risk.

Banks, businesses, corporations, lawyers, brokers and the various kinds of financial services devised schemes to maximise their power base, income and bonuses. The rich and powerful exploited the goodwill of 99% who were left completely in the dark about the corrupt intentionality of banks and wealthy investors. Greed changed the amoral into the immoral.

Property owners realised they could not pay their mortgages. Houses up and down the country became empty. Prices began to fall in the effort to resell them. House prices dropped to the point that home owners found themselves in negative equity. A home in some districts in the USA became worth half of what the house had been bought for. The slide turned into a crash.

The desire to make money had left the banks, investment banks and private investors with empty properties and massive debts due mostly to these subprime mortgages, as well as hugely ambitious takeovers. Investors worldwide did not want to buy the bonds of the banks and the investment bankers.

Big banks, investment banks, and insurance companies went bankrupt. Greed took the nosedive into public anger and from anger the government propaganda machine went to work with breath-taking speed to tell citizens that the banks were "too big to fail." Corporate authoritarianism had to be maintained.

When I took out my mortgage, my bank, Nat West, suggested that I pay a little extra per month then I would receive around £3000 plus at the end of the mortgage at the age of 63. A year before the end of my mortgage, the bank wrote to me to say that I would not receive this bonus due to changes in the financial markets. Situated in Totnes high street, my bank told me that I still owed £6700 on the mortgage after paying the mortgage off for 24 years. They suggested I pay the £6700 off over 25 years at £50 per month.

More than 1.5 million customers with the Nat West bank found themselves in the same position. The bank had gone virtually broke. It had totally mismanaged the finances of its customers. The government said the Nat West bank, as part of the Royal Bank of Scotland, was too big to fall and gave the bank £20 billion of taxpayers' money to prop it up.

I disputed this demand for £6,700. A lawyer (a friend) told me that I would have to prove that the bank deliberately misled me in 1982. He said the small print covered the bank in case of not meeting the anticipated amount. In 2018, the head office of Nat West closed my local branch abandoning hundreds of residents and visitors, as well as firing the loyal bank staff.

The British government gave the main banks a total of £37 billion. Other European banks engaged in similar rescues amounting to €969 billion. HBO and Lloyds received 17 billion. The US government gave $700 billion to its banks in its rescue package. The burden fell on ordinary taxpayers to pay for the billions of dollars rescue package. The corporate criminals steal the money, homes and peace of mind of millions of customers. They also colluded with the government to use taxpayers' money as well, instead of using the money for various kinds of social services.

Businesses have always used their lawyers to pay as little in the way of taxation as possible whether through tax havens or secret agreements with the Inland Revenue so the 99% had to pay for the shortfall or face cuts to their services. This has caused immense hardship to millions. The world of high finance has no obvious social values and employs very few people.

Most economists, financial experts and traders did irreparable harm to the economy through grasping after short term profit with no vision of the future consequences. They harmed the lives of millions of people. All the economic graphs and charts on the computer screen meant nothing, nor did the years of training in economic management in top business schools because the desire, the greed to become filthy rich mattered more than ethics, and more than reality.

The big banks and big business hid their greed behind a cloak of legitimacy and an economic language incomprehensible to citizens on the high street. Ever since Ronald Reagan and Margaret Thatcher lightened all the regulations for making money, the gap between the haves and have not has grown. Inspired by a 1980's Hollywood movie, the mantra for Wall Street became "greed is good."

Entertainment serves as a tool for propaganda. The Americans always win against their enemies. Governments and corporations make mistakes, but justice always comes through in the end. The little guy overcomes all the odds stacked against him or her. Living in the desire to pursue profit, the filmmakers will reject the notion that they serve to promote propaganda.

You will see in numerous films in the West an irrelevant reference to cigarette smoking, eating junk food, see the US flag or hear irrelevant references to the USA in European films. Film makers believe that their movie must mention the USA so that Americans pay money to watch the film. Many rock bands and ballad singers from the USA or the EU have had to write and sing a song about New York or California. Propaganda. Do you know any songs about London or Paris? The USA appears like a country obsessed with itself. The entertainment industry must show deference to the US.

I remember my communication with a wealthy businesswoman running a capital investments company in the USA. About a year before the 2007/2008 Wall Street crash, she mentioned that Wall Street traders had invited her to ring the bell to start morning trading. Business leaders regard the ringing of this bell as an honour to receive such an invitation. I emailed the businesswoman, a long-standing supporter of the Dharma and teachers, about this invitation. Coincidentally, my emailed arrived on her Blackberry while she was sitting in a limousine on her way to Wall Street to ring the bell. This is what I wrote:

Dear   ....
Have you thought about ringing the bell only after shouting out to them in the pits below something like "For Whom the Bell Tolls, it tolls for thee - until you take greed out of the equation of venture capital?!" A bit of hell, fire and brimstone would be good for the epicentre of world capitalism. You would make it to the front page of the Wall Street Journal. Meditate on it. You are strong. You can take the subsequent heat or take refuge in my house! Always a delight to hear from you.

Three Bows
In the Dharma
Christopher

I regarded it as an opportunity to trigger a great debate on greed. She declined my invitation. A pity, I thought. The thought arose that such a change in attitude could have prevented the 2008 financial global crisis triggered by crude desire in Wall Street and the London Stock Exchange and the whole mass of suffering that followed. The mathematical formulas of countless respected economists that predicted relative stability and growth proved to be a mass delusion in the corridors of power, a blatant arrogance and absence of understanding about the nature of the arising and falling of situations, one of the chief characteristics of existence as the Buddha stated often enough. The Buddha expressed his deep concern about certain dynamics in society. He said: *"Enraptured with greed, enraged with blame, blinded by delusion, overwhelmed with the mind ensnared, people aim at their own ruin, at the ruin of others or the ruin of both. They then experience suffering and grief."* (AN 3.55).

The pursuit of profit gripped consciousness of people in finance, as they milked the system not only robbing people of their savings but also getting people to horrendous levels of debt costing livelihood and even the lives of workers worldwide. The God of Money took first place.

Nothing mattered but making money. A thoughtful government would institute severe penalties to CEOs and boardrooms for wilful evasion of tax payments and behaving in utterly irresponsible ways to the exploitation of the 99%. CEOs barely received a rap on the knuckles from the government.

The myth of a balanced trading floor, stable, moral and self-correcting, has shown itself to be unstable and often immoral. The market of credit found itself utterly unable to correct itself, so bankers had to run with a cap in hand to their governments and business friends in government to get themselves out of the hell hole of the credit crisis.

Causes and conditions for the collapse of the banks included:

1. *Sheer wanton greed to make huge sums of money for empire building, personal aggrandizement and to inflate the ego of self-importance.*
2. *Poor judgement, poor decisions and living in a Darwinian world of dog eats dog. Bank executives displayed frequently flaws in their analysis and a disregard for the suffering they caused people in their personal striving for riches and power.*
3. *Lack of ethics, responsibility and vision due to obsession with short term gain.*
4. *Credit Default Swaps and Collateralised Debt Obligation and the use of leverage amounted to sheer speculation about future gains.*
5. *An arrogance that the heads of capitalism could handle the market better than a regulated system that had developed over generations.*
6. *Blind to the reality of the huge ongoing losses in their credit trading schemes the banks incurred even as they sought to expand their empire further.*
7. *The desire to become an even bigger player in the field of finance through the determination to take over other banks and financial institutions or engage in billion- dollar mergers to dominate the market.*

The government used the people's money for massive bailouts plus several hundred billion pounds more provided in loans and guarantees. Governments refused to take any responsibility for treading lightly with bank regulations, credit transactions and speculative deals.

Instead, the banks blamed market changes in other parts of the world for the crash.

You will not hear a word about business ethics from mindfulness leaders working in the corporate world. Mindfulness coaches show no interest to guide bankers and management towards integrity. The guided meditations offer a temporary relaxation of the body/mind devoid of any lasting insights into the ideology of the corporate 'selfie' culture.

Third and Fourth Noble Truth of the Resolution of Suffering and the Way to the Resolution applied to the Credit Crisis

Dharma practice includes equally the inner transformation of desire, greed and exploitation into wise intention and wise action. Every link in the noble eightfold path (see chapter one) applies to the bankers and investors, as much as anyone else. A change of heart and a change of view is what matters. The Dharma also addresses equally the form, namely the structures, systems and the organisation that perpetuate suffering in all its faces.

The Buddha explained that consciousness depends upon name and form and name and form depends upon consciousness. Consciousness cannot exist outside of name and form and name and form cannot exist outside of consciousness. If consciousness undergoes transformation, then the relationship to name (the language, mentality and psychology) also changes. If the form employed becomes a primary condition for suffering, then the change of the forms changes consciousness. What does this mean? In his analysis, the Buddha compared this to two sheaths of wheat mutually supporting each other.

The teachings do not start off with the repeated view that first you must work on yourself and then you work to make external changes. It is a false dichotomy since a human being constantly lives in a relationship with the presence of others as well the often-dominating factors of form and structures that support ideologies, political, economic, scientific, and religious.

The application of wisdom, inwardly and outwardly, expresses itself through the critique of the problem, the causes and conditions as well as the resolution and the way to it. It is the unshakeable principle of the Dharma. From the standpoint of the Dharma, it is an inadequate response to focus exclusively on the desire, greed and its painful global consequences of the credit crises. It is equally important for an analysis of the causes and conditions to be named. What led up to the crisis? What are the forms and structures that need dramatic change? What is the resolution?

If you change the corporate rules, structures, hierarchy, ethics and regulations, you change the consciousness of the entire staff and the customers.

In the face of widespread and wholesale suffering and hardship for millions of people, capitalism must change. As the primary global ideology, founded on the belief in economic growth, the exponents of capitalism perpetuate heartache and anxiety especially for the poor. The credit crisis, the huge debts of nations, will stay with much of the world's community for many years ahead. Future generations will struggle to forgive the generation born in the last century.

The Way to Ethics and Mindful Action with Banks

I believe this would include the:

1. *Appointment of truly independent inspectors for any merger*
2. *Break up the big banks*
3. *Elimination of credit default swaps and collateralized debt obligations*
4. *Enabling of representatives of workers to have equal representation at board meetings*
5. *Making available information on all salaries and bonuses to the entire work force*
6. *regulations only to allow high street banks to engage in high street business*
7. *regulations only to allow investment banks to do business on behalf of investors*
8. *regulations to ensure the law holds bank bosses accountable for their decisions*
9. *Stop tax havens and make them illegal*
10. *Tax all financial trading, derivate, stocks and shares*

11. *The setting of real limits on pay. Just as there is a minimum hourly rate in most Western countries so there should be a maximum wage as well – say 20 times more than the minimum wage in any business*

12. *The setting of real limits to bonuses with distribution to include workers*

While rioters, burglars and handbag thieves get sent to prison for years, 99% of the bankers who plundered people's finances continue to work as if they had not engaged in any ongoing criminal acts. Investment banks had long since lost contact with the real world of people and their peace of mind. The commercial world of pursuit of profit, property and other commodities became their only reality. Their desire, fear and greed affected the price of oil, crops, copper producing insecurity for farmers and workers worldwide.

Financiers would switch their attention from one part of the world to another to create new markets and abandon other regions of cheap labour - in the name of globalisation. The markets had no interest in the consequence of their trading on the lives of ordinary people.

The big banks had lost interest to use their profits for the welfare of communities and concentrated instead on capital investments. Is it any wonder that skyscraper buildings of big banks, corporations and insurance companies - with their lavish marble interiors and extravagant fountains, dominate they skyline of our major cities? Personal and corporate aggrandizement mattered more than the upliftment of citizens and their environment. The people who ran big banks into the ground leave their positions with considerable wealth while the middle classes and the poor pick up the bill. Never was so little done by so few for so many.

The Buddha and Wealth

The Buddha examined the making and use of money through the lens of right understanding, wise leadership, responsibility with inquiry into causes and conditions. He stressed a healthy, pragmatic and insightful approach to wealth. Wealth brings responsibility.

He detailed four responsibilities for the wealthy:

1. *An ethical foundation for the product or service*
2. *To earn enough to support of themselves and their loved ones*

3. *To save money for the future, avoid financial risks and debts*

4. *To give generously (dana).*

This Buddha makes clear that the wealthy ensure they inquire into any exploitation to create and increase wealth. They ensure their money does not support corporations such as the defence industry nor cause harm to people, animals and the environment.

Personal prosperity and happiness in daily life fuse together through kindness, friendship, and compassion. The wealthy need to realise the importance of substantial acts of generosity for others and themselves through the sharing of wealth, knowledge, expertise and skills. With wealth comes responsibility for the welfare of others, near and far. A greater wealth signifies a greater responsibility for others, who are less fortunate. Though the super-rich enjoy setting foundations and trusts in their name, they must dig deeper into themselves and their pockets than that. Genuine compassion takes real sacrifice and dedication, often at the expense of comfort and security.

A wealthy US businessman, who travels into Burma annually to support the desperately poor, oppressed tribes and numerous refugee families, takes risks with his health and safety. He carries with him substantial wads of Burmese currency. The military regime running Burma, a Buddhist country, does not take kindly to such acts of compassion from a Westerner.

The Buddha did not have a problem with people becoming wealthy providing the wealthy individual or family examined the means employed to make money and the impact it had on others. The wealthy employer has a duty to ensure the real welfare and financial support for the management and workers and safeguard against huge differentials in pay. Rather than an aloof relationship to staff, business leaders and employers can experience a genuine happiness and contentment through the development of empathy with everyone employed and the needs of their families. The Buddha stated that "happiness is the greatest wealth."

The Buddha said that when you plan to do something, you should reflect thus:

- *"Is this action unskilled?*
- *Does it lead to problems for others?*
- *Does it show inner skill?*

- *Does it lead to happiness for myself and others?" (MN 58).*

Politicians, bankers, financiers, investors and economists have a lot of soul-searching to do to resolve the widespread suffering around easy credit and debts. It will require a root and branch change in both the psychology of big business and capitalism to develop a culture of wisdom and co-operation.

The Buddha spelt it out: *"When this (causes/conditions) exists that comes to be. When this (causes/conditions) does not exist, that does not come to be."* (MN 79.7) Any projection, distortion or fetish around money, position and ownership become the causes and conditions for painful consequences including living in delusion.

The Buddha commented: *"It is not for the sake of pleasure that one lives. There is something higher and more sublime than that. When one knows and sees thus, the mind is liberated from greed, blame and delusion. For the sake of this freedom, one lives."* (MN 79.28.44).

7. ETHICS AND INSTITUTIONAL CHANGE

Many Dharma teachers in the Theravada Buddhist tradition explain the five precepts at the beginning of Buddhist retreats, East and West. Participants will start the retreat hearing about living with virtue through making a commitment to observe ethics, both on retreat and in daily life. Retreat often provides a precious and supportive environment for ethical and mindful activities while application into daily life often poses a challenge.

The practice and understanding of ethics/virtue (*sila*) serves as a bedrock for the Dharma. As teachers, we offer the basic five precepts, often with a short explanation of them for 10 to 15 minutes at the beginning of retreats. The best of the tradition extols the importance of non-harming with care and respect for all, humans and animals alike. Some people work deep within themselves to realise a change of heart, a change of attitude and a different intentionality to live in accordance with such a virtuous way of being.

Real inner change matches our commitment to uphold and protect the ethical guidelines. For example, some Buddhists commit themselves to the ethics of diet resulting in the decision to refuse eating anything with a face – such as animals, birds or fish. Such ethics confirm an austerity, the deliberate refusal to eat certain kinds of food. Ethics and austerity support each other.

In his extensive teaching of around 10,000 discourses, the Buddha only made a handful of references to the five precepts as a single category. He made numerous references to each one of the precepts but very rarely formed them into a group, presumably to safeguard the precepts from being interpreted as commandments. Precepts serve as the most common translation for the Buddha's use of the Pali word '*sila*' which combines ethics with virtue. Ethics expands much further in the Dharma teachings than just practice of the five precepts. *Sila* has a significance alongside mindfulness, truth and freedom.

Familiar to many Buddhists, the five precepts consist of the training in:

1. *Not taking life,*
2. *Not taking what is not given,*
3. *Not engaging in lust for pleasure, including sexual*

4. *Not lying, nor engaging in abusive, malicious speech or senseless talk*
5. *Not becoming heedless through indulgence (in alcohol and drugs).*

The Buddha warned that those who violate *sila* live fearfully, invite the anger of others and suffer hell during their lifetime. They will experience dread through the wrath and punishment of others. While those who engage in the ethical training to live respectfully, and in accordance with the same precepts, live at ease with themselves and with others (*AN, Book of Fives*). It is a simple evident truth worth remembering.

During my years as a Buddhist monk during the 1970's, we used the word *virtue* as the translation for the word "*sila*". In recent years, Buddhists have quietly dropped the word "virtue" as the translation for *sila* and replaced the meaning with precepts or morality. There is a significant difference between the meaning of virtue/ethics and morality. Western liberal values have become preoccupied with the morality of social, religious, political institutions and create legislation to uphold morality. Morality, laws, rules, precepts, rights and obligations become a means to control behaviour.

It is important to distinguish ethics from morality. In its Buddha Dharma sense, *sila* refers to an ethos of virtuous action to reduce and resolve suffering through changing the conditions in order to stop its arising inwardly and outwardly. In common parlance, morality belongs to a code of rules brought about through a collective agreement, religious, secular laws or a personal viewpoint. Laws and morality invite blame and punishment. In Dharma language, the concept of morality represents forms of conduct, cultural agreements and set of rules. A person or group may approve or disapprove of a given moral code. Sila serves as a practice to develop a non-harming, non-exploitive way of life of benefit for oneself and others. Morality and rules certainly can benefit society providing the morality shows kindness and compassion. There is the danger that identification with a certain morality can feed into notions of superiority and inferiority of others.

Virtue and ethics in the Dharma supports an action emerging from the depth of our being that stays true to its ethos of empathy, despite any proliferations and reactions from the conditioning that generates self-interest.

Ethics, ethos, ethnic, ethology bear the same root - from the Greek word *ethos* meaning *character*. We develop a clear-minded character through virtuous ethics. Society develops a code of morality (from the Latin *mores* - rules to hold together) through the judiciary, political/social/religious priorities and collective conditioning. While having a useful place in society, morality can easily turn into a moralising tendency, self-righteousness and intolerant attitudes. In the Latin, morality suggests agreeing to a proper form of behaviour in conjunction with the mores of society.

Morality often shows conformity to an outward regulation, a kind of agreement within society while a virtuous action does not depend upon such social norms.

Four Major Kinds of Financial Corruption in Business

We need to uncover the profound significance of ethics and virtuous action in our personal lives, social lives and working lives so that we can respond to the issues of our time.

Ethics, values, mindfulness and concentration co-operate. Let us say that a mindfulness teacher offers a workshop in a major corporation. A team of managers sits together in a circle. The teacher gives a guided meditation. After the meditation, the teacher asks the group what arose in their mind during the meditation. One of the managers said that he became very mindful of a deception that his company deliberately perpetuated on millions of their customers regarding their best-selling product. He told the teacher and co-managers that he needed to speak up about this deception. Other voices also spoke up. Between them, the managers share their concerns about areas of corporate corruption.

The teacher facilitated the discussion rather than moving back into formal meditation. Thus, the meeting concentrated on ethics, values, mindfulness (of corruption), values and concentration. This focus excluded other themes, practices and topics. The Dharma of ethics/virtue addresses corruption head on.

Corruption violates ethics; it can reduce or deprive millions of people of their hard-earned income and breeds an atmosphere of mistrust in the office and on the factory floor. As the public knows, corruption operates widely among the most influential people in society including presidents, prime ministers, ministers, CEOs and members of boardrooms. Corruption reveals itself in the attempt to maximise gain regardless of the widespread suffering.

The Duties of Kings, Queens, Presidents and Prime Ministers

The Buddha described the position of the King as a social contract between the King and the people. He said that the people should censure the King, if he engaged in actions that caused suffering. The King would then deserve to be banished. In return, the people would pay taxes to a 'capable' king. He said that the people should choose the King (Maha Sammata).

Thus, the people appoint the King through common consent and a democratic election (DN iii 92). He said that the most important duty of the King reveals itself through upholding the Dharma (the noble eightfold path). A King knows what is to be done for the welfare of the people and what is not to be done, because it brings woe to the people. This is the duty of the King (DN iii 61).

The people paid money to the king through the levied taxes on food and goods. Government officials (referred to as Kammika) had offices at the exit gates of the cities, river crossings and on the roads to tax merchants and caravans (Vin iii 52). Corrupt monks, however, would smuggle in their robes such items as jewellery and precious stones (Vin iii 62).

The Buddha reminded Kings that if they failed in their duty, it would be a disaster for the citizens of the country. If the King ignored ethics and wisdom, then his ministers would also act in harmful ways. The Brahmins, the priest and people in the cities, towns and villages would then act in much the same way. People would live in conflict, become weak and sickly (AN ii 74-75). One King, named Ajatasatthu, needed 24 hour a day protection in his palace and could only travel in secrecy due to his fear of being attacked. The word got out that the King plotted to kill his father (Vin ii 190).

The duties of those in positions of power include support for the priests, military, merchants/business people and workers. The duties are to:

- *Provide lawful protection*
- *Provide safety*
- *Provide accommodation for all citizens*

- *Support for animals, including birds and fish*
- *Address crime*
- *Give money to those in need*
- *Support people in cities, towns and the countryside*
- *Develop the wholesome and overcome the unwholesome*
- *Know what will lead to harm and suffering*
- *Engage in what is wholesome.*

This is the duty of a wheel turning (evolving) ruler.

The Buddha said:

- *One ruler did not give wealth to the needy*
- *As a result, poverty became rife*
- *From poverty came theft*
- *From taking what has not been given came an increase in the use of weapons*
- *From weapons came an increase in the taking of life*
- *From taking what has not been given and use of weapons, lies and sexual abuse increased*
- *And all this shortened people's lives and their beauty.* (DN 26)

A thoughtful board, senior managers and workers need to explore four major kinds of financial corruption running rife in the business. The same principles apply to government ministers and social, political and religious organisations. They need to hold regular meetings to agree upon an action. Areas of corrupt practices are often inter-related. They include:

Deception

Corporations and smaller businesses will overinflate their charges to squeeze as much money out of consumers. Banks and corporations will take risks with the savings of clients. Large businesses engage in reckless gambles to swallow other businesses. Businesses will produce sub-standard, inferior quality goods. Corporations will artificially drive up prices for a few weeks then drop prices to announce a sale. Corporations will engage in various marketing strategies to persuade customers to go into debt in the short and long term. Sports stars will take banned drugs to win matches, thus deceiving their competitors, as well as the public. Sports officials, along with sportsmen and women in athletics, football (soccer), cycling, boxing, tennis and other sports have engaged in corrupt practices, such as the use of drugs in the addiction to fame, power or money or all three.

The Buddha referred to five kinds of miserliness (contemporary examples in brackets):

1. *Dwellings (houses, work environments, health care, city and rural etc.)*
2. *Families (income, living conditions, social political support etc.)*
3. *Gains (profit, avoidance of payment, avoidance of taxes, overpriced goods/services)*
4. *Praise (capacity to accountability, ethics and a moderate lifestyle)*
5. *Dharma (ignoring body of teachings, confining Dharma to mindfulness in the moment).*

CEOs, Bankers, Business Leaders and those engaged in the Financial Markets could question their level of miserliness. The superrich have little opportunity to make donations. They may give substantial sums of money to various charities and foundations. These sums of money constitute some of the return of the money back to society through exorbitant charges. It is questionable whether using one's name for a Foundation constitutes a gift. The substantial sum offered enables the superrich to feel good about themselves. The best of gifts is anonymous, not back up with public relations experts paid to make the donor into a kind and generous human being.

1. *Do their factory and farm workers live and work in decrepit, crowded and unhealthy environments?*
2. *Do the families of factory and farm workers have to live in gross conditions due to low salary paid to the worker(s) in the household?*
3. *Do the profits of corporations come at the expense of low paid workers, overcharging of the products and obsessive desire to accumulate as much wealth as possible?*

4. *Do the bosses and financial consultants avoid giving praise to those who apply ethics in employment, call for change in institutions and/or use the tactics of the bully with regard to staff?*
5. *Does the desire to hold onto power and increase wealth get in the way of teachings of a truly humanitarian attitude and application of wisdom?*

Bribery

Certain Corporations will pay significant sums of money to influential individuals in other corporations and governments to win a contract. Bribery also includes payment to elected offices in government to act or vote on their behalf. Such officials place the interests of the corporation way before the interests of the public. Bribes also go to public servants to secure a business license or permit corporations to pay money to politicians, national or local, to rush through a contract. Gambling syndicates will pay sports stars to lose matches. Lawyers will arrange for large sums of money to go to certain individuals or businesses to buy their silence. Organisations and institutions will 'grease the palm' of officials to get through paperwork quickly.

Fraud

Businesses misrepresent facts for personal or corporate gain. Corporations engage in fraudulent ways to persuade people to part with their money. Bosses and senior executives will award themselves large salary increases, significant bonuses and five star all expenses paid excursions through fraudulent claims about their products and services. They operate with a sense of entitlement at the expense of lower paid workers and consumers. Bosses and executives ensure that they receive substantial pay-outs when they must resign due to their mismanagement.

Embezzlement

Embezzlement is the act of wrongfully appropriating funds entrusted into the care of a business, big or small. Corporate embezzlers deliberately withhold financial assets for individual or corporate self-interest. It is a pre-meditated crime. Embezzlers in corporations steal assets, savings and funds. Corporations and banks rarely report such thefts to the police because of fear of bad publicity. Corporations engage in a form of embezzlement of the public purse through the evasion of taxes, sometimes amounting to billions of $$$, year after year. Theft from the public purse shows a deliberate intention to under-report annual income to the tax authorities or to employ tax loopholes, or use tax havens, or all three. These huge sums of unpaid taxes would support the poor, sick, elderly, single parents, young and the unemployed. These corporations show a cold, heartless determination to maximise profit, no matter who suffers. These corporations have deliberately embezzled the money of the people.

CEO's will claim that they have a lofty position, so they cannot expect to know of corruption in the company. They will find fault with others for not informing them of financial misconduct. The bosses decline to take responsibility and instead refer to misconduct in the corporation as 'control failings,' 'multiple poor decisions' a 'system failure" or a 'failure of implementation'. Such jargon becomes an excuse for breaking the law, financial abuse, gross misconduct and corrupt practices. The employment of a language of excuses blocks culpability. By claiming that everybody in the corporation must take responsibility, it means that nobody ends up taking responsibility. The blame falls conveniently on human error and not on the corporate individuals, who manipulate the system for power and profit.

Bankers receive breath-taking bonuses to satisfy their lust for money while taxpayers see their hard-earned money used to bail them out after their gross mismanagement. Public relations advisors, lawyers and accountants have become masters at shifting responsibility.

The application of mindfulness includes ethics and accountability. Caring staff cultivate empathy for the less fortunate and challenge those who wilfully engage in corrupt practices - from supporting wilful tax evasion to harmful commercial enterprises. The mindfulness industry ignores corporate corruption. Mindfulness of corrupt practices remains far outside the remit of the workshop mindfulness leaders, even though corruption feeds stress, greed and fear – the factors they aim to reduce in the first place by teaching mindfulness.

The application of mindfulness includes the development of responsibility, cultivation of empathy for the less fortunate and the application of action to harmful practices. Real change comes when there is the collective agreement to move from the unspoken to the spoken. This is the first step towards ethics and personal responsibility. Employees often know what is going on behind closed doors but fear to become a whistle-blower because of the consequences. Authentic mindfulness practices inspire confidence, fearlessness and a liberated voice.

Overview of the First Training Rule

Serving as the basic training guidelines, each one of the five precepts stands worthy of reflection and inquiry, as an indispensable feature of lifestyle. Gross and subtle aspects of these guidelines challenge our views, conditioning and attitudes. *Sila* is vital in the practice of waking up and indispensable from a life of mindfulness and wisdom.

'Bad' things happen in this world. There is what is 'not good', 'bad;' there is 'terror,' and 'acts of evil.' Our views about others constantly affect our judgment. Blame, retaliation and retribution can serve as a basis for our morality. Mindfulness and loving kindness meditation can develop at the expense of inquiry, a passion for change and awakening to reality. The neglect of ethical practice generates more stress and suffering than anything else.

Outside of such meditations, the mindfulness practitioner may pursue personal, social or corporate goals that harm others or themselves in the short or long term. Identified with a nationality, the mindfulness practitioner can wholeheartedly believe in the nation's right to attack others and punish their citizens, armies and governments.

The first training in non-violence stands in contrast to a reaction: "You have hurt me (us) so we will hurt you" The reaction gets justified as a morality of like for like. "You have used weapons to kill and maim our people. We will use weapons to kill and maim your people." In conflict with each other, organizations and nation states use similar means to inflict suffering on their enemies. The organization and the State share more in common that what separates them. Unable to cope with the suffering and humiliation of a terrorist attack, we demand that the military make others on the other side suffer. Both sides offer their supporters a moral justification for inflicting suffering on the other side. Both sides perceive the other side as 'evil'. The same justification takes place for smaller crimes and unethical behaviours. People adopt a self-righteous standpoint about the unethical behaviour of others to justify inflicting pain on them. We do not see the link about our attitude and the attitude of others who created pain. We confuse revenge with morality.

I recall attending a meeting of Dharma teachers in Switzerland. The facilitator for the session gave us one to two minutes each to share our views on war. Some teachers felt war might be necessary at times. Others felt a country had a right to defend itself. Others were not sure what their feelings were about war. Others would only consider non-violent strategies to deal with war. It was clear there was no consensus of views. Our discussion lasted an hour before we moved onto another topic. It seems unfortunate that the seniors in the Sangha waver on such issues on the morality of war and the significance of the first ethical guideline of the Buddha.

For numerous generations, human beings have introduced laws, commandments and legislation. Such legislation, secular or religious, aims to determine people's behaviour. Laws and the religious commandments endeavour to stop what we perceive as 'bad', 'wrong' or 'evil.' National or international legislation can protect people from suffering or violation of various agreements. Moral codes, religious and secular, ancient and modern, continue to matter with or without general approval.

These codes include ancient religious texts, such as the Torah in Judaism or rules of the Vinaya in Buddhism or the charters for human rights, the American Constitution and EU agreements. The Buddha also employed rules for the ordained to develop an austere, nomadic lifestyle.

Rules of morality of religion or the nation state or both can sanction killing and violence. For example, the first precept of the major religions focuses on not killing. *'Thou shalt not murder'*, says *The Bible*. Religions define this commandment to apply to individuals of society, but do not apply the same injunction to the aims of the nation state. This enables a military commander or soldier with religious faith to kill while sustaining his or her religious beliefs. The religious and social injunctions do not apply to people outside of the country.

The military and their political/religious leaders treat warfare as a moral duty. The distinction between morality and ethics/virtue is significant.

The Construct of Self and Other

No one can keep the precepts or any other code of morality to perfection. No one can observe such a high moral standard. Neglect of one or more of the precepts may arise due to identification with the cultural mood or predisposition of the culture in the pursuit of pleasure, regardless of the cost. Ethics easily depends primarily on a sense of *self* and *other* with a view that one is right and the other wrong.

The judge, namely the self, and the judged, namely the other, have the potential to learn much from each other to enable mutual understanding to develop. We cannot see clearly the person or the people when we place them firmly in the category of the '*other*' and different from ourselves. Wise judgement requires an exploration of what we share and what constitutes differences.

The threefold training for practitioners consists of virtue/ethics (*sila*), meditative concentration (*samadhi*) and wisdom (*panna*). All Dharma teachers need deep commitment to train their student in the practice of application of ethics. We need to make the range of depths of ethics explicit rather than unspoken. The inclusion of ethics into one's practice matters as much as any mindfulness or meditation practice. Yet questions arise around virtuous actions:

1. *Are the current teachings of the five precepts addressed in depth?*
2. *Have the teachers failed to address many ethical social and political issues?*
3. *Is there a preoccupation around sexual ethics that overshadows the other precepts?*
4. *Do we use the five precepts to leap onto the throne of moral self-righteousness?*
5. *Have the five precepts become a ritualist language rather than fields for practice?*
6. *Have teachers failed to point to ethics outside of the five precepts?*
7. *What confirms a real expression of virtue/ethics/action?*

Teachers/mentors/facilitators of mindfulness and meditation can live in a comfort zone regarding the five trainings through only offering a simplistic view. *"I don't commit murder. I do not rob people. I do not rape others. I do not lie and deceive. I am not addicted to alcohol and drugs. Therefore, I observe sila and only need to develop my meditation practice and understanding."*

This interpretation of the five virtues only addresses some aspects of ethics. We need to explore deeply the five ethical guides to shed light on contemporary issues. Thoughtful Buddhists need to engage in deep analysis on the moral issues of our time. We can learn from the analysis on ethics by certain Buddhist academics, scholars and activists.

The Buddha compared a tradition to a line of blind men holding each other and following on from the first blind person who started the tradition *(DN 1.240)*. Much energy gets siphoned off to preserve a tradition or an ancient code of Buddhist discipline *(Vinaya)*. Spiritual/religious teachers often appear unwilling to offer a view on war, conflict and corruption for fear of sounding judgemental, moralistic or coming across in an absolutist manner.

Four common responses emerge from Dharma teachers or practitioners to specific questions on ethical issues:

1. *Yes, this is breaking a precept*
2. *No, this is not breaking a precept*
3. *It depends*
4. *I do not know.*

A worthwhile training makes us mindful of the significant issues of humanity and to reflect on ways to end suffering or knowing what eventually leads to suffering. Here are examples of ethical issues involving each of the five precepts:

First Precept

- *Is support for the nation state engaging in acts of war a violation of the first precept?*
- *Is an abortion or support for an abortion a violation of the first precept?*
- *Are experiments on animals showing a disregard for this precept?*
- *Is embryonic research a violation of the sanctity of life?*
- *Does eating animals, birds and fish reject the Buddhist commitment to saving all sentient beings*
- *Does the eating of animals have far reaching consequences for our health, the suffering/death of animals and the environmental impact on other creatures to clear land for farm animals?*

Second Precept

- *Is the maximisation of profit through investments in unethical stocks, such as the defence industry, destruction of rainforests and harmful pollutants contributing to the harm of people and animals and robbing us of security and health?*
- *Is the excessive pursuit of wealth a form of stealing from the world's poor?*
- *Is withholding taxable income stealing from the national purse?*
- *Is the illegal copying of software, music and film CDs a form of stealing from those who own the copyright?*
- *Is spending money on luxury goods, gambling or extravagance in lifestyle a corruption of mind at a cost to others who need our support?*
- *Is the excessive use of natural resources a form of taking of what has not been given?*
- *Is living beyond our means causing suffering now and depriving future generations of resources?*

Third Precept

- *Is there an obsession with the third precept that overshadows the equal importance of the four other precepts?*
- *What is sexual freedom and what is sexual irresponsibility?*
- *Are a teacher and yogi, or guru and disciple, making love inherently sexual misconduct?*
- *Does violation of this precept always require harassment or manipulation?*
- *Is taking a lover while in a marriage always a violation of the third precept?*
- *Is three or four people making love together sexual misconduct?*
- *Is having more than one partner, including several partners, sexual misconduct?*
- *Is a monogamous relationship with a long-term commitment a Judeo-Christian value, a personal preference or an ethical ideal?*
- *Is watching pornography showing a disregard for the third precept?*

- *Is using sex to market products an abuse of the precept?*
- *Is working in any capacity in the sex industry an abuse of the third precept?*

Fourth Precept

- *Is the selling of goods (a house, car, policies, shares, goods) that knowingly can result in deep distress for the consumer a breaking of the fourth precept?*
- *Is lying ever justified?*
- *Is secrecy a form of rejection of the fourth precept?*
- *Is going into a country or occupied territory and claiming tourist status when one is going to teach the dharma a lying to the immigration authorities?*
- *Is teaching about renunciation and a simple lifestyle when one is living a wealthy lifestyle revealing a lack of integrity?*
- *Is using the dharma to maximise a certain lifestyle acting falsely?*
- *Is secrecy a form of suppression of freedom of speech and a violation of the spirit of the fourth precept?*

Fifth Precept

- *Is the taking of mind altering drugs for recreational purposes a violation of the fifth precept?*
- *Is the taking of mind altering drugs for spiritual exploration a violation of the fifth precept?*
- *Is the taking of such drugs giving support to the worldwide drug mafia that ignores all five trainings.*
- *Do we find out about the way drugs develop such as experiments on animals?*
- *Do we express our concern about the massive profits made from the ill-health of citizens?*
- *Why are the drug companies doing nothing to change the behaviour of the food industry which harms the health of citizens of all ages?*

- *Is a problem with alcohol or drugs an abuse of the fifth precept or, if there is respect for the precept, is it an addictive problem, rather than an ethical issue?*
- *Is smoking cigarettes a violation of the fifth precept? Nicotine is the most addictive of all substances with a dangerously substantial risk of eventually causing cancer as well as much heartache and suffering for oneself and loved ones while precious land is wasted on tobacco crops.*

There is no room for complacency. Virtue, ethics and mindfulness flow naturally together. The exclusion of ethics inhibits the opportunity for profound insights. The restriction of teachings to methods of mindfulness and meditation keeps mindfulness trapped in a narrow remit. Mindfulness cannot then serve the deeper needs of society but works as an agent to preserve the status quo and the current conservative application of mindfulness.

The Buddha said that those who uphold *sila* make wisdom shine and those who uphold wisdom make *sila* shine. No single precept is more important than the other ones. The practice of virtue in body/speech/mind and our actions work as a liberating force since it liberates us and others from fragmented and distorted perceptions.

Virtue/ethics and mindfulness act as a backbone to the power of the voice to speak up and express concern about issues that violate a virtuous way of being.

The Buddha refused to settle for five precepts as the only definition of ethics. Here are some examples of the Buddha's teachings on ethics. In the Noble Eightfold Path, he stated that ethics consisted of Right Action, Right Speech and Right Livelihood (usually translated as 'right,' *samma* literally means to be *'properly connected to/conducive/fulfilling* on the path to an awakening life). The other links consist of Right

View, Right Intention, Right Effort, Right Mindfulness and Right Concentration

Ethics as a Force for Change

The Buddha firmly placed our livelihood in the field of ethics, namely forms of skillful employment clearly in accordance with wise intention, deep values and beneficial results for all. The coupling of virtue/ethics with mindfulness in the powerful committee rooms and corridors of political and corporate power would initiate a revolution.

Bosses, management, office and factory workers would find themselves engaged in a depth of sharing to generate a transformation in the values and priorities of a business.

The Buddha also taught *sila* as:

- *restraint of the senses (indriya-samvara-sila)*
- *wise use of food, clothing, shelter and dwelling place (paccaya sannissita sila)*
- *wholesome action (kusala sila) of body, speech, mind and livelihood*
- *not clinging to ethics, codes of morality, rules, methods of practice and rituals (silabbata-paramasa).*

He advocated skillful means to evolve as human beings. The break out of a limited view of ethics as confined to precepts opens our minds to an exploration of *sila* in its wider sense. The recognition of the co-arising of mindfulness with ethics shows concern for the welfare of present and future generations. The practice then questions deeply conditioned attitudes. The exploration of mindfulness-ethics applies inwardly and outwardly to find the truth of situations. We would then inquire into:

- *the ego of desire for sense satisfaction and the impact of suppression*
- *obsessive behaviour around basic needs*
- *the pursuit and ownership of more requisites*
- *getting lost in time, money and energy devoted to acquisition*
- *neglect of a lifestyle in accordance with deep values*
- *private and public moralizing around behaviour*
- *harmful behaviour of religious/political/corporate/social institutions.*

Ethics supports healthy thoughts, beliefs and actions. In religious and secular life, the clinging to the concept of what is right may become an instrument to slag off individuals or groups. Grasping onto rules generate rules within the original rules, and rules within those rules. The Buddha said "Trifling and insignificant are the minor details of rules of morality" as observed in the code of monks and nuns. (AN iii 9.85). A moralist interpretation of an event inhibits the mindful inquiry into the conditions for what ethical issues arise.

The accusers can violate ethical issues as much as the accused. The one who points the accusing finger can forget that he or she has three fingers pointing towards themselves. Ethics examines our intentions in the treatment of others.

People's lives change through awareness, exploration of suffering and the factors, past and present, influencing behaviour. The application of skillful means and deep insights reveal a movement into the right direction. A capacity for a radical non-acceptance of our socialised mindset has a profound significance on virtue preparing the way towards fearless living.

'Good' and 'Evil'

In a major conflict, home or abroad, wise action becomes a public statement of an ethical standpoint regardless of any ridicule, bemusement or doubts of others.

To label individuals, organisations or leaders of nation states as 'evil' blocks the inquiry into causes and conditions that trigger expressions of 'evil'.

Are ethics inseparable from our mind's constructs of good and evil?

Are there ethical actions not bound to notions of doing good and overcoming evil?

A person who claims to have made -up their mind about others often wants retribution. The dark perception of *evil* endorses the dark force of revenge and the desire to inflict suffering on so-called "others." We employ different languages but the desire to inflict suffering remains the same.

Carrying the arrogance of claims to the Western civilization, we bring to bear on *others* our ideology of liberal democracy, secular culture and consumer values, as the only fit way to live. Imposing our version of what is *good* for others, we act upon the belief in differences between ourselves and *others,* as if the perceived differences revealed true reality. We want to change people to make other countries more like us which reveals a demand for sameness.

We believe that we know what is *good* for an individual, a community and a non-Westernized nation. We split our inner life into two, namely *self and other* or *us and them* and act on the belief. We make war on others with a view to making them submit to what we want from them. Citizens have very little choice in terms of influencing major decisions. The influence of social media, the funding of political parties and the lust to hold onto power weakens year by year the body of the democratic processes. Cynicism and disillusionment has become rampant in democratic countries. We live largely under the control of rich and powerful institutions and individuals.

The situation may or may not have been similar at the time of the Buddha. Kings ruled their kingdoms in a hereditary system, which Prince Gautama would have benefitted from as heir to his father's throne if he had stayed a Prince. Gautama, the Buddha to be, advocated democracy to replace the hereditary system, which would have displeased the royal families in the kingdoms, where he gave teachings. The Buddha knew the power of those at the top in society, so he reminded them of their responsibilities.

The countries of north India consisted of monarchs, republics, city and urban councils, confederations and tribal co-operation. The Buddha appreciated the Vajjian people. They held frequent, well-attended meetings that were peaceful, orderly and well-conducted. The councils paid respect to the wisdom of the elders, respected women, took care of the shrines in the country and implemented decisions for the welfare of the people (DN ii 73). The Buddha observed that the whole country prospered because of these meetings.

The Buddha established his large nomadic Sangha based on the assemblies of citizens' meetings to come to common agreements. The Buddha respected a republican model and expressed his concerns around Kings and Gurus dominating the lives of their subjects or disciples.

Words become highly politicised. Take words like *American, Arab, asylum seeker, black, Christian, European, Jew, immigrant, Muslim or white*. We cannot see clearly the person or group of people having placed them in the category of *other*. An American is not an American. A Muslim is not a Muslim. A black person is not black, and a white person is not white. 'They' are not who we think 'they' are. 'We' are not who they think 'we' are.

Human beings express themselves in infinite ways with infinite presentations. The expression of black, white, European, Asian, confines human beings to the finite and entails a failure to recognize their diversity. Those who confuse labels with reality miss the opportunity to live in the real world.

Politicians and the media also hide behind the self-delusion that they report reality rather than acknowledging their employment of labels and concepts to describe their version of reality. We experience authentic ethics when we are grounded in awareness of the contingent factors to whatever situation arises and wise steps to take. Then there is no possibility to deliberately inflict suffering on others in the name of a necessary action. Ethics take priority over personal views of good and evil.

Ethics Beyond Good and Evil

The Buddha has offered wise counsel on a wide range of ethical issues.

In alphabetical order:

1. *Action*
2. *Livelihood*
3. *Judgments*
4. *Moralising*
5. *Lifestyle*
6. *Making money*
7. *Sensual pleasures*
8. *Ethical goods*
9. *Use of resources*
10. *Diet*
11. *Travel*
12. *Codes of morality*
13. *Upkeep of outdated religious rules*
14. *Law and punishment*

The Buddha stated: "Having abandoned formal practice and actions both *'good and evil'*, neither striving for *'purity'* nor *'impurity'*, one abides without adhering to either extreme." (Sn 900). Ethics include inquiry into the insubstantiality of the ego, wisdom and liberation. It is the *sila* of the *sila*s – the greatest act of virtue of that a human being can express with such a deep, ongoing interest.

Through grasping onto the identification with any system of thought or form, including formal meditation practice, the self easily becomes bogged down in notions of purity and impurity, right and wrong, progress and regress. Depending on our belief in what is *good*, we then fix what is *not good*. Identification with the '*good*' precedes the '*not good*', the '*not right*'.

Naively, we believe evil comes from evil or from unhealthy and destructive influences of the past. Good men and women, who have had a loving and supportive upbringing, with caring parents and loving family members, commit the obscenest evils – especially in war. Why? *Evil* emerges from identification with the *good*. If we project the notion of the good onto the nation state or religion, and political/religious authority figures, then the *evil* of intent can follow. The common belief that emotional and mental health issues originate in childhood confirms a dogma rather than insights. Far too many exceptions refute the belief.

Fear of *others* obstructs the virtue of ethics. Ethics requires inquiry into the encounter with events. *Sila* thus provides a profound challenge to step outside our conditioned mind, and identification with secular or religious ideologies to act from a fresh perspective.

A constricted, fragmented and defined sense of the world determines our limits as humans robbing us of our potential for the immensity of realisations. An inquiry into ethics, outside of mental constructs and conditioning of 'good' and 'evil,' challenge our habitual perceptions and views.

Virtue or Control of Behaviour

The view of "breaking rules" does not apply to the spirit nor to the literal meaning of the meaning of *sila*. *Sila* is a practice, a training (*sekha*) to develop the heart and mind. The infliction of harm, exploitation or abuse of other shows a lack of self-knowledge, unresolved reactivity of the mind or irresponsible obedience to the will of authority. Generosity, kindness, right livelihood, non-harming, sharing and moderation in lifestyle show an immense virtue in lifestyle. You cannot legislate for that. You cannot force people into such a way of being.

Authentic virtue and ethics comes through love and the wisdom of deeply rooted responses to a noble way of life. The world of *do and do not* imposes upon us a mechanical obedience, commandments and morality but compliance to rules does not confirm virtue. The development of a virtuous way of life ensures respectful action towards others and ourselves.

Rather than slipping into a moralising attitude, we practice developing a language and understanding that pays respect to the diversity of exploration so that virtue, mindfulness, and wisdom can develop for all. The five guidelines for inner development point in the direction of the resolution of suffering. Ethics includes a deep exploration and change to the conditioned arising of problematic situations to dissolve fear and blame between people.

This ethic reveals a clear encounter with any situation to realise the infinite potential of it. Any situation, large or small, personal or global, reveals a range of feelings, perceptions, thoughts and knowledge. This composition carries within it the potential to reveal a truth that develops a faithful response to wise resolution of the encounter. Ignoring this ethic, we become corrupted through settling for something less in life, namely pursuit of self-interest, the finite and transitory.

Inquiry offers limitless potential for insights and realisation while putting aside the blind adherence to rules and rigidity of views. The adherence to rules of behaviour belongs to a social mores having little or nothing in common with virtue, ethics and a dedicated action. Those who identify most strongly with vows, laws and the social order may restrict the capacity for engaging in the ethical act.

Western culture subscribes to human rights without realising how selective, rather than universal, these rights are. For example, some might consider it a human right to be free to travel anywhere in the world. Such people wish to choose to stay in any country, anywhere in the world, for as long as they wish, whether to work, marry, rest or simply experience. Nations often block this right to travellers, pilgrims, migrants, refugees, asylum seekers and families searching for a new place to live or spend time in. The demands of the nation state take precedent. The human right to travel anywhere and stay anywhere rests on the principle that the Earth belongs to everybody. Governments block freedom of movement, except for the exceptionally rich who can travel wherever they wish to and stay in a country for as long as they wish to.

The Buddha reminded us that clinging to views conditions the mind resulting to end up in extreme standpoints. If the mind clings to the idea of the *good* as success, praise, gain and pleasure, then the more the mind resists failure, blame, loss and pain. The *good* entails the shadow of the *not good, the bad, the terrible* thing to happen and the *evil*. Due to the conditioned perception of situations, the *good* becomes the '*not good*'.

We also name the other as evil, so that we feel good about ourselves. Owing to failure in an undertaking, we can feel to be a victim. This can lead to despair. We can drive ourselves harder to try to achieve our idea of what is good. Ethics contribute to the release from clinging to concepts of good and evil to know another kind of knowledge.

Harsh punishment attempts to take away others' sense of self-worth, demonise their character and make them change their mind-set. The punishment of other makes us feel that we are better than they are. Others must suffer because we have identified with the good and projected the blame, the evil elsewhere.

Respect reveals itself through a willingness to stay steady when faced with a challenging encounter and examine causes and conditions for behaviour.

A Profound Ethic Means to Stay Faithful to Wise Action

Between early 1967 and 1970, I spent years travelling on the road taking me through various Asian countries. While making the journey through southern Thailand, I stopped off at *Wat Suanmoke* (Monastery of the Garden of Liberation), near Chai Ya. I asked Ajahn Buddhadasa questions about life, about Buddhism and so on. After I had been there for some days, I knew I wanted to become a Buddhist monk, practise meditation, reflect on my life and subsequently lived in the forest with him as my teacher. He responded coolly to my request. "Anybody who changes their religion does so because they haven't understood their own", he responded to my surprise. He then took down a copy of the Bible and turned to the first pages of Genesis. He then read out a verse "Do not bite off the tree of knowledge of *good* and *evil*."

"If you understand that statement in The Bible, then you have understood the deepest meaning of religion. That is all you have to understand", he added. He looked serious. I could see that he meant everything he said. He showed no interest in giving me any support for ordination and sent me away. I left the monastery, travelled northwards into the far north of Thailand, crossed the River Mekong into Laos, witnessed features of the war, and then with a renewed determination returned to the monastery. Ajahn Buddhadasa could see for himself my single-pointed determination to ordain and set in motion the wheels for it. He was right. The non-grasping onto the tree of knowledge of good and evil lies at the heart of human inquiry. Non-grasping is a liberating ethic enabling the capacity to stay true to wise action.

We create an identity of being a victim through feeling sorry for ourselves. A *victim* experiences a living death. In time, the victim could become the victimiser, who inflicts suffering on others, and then they become victims. Insight into the process of feeling sorry for one '*self*' and insight into the self making others feel sorry for themselves springs from an ethic and virtuous actions for another.

The commitment to a life of virtue contributes to eliciting the truth out of a situation. Truth becomes obscure in the belief in the *good* and the determination of what is *evil*. The quest for truth, the real and the authentic requires a faithful endurance.

The Guardian, a daily newspaper in the UK, reported the story of Ruqia Hassan, a 30-year old Kurdish woman, who repeatedly criticised ISIS on her Facebook page. Fearlessly, she commented on the brutality of the regime in occupied Syria. *"None has shown us any compassion but the graveyards"*, she wrote. Referring to air strikes from the West, she wrote: *"People in the market crash into each other like waves, not because of the numbers, but because their eyes are glued to the skies…their feet are moving unconsciously."*

On the air strikes, she wrote bluntly: *"May God protect the civilians and take the rest."*

"Today (the ISIS police) launched random detentions. God, I beg you end this darkness and defeat these people."

"Every day, they ban, ban, ban."

Ruqia, a graduate of philosophy, would not stop putting out her messages on Facebook despite pleas from her family and friends. Mindful of the risks, Ruqia continued her Facebook dissents exposing the truth of ISIS. She reported about the reality of life in Raqqa remaining faithful to the ethics, staying true to reality, beyond considerations of self and other, good and evil.

ISIS arrested her, imprisoned her, and then executed her. Rather than closing down her Facebook page, ISIS left it open to trap her friends. They arrested five of her Facebook friends and executed them.

Such mindful and fearless actions require a depth of commitments, sometimes beyond the comprehension of the ordinary mind. The Buddha spoke of the goal of such ethics, to bring about the end of the harmful action.

A steadfast commitment to meaningful changes expresses a lifelong practice, which makes contributions to a liberated way of life.

Ethics and Truth

If we believe we have the Truth, we make it into a possession to promote, sell or for the conversion of others. We cannot possess the Truth. For as soon as we adopt that view, that Truth becomes the *good* and those outside the view of the *good* become ignorant, the foolish, the infidels, the evil. We engage with a situation to elicit the truth from it. The wise response triggers a break away from the past, namely a belief in the *good* and the not *good*. We explore ways to free us up from the reactive and possessive mind.

A commitment to truth offers a potential to uncover anything hidden. The truth reveals itself via the inquiry into a situation enabling an opening up of the issue. Awakening to the truth provides us with the ability to respond to the reality of the situation. Ethics, mindfulness and truth work together to enable deep discoveries that were previously hidden from perception. Along with reflection, inquiry and clear comprehension, the invaluable insights enable a genuine breakthrough.

Vigilance ensures that the mind steers away from grasping onto these insights that build of egotism, such as the view *"I've got it."* Treasures of understanding then end up becoming subservient to the ego. The Ego then holds onto one or two realisations and forgets the infinity of possibilities. The grasping of the mind keeps insights to the finite. We are then unable to see more.

The wise attribute significance to the here and now only when a truth emerges from it. The Buddha exposed the emptiness of the here and now, as something of itself, possessing an inherent existence. We cannot equate truth with the here and now. The Ego quickly highlights the *Now* as the confirmation of truth, as if abiding in the *Now* or *Being* meant the same thing as the realisation of truth. The ego makes us think that being in the moment is the same as knowing the truth.

Ethics contributes to the discernment and inquiry into the truth of suffering and its resolution. One stays faithful to this inquiry and refuses to cling to an absolute or relative view of a situation. The ethics of commitment to the reality of what unfolds takes priority.

Non-reliance on a positive outcome confirms fearless ethics. The absence of any ultimate guarantee for actions provides the very condition for the possibility of an ethical act. If we limit ourselves to a dependency on positive outcomes, we neglect our potential to express what matters.

The Buddha on Mindfulness of the Importance of Ethics

The Buddha's awakening under the Bodhi Tree includes the positive. His awakening inspired men and women for more than 100 generations to engage in the quest for truth with the willingness to make sacrifices for that deep investigation. On the negative side, some seekers pursued a single experience to confirm truth and reality without thinking that any later realisations are necessary.

The Buddha came across many insights during his 45 years of teaching through reflection, inquiry, meditation, and first-hand experiences. Fresh insight, realisations, discoveries and countless treasures emerged throughout his life. He showed the way to a wise freedom of being and freedom of action.

Nine Ethical Values on the Noble Path to Awakening:

1. *Right Understanding or Right View explores the nature of suffering, causes, resolution and the way*
2. *Right Speech namely truthful and clear with a wise attitude*
3. *Right Action, namely freedom of causing harm, exploitation or abuse*
4. *Right livelihood, namely skillful work and lifestyle, respectful and sustainable*
5. *Restraint of the senses (indriya-samvara-sila)*
6. *Wise use of food, clothing, shelter and dwelling place (paccaya sannissita sila)*
7. *Wholesome action (kusala sila) of body, speech, mind*
8. *Not-clinging to and exaggerating rules, methods, techniques, forms, rituals (silabbata-paramasa)*
9. *Dedication to the depths of insight and realisation.*

Ethics influence our thinking, beliefs and actions. In the dynamics of our existence, our ethics have an enormous impact upon every area of life. These days, there is an insufficient exploration and education around virtue/ethics, either in religion or secular culture.

We make a short journey on this earth before departing from this realm. We can explore what arises, stays and passes including experiences and situations. We face presence and absence, what exists and does not exist. We look at the world to find out what matters. We develop the courage to express our voice.

Do we comprehend what shapes our views and standpoints and what shapes the views and standpoints of others? We need to explore the influence our cultural upbringing has on us and to inquire how deeply entrenched it is, so that we can increasingly loosen its grip on us.

We may not know or understand the underlying conditioning of those with whom we strongly disagree. Others may have a different perception owing to the taking up and adoption of a different presentation, or appearance, from the other. Others will have a different perception of themselves than our perception. A myriad number of presentations, and a myriad number of interpretations only confirm the emptiness of any essence of the other, as well as ourselves.

If we stay wary of the other expressing an intrinsic difference to ourselves, this makes for the possibility of the recognition of the commonality of both. Wisdom responds to unity and differences between people. The heartfelt sense of the commonality between the self and the other will release a genuine empathy. Empathy confirms the authentic connection rather than identification with the mental construct of ourselves as superior and the other as inferior.

The Language of Choice

The dissolution of divisive views leans towards the repudiation of the idea of the good, of doing good and behaving in a good way. The inflated self of the individual can manifest in the dangerous belief: "I had no choice." Such a standpoint, particularly regarding actions involving harm, shows a mind in its contracted state, narrow and dogmatic. Our politicians tell us: "They (the enemy) left us with no choice. We had to invade to protect ourselves." Such a warped mind fails to explore alternatives to the presiding view with all the painful consequences imposed upon the other.

We think that we cannot imagine living in a world without self and other. It becomes hard to imagine any substantial significance to the *self-other* construct. The same principle applies right across the board. There is no substantial difference between life-and-death, being and non-being, existence and non-existence, presence and absence. The capacity to remain free from attributing any kind of substantiality between one side and the other side releases this exceptional freedom of movement.

The self finds itself composed of corrupt thoughts, proliferation of tendencies and a motley collection of assumptions - as if these warped perceptions give an authentic sense of reality. This impregnation obscures the real. Yes, there is the truth of what obscures, the stress and numerous problematic conditions of life, but it would be foolish to ascribe too much of the real to the various manifestations of the unresolved issues in the mind. There is the potential to see these diverse expressions of internal life, often impacting upon the body as well, without ascribing the real to these presentations.

A noble ethic sees the emptiness of a single claim upon a presentation, acknowledges the possibility of infinite presentations and the far-reaching discoveries to enable noble action.

The primary task of a conscious human being requires faithfulness to fearless action through suspending our tedious preoccupations with ourselves and projections onto others. These preoccupations get in the way of the apprehension of deep insights shedding light on situations. Ethics, mindfulness and concentration require a certain austerity to stay focussed on the essential priority.

The emptiness of essence of any self-existence, any single perception, makes it possible for genuine freedom to respond. We need a new kind of human being to evolve.

8. GREED IS **NOT** GOOD

Powerful corporations reveal themselves to be the contemporary equivalent of dinosaurs. These businesses trample everything underfoot. Young people need to boycott jobs in the corporate world if they want to have a worthwhile life for themselves and the next generation.

Companies remain intent on maximising profits, personal salaries, bonuses and career opportunities. Conferences on mindfulness, ethics and vision seem little more than exercises in public relations. These gestures seem trivial in comparison to the core aims of corporations. A meteor will land one day and extinguish them.

Around 90 global corporations generate two thirds of greenhouse gas emissions, polluting the Earth and producing climate change with nightmare consequences. The same corporations exploit the welfare and health of people, animals and the environment. They violate the Earth and its resources and show little or no regard for present or future generations.

A large business often interprets ethics as upholding the laws of the nation state. Yet, we cannot even take much comfort in the moral responsibility of corporations to uphold the laws of the country. Lawyers have found ways to keep technically within the law while deliberately ignoring the spirit of the legislation. Taxation loopholes demonstrate a clear example of manipulating the law. A small team of corporate lawyers and accountants will collude to detect loopholes in taxation to avoid paying corporate taxes. They could not care less about the loss of tax revenues for governments to support the poor and the environment. Corporate behaviour shows insensitivity and lack of respect for communities worldwide. They show little or no interest for a sustainable way of life.

The fetish for power and profit reveals a dark insensitivity from corporate leaders enslaved to the aims and objectives of the corporation. Corporations resist legislation and government regulations. They lack the necessary values for a genuinely considerate way of conducting business. A company can always find ways to modify rules of behaviour to suit its own economic advantage, regardless of the cost to its own workers worldwide.

Campaigns to force companies to change their harmful and destructive behaviour flounder due to the resistance of the bosses to implement meaningful change. The psychological dynamic of the bosses plays a determining role in the way they run a corporation. We can compare modern day CEOs who exercise power over their little corporate kingdoms to the kings/dictators of ancient India. The Buddha observed that if the King failed in his duty to observe wise governance, it would lead to disaster for all his subjects. The Buddha said: *"When the King is unrighteous, the ministers also become so, and so do people in the cities and countryside become unrighteous. The seasons proceed off course. The winds blow off course and at random. Sufficient rain will not fall. The crops ripen irregularly. People become ugly, weak and sick."* (AN ii 74-5).

Just as the kings/dictators of 2600 years ago, some CEOs today do have a wide variety of issues to address to support millions of customers or employees to live a righteous way of life. As the Chinese proverb states: "The rotting fish starts at the head."

Do we, the consumers, get the corporate masters we deserve? The same principle applies to our mediocre political masters. Do the government and the opposition parties reflect on the mindset of the owners of the media and the people? The Buddha emphasised the consequences of abuse of power from the top down, but we also stay mindful of our responsibilities for allowing such abuse.

Some of the areas that CEOs, boards of directors and shareholders might need to investigate include:

1. *Addictive substances in drink and food*
2. *Arms deals*
3. *Child labour*
4. *Construct of personal and private property so society consists of individuals to target*
5. *Consumption of oil, minerals and rainforests*
6. *Corporate cartels to keep the price of goods high*
7. *Corruption*
8. *Destruction of habitat*
9. *Experiments on humans*
10. *Food with excess of salt, sugar and fat*
11. *Forced Labour*

12. *Gambling*
13. *Globalisation*
14. *GM crops*
15. *Health and safety issues*
16. *Intellectual Property Rights (IPR) to possess certain words, designs and trade marks*
17. *Food with excess of sugar, salt, fat*
18. *Lies, deception, cheating, manipulation, exploitation*
19. *Manufacture of weapons*
20. *Marketing of harmful products such as tobacco, alcohol, weapons and junk food*
21. *Massive wage differential between the highest paid and the lowest paid*
22. *Outsourcing to secure the cheapest labour possible*
23. *Overpriced goods for the benefit of bosses and shareholders*
24. *Pharmaceutical companies often prevent other companies making the medicine cheaper and better available for more sick people*
25. *Pollution*
26. *Pornography*
27. *Powerful influence over democracy and governments/opposition*
28. *Pyramid schemes*
29. *Spam*
30. *Subliminal messages*
31. *Suppression of information*
32. *Surveillance of citizens*
33. *Swallowing up of smaller companies*
34. *Targeting of children*
35. *Tax avoidance*
36. *Violent video games*

37. *Wages, hours of work*

38. *Widespread use of sex to sell products*

39. *Work conditions*

40. *Workers' salaries*

To take one example of harmful action from the above list: millions work as forced labourers under daily mental or physical threats or both. Employers abuse workers, dehumanise them and treat them as a commodity. Often referred to as modern slaves, workers have tight constrictions imposed on them in the workplace with immense pressure to maximise production to keep their jobs and satisfy the demands of the corporation.

The Noble Eightfold Path of the Buddha can serve as a guideline for the ethical behaviour of a company/business/corporation since every link supports every other link to ensure the integration of ethics, mindfulness and wisdom. Every link has an ethical component to it.

The application of:

1. *Right Understanding*
2. *Right Intention*
3. *Right Speech*
4. *Right Action*
5. *Right Livelihood*
6. *Right Effort*
7. *Right Mindfulness*
8. *Right Concentration*

Coupled with the other links, right mindfulness ensures the health of the company based on a depth of inquiry leading to governance through wisdom. In the USA and other nations, the state treats a corporation legally as a person such as in the right to possess property and to pay taxes. This means that the application of responsibility applies to the entire corporation, as a person, as much as to the CEOs, directors, and employees.

The basis for personal behaviour of the corporation needs inner development, reflection and a meaningful education from the first grade of school to the end of university studies. Desire, obsession with competition and blind pursuit of profit obstructs the willingness to sit down and address every link in Noble Path, so that everybody, from CEO's to the lowly paid, can address the shortcomings of the company. The Buddha offered a Path of transformation, so business leaders and employees realise they have wider responsibilities than aiming for and keeping massive profit margins.

The Buddha pinpointed the desire and determination to get one's way as a major cause for suffering. He reminded the rich and powerful of the corruption due to greed and its impact on society. He knew that the super-wealthy often escaped punishment for their behaviour. The Buddha employed the language of right intention, right action and right livelihood as well as speaking of the power of the people to censure the corrupt, to hold the corrupt accountable and take steps to make changes. Compelling desires and aggression also affect the mind of the poor and needy when there is a lack of charity (*dana*) to support their daily needs.

In the Buddha's era, those who engaged in violence, exploitation, plundering, theft, sexual abuse, paedophilia, and financial manipulation faced the death penalty. They might have gotten away with a lighter sentence, namely having all their property and wealth confiscated or they faced banishment from the cities and towns (MN i 87; DN I 52; SN iv 349; AN I 154).

Those on trial appeared before the Officers of Justice. The King consulted these Officers on the punishment for monks who ordained army deserters (Vin I 74.4). King Pasenadi of Kosala expressed his frustration to the Buddha at the lies and deceptions stated in the courts by Brahmins, the rich and the powerful, as well as various witnesses (SN I 174).

As with our courts today, citizens are not equal under the law. A poor man who killed a goat to eat for his family could end up in prison or be flogged while the butcher would have to beg a rich man to pay him for the goat or return it (AN i250 -253).

The influential American economist, Milton Friedman (1912–2006), a staunch supporter of corporate capitalism, claimed that corporate executives have the responsibility to "make as much money as possible while conforming to the basic rules of the society." This well-known statement continues to influence corporate thinking, as if a corporation had an enclosed self-existence with minimal regard for the local and global consequences of their actions.

Corporations appear motivated to get away with whatever they can. They worship at the altar of profit. Major corporations continue to accumulate vast profits. Profits run into billions of $$$ through tax avoidance, exploitation of workers, overpricing of goods and services.

The Institute of Business Ethics in the U.K. believes that an organisation cannot be genuinely "responsible without an embedded and inherent culture that is based on ethical values such as trust, openness, respect and integrity." These are fine statements which would need a radical change in perception, values and attitudes in the world of big business. There is no sign of such an embedded culture in our corporations. A small modification in corporate behaviour only occurs through an intensity of concerted and continuous public pressure. Big corporations have become too powerful. They cause too much harm and suffering. They need to be broken up.

Teachings from the East enter the Marketplace

Drawing on teachings from India and the Far East, the practical philosophies of the Buddhist, Taoist and Yoga traditions have entered into the market place but at a heavy cost: namely major changes in the DNA of these ancient teachings. Corporations select suitable aspects of these teachings that do not threaten the fundamental politics of the business.

Businesses have come to believe that selective /psychology/mindfulness courses can fill the void in the lives of their stressed office workers. This brand of spiritual practices circumvents the practices for radical change within the set-up and structures of a corporation. For example, corporations show no interest to develop the noble eightfold path. The corporate world endorses practices that offer the feel-good factor. Meaningful change in governments, businesses and society starts to take place when people experience strongly the 'not feel good' factor about a critical issue. Then the people in power sit up and take notice or face a rebellion on their hands when citizens and employees start to express their concerns and pursue a different agenda.

Regardless of income, many office workers have become tired of the tyranny of the constant striving to achieve goals and targets set by their bosses. Company psychologists have long since realised that if management and office workers enjoy together an environment of reduced personal stress, then inner resistance and office conflicts will reduce. Staff will have more energy available to concentrate on the aims of the bosses.

Workshops on the inner life enable the staff to get in touch with their 'spiritual side' through attending company sponsored courses and workshops, with the emphasis on the self of the individual, rather than abusive self of the company. The privatised self in the office ensures reduction of criticism of employers, since workshop leaders will point out that finding fault with the corporation shows a reactive and judgemental mind. Employees then think: "My criticism of the corporation is my negative mind. It is all my unresolved stuff." Such modes of thought and speech confirm the privatisation of the self in the office.

The language of psychology and mindfulness then functions as a means of suppression of freedom of speech, of Orwellian style thought control. The staff fears to speak up especially if they practise being in the here and now without sounding judgemental. Self-mastery over thought and speech easily ends up contracting the inner life to a pleasing, submissive state of being rather than freeing up the voice to have the willingness to question authority. The current approach suits the business agenda since those who engage in such activities show little or no inspiration to question the ethics, value and policies of their employers. Employers only want to reduce stress so that staff relax and enjoy themselves without so much reliance on alcohol and drugs, both recreational and prescribed. It is the equivalent of dancing on the Titanic with a huge iceberg penetrating the ship.

Limbs of Awakening

The Buddha referred regularly to the seven limbs of awakening:

- *Mindfulness*
- *Inquiry/reflection/investigation/inner and outer*
- *Happiness*
- *Calmness*
- *Meditative Concentration*
- *Energy*

- *Equanimity*

All seven limbs in the body of the teachings and practices (the *Dharma*) support each other while businesses show a noticeable absence of any real wish to inquiry/reflection/investigation/introspection into their practices, yet corporations approve of the other six limbs!

Psychology/mindfulness teachers find themselves welcomed into the corporate world providing that they exclude the second limb of inquiry into the body politic of the corporation. Corporate leaders can subsume the other six limbs to increase corporate goals and simultaneously reduce stress. This has little to do with the goal of an enlightened way of living but confirms an unenlightened approach to the end of stress and suffering.

There is a dark underworld in far too many powerful businesses that stays excluded from comprehensive mindfulness and inquiry. Some of these corporations have hired secretive intelligence firms collaborating with government intelligence agencies to spy on non-profit organisations, groups and activists. Corporations will send an observer to attend company workshops and report to the bosses whether the facilitator engages with staff in inquiry in any areas of questionable corporate practice. Facilitators, who dare to mention business ethics, will find the corporation politely declines to make further invitations to the facilitator to lead workshops.

The Centre for Corporate Policy (CCP) in Washington, D.C., says that corporations spy particularly often on environmental activists, though this is not an exclusive focus. This corporate abuse of power undermines democracy and the important work of non-profit organisations. Activists and whistle blowers campaign for social and environmental justice, as well as trying to hold corporations accountable for violent and corrupt practices.

If an office member had an authentic awakening, then that company would hear a free-spirited voice engaging with staff and bosses in an inquiry into such areas as ethics, karma, ego, greed, competition, control, pollution, generosity, the goals of an enlightened business community and truth. The potential for an enlightened business community is there but, without such motivation to question, nothing can develop. It is no wonder that insightful Buddhists have emphasised for 2600 years the importance of motivation and the freedom to enquire.

With few exceptions, teachers/facilitators working in corporations seem to lack the motivation to address all the seven limbs of awakening.

Yet, facilitators offer genuine benefits to officer workers with much evidence, based on people's experiences, to confirm significant levels of stress reduction. The benefits contribute to a certain level of inner peace and harmony in and out of the office. But the benefits do not go deep enough. Some of the benefits from psychology/mindfulness workshops for staff include:

- *A calm abiding reducing reaction and angry outbursts*
- *A greater ability to negotiate decisions*
- *A relaxed atmosphere*
- *A willingness to be vulnerable*
- *A willingness to listen*
- *Application of exercises, such as mindfully breathing in and out to relax*
- *Development of new friendships and empathy for the difficulties of others*
- *Less gossip, less backbiting, less distortion of statements*
- *More energy and creativity*
- *Mindfulness of speech, including tone, attitude and content*
- *One minute of silent meditation at the beginning and end of a meeting*
- *Reduction in caffeine. Stimulants and hurried eating*
- *Reduction in levels of control and its shadow of fear*
- *Reduction of stress*

Businesses might conclude that they do not need any more for their staff than the bullet points listed above. They might not see that the above developments just scratch the surface of true well-being. Through co-operation, staff can apply together wisdom and compassion to every aspect of policy.

There is a need for

- *reduction of the wage differential between the highest and lowest paid,*

- *frequent examination of ethics of the products and services,*
- *use of materials and impact on the environment and animals.*

The heads of business would give priority to an ethical and enlightened company with a willingness to reduce the profit margin and endless desire to grow the business to develop in that direction.

Depth of Inquiry

We endure reading or listening to absurd claims and a huge amount of hype from certain leaders in the world of mind/body and spirit. To take one example of naivety: in the closing sentence of his introduction of *Practicing the Power of Now,* Eckhart Tolle, a well-known spiritual teacher in the West wrote: "It is inner stillness that will save and transform the world."

How does inner stillness resolve differences in perceptions, views and vision of varying groups of people? Discussion, listening, inquiry, love and motivation serve as some of the basics for a resolution. Human beings resolve their differences and misunderstanding through negotiation. Surely Eckhart Tolle does not imagine that two people, a team of facilitators, a group engaged in negotiation, diplomats or presidents/prime ministers of nation states or corporate leaders and environmentalists, simply sit in stillness as an answer to disputes, conflicts, wars and climate change. Does he imagine they will all agree if everyone speaks from stillness? How will that guarantee wise action when thoughtful people still have different perceptions of the way forward?

Sadly, these so called enlightened teachers, their methodologies and those who market them, have failed to engage in a collective investigation into any exploitation of big business of people and environment, let alone transform the consciousness of the boards of directors. There appears to be no evidence to show any depth of inquiry leading to real transformation of any big business. For a start, the inquiry would have to address:

- *Ethics*
- *Redistribution of income*
- *International co-operation to safeguard the Earth for present and future generations*
- *Making things last, sustainability and recycling*

- *Workers' rights to address salaries, working hours, health, safety and holidays*
- *Inquiry in the workplace of any abuse, harassment or discrimination.*

Without inquiry, we cannot expect people to take real steps forward for the resolution of suffering brought about by corporate greed, violence upon people, animals and the earth and the delusion inherent in ambitious businesses. A small but growing number of mindfulness teachers take risks to bring mindfulness and inquiry to the work environment. At times, these teachers must face rejection. They are the exceptions to a submissive, cap in hand, mentality. One mindfulness teacher in Europe wrote to me:

"The two bosses asked me to work for them in corporate training as a mindfulness teacher. After they showed me their concepts, I started to ask quite a lot of questions. They just wanted to sell 'mindfulness' as a new inspiration to their business clients.

"I got them to reflect on their intentions and I could see how they started to feel affected by my questions. I asked them if they really want to support the very sick system (especially in large companies) any longer.

"Mindfulness can come along only with roots in ethics and values for wholesome intention. I said I can teach these topics, but only if the whole training concept will address inquiry.

"These two guys became increasingly silent. Somehow, I had the feeling you have been just sitting next to me. It was a bit like a Dharma talk. I left the meeting with a satisfied sense. I am sure, something touched them, and it will make a difference in the future."

The two bosses did not get back in touch with the mindfulness teacher. In my reply to her, I wrote: *"Do not put yourself out of a work opportunity by being too direct, too early. You can explore ethics (sometimes the word 'values' sounds easier on the corporate ear) in your workshops."*

A US teacher of mindfulness said in an article in her e-News: *"I feel strongly that Dharma teachers must not distort the path by pandering to the fickle desires of the marketplace or settle for the fragments of mental development that can be measured by researchers."*

A mindfulness teacher in Germany wrote to me: *"Mindfulness is particularly requested and used in the business sector as an efficiency-enhancing tool. Mindfulness for me is no module for performance enhancement in the rat* race. Mindfulness is part of a cultural change in a company. I would like to make my work available for companies who wish to promote the development of the individual and society."

It is these voices that matter. They express the voice for real charge. Such facilitators show a willingness to address the very thorny issue of ethics, values and responsibility. These voices contribute to an empowerment of employers and employees to examine every area of business life in mindful and sensitive ways.

Corporate Consumerism and the Buddha Dharma

Corporations or spiritual coaches will invite respected Tibetan lamas, Thai Ajahns, Zen Masters, Taoist adepts, Indian gurus and charismatic Western teachers of Eastern teachings to visit corporations' head offices to add a little mystique to the company and their products. The market consultants can then sell a company or product as having an exotic image. We find Buddha images in the offices of corporations with questionable business practices.

The Dharma offers a different world view from exploitive political/corporate/capitalist/pharmaceutical/media/religious/spiritual and educational institutions driven by self-interest.

Thoughtful citizens then have choices to make. Here are some examples:

- *A Political, Party or Non-Party Politics/Social Justice*
- *Being in the Now or Inquiry into Suffering*
- *Competition or Cooperation*
- *Consumerism or Sustainability*
- *Hierarchy of Power or Networks for Change*
- *Individuality or a Collective Active*
- *Pursuit of Wealth or Sharing Benefits*
- *Self-Interest or People/Animals/Nature*
- *Privatisation or Public Responsibility*
- *Pursuit of Status or Seeing the Emptiness of Egotism*
- *Stress Reduction or Stress Destruction*
- *Sleep Walking through Life or an Awakened Life*

- *Self-Compassion or Compassion without Limits.*

Governments and corporation are part of the crisis on Earth, not part of the cure. Our institutions often seem like a helpless baby who has not even learnt to crawl, let alone stand up and walk the Path of Awakening. Like babies in a pram, they clutch at attractive things in the material world regardless of the cost. If they could find an inner depth and empathy for people of all ages, they might launch a passionate interest in an expansive vision. The release of such passion would encourage citizens to explore:

- *The Nature of Desire*
- *Causality*
- *Emptiness of I, Me and Mine*
- *Inquiry into Our Relationship with People, Animals or Environment*
- *Sustainability of Resources*
- *Right Livelihood*
- *Right Action and Results*
- *Love and Liberation*

Working with Stress

There is widespread appreciation in the medical profession for the way the daily practises of mindfulness reduce stress in the body/mind process. These practices truly work for many. MBSR (Mindfulness Based Stress Reduction) trainers and their clients can offer evidence of the benefits of mindfulness to improve health and mental well-being. MBSR courses have changed the attitude and outlook of people's lives.

It is a different story in terms of mindfulness in the business world. The reduction of stress in the office certainly has much merit, but there is no parallel evidence to show that mindfulness courses have changed the attitude and outlook of a single corporation. These business workshops offer no challenge whatsoever to the impact of corporate control upon the people and the Earth. The Faustian Pact of corporate/consumer ideology threatens all sentient beings.

Activists, campaigners, dissenters, critiques and polemics continue to offer the strongest voices for change to the corporate empire.

Thoughtful people apply their skills out of passion and conviction to support life on Earth and to transform the culture of corporate consumerism. Campaigners put an immense amount of time, energy and resources to team together in order to put real pressure on governments and corporations to change their behaviour.

Workshop leaders working with business men and women also need to develop the inner empowerment to inquire deeply into corporate values. Mindfulness courses need to expand the vision to address institution problems not just personal stress in the workplace. There is the sickness of greed and aggression in capitalism. Have courses, workshop and programmes become another marketable product to avoid challenging business ethics and policies?

The First Question to Address Ethics

For example, inquiry can begin with a simple explicit question: *"Are there any actions in this corporation that cause harm, or the outcome of which is harmful?* Once the facilitator raises such a question, then ethics and mindfulness/psychology have a relationship.

This principle does not apply to people seeking support from mindfulness programmes in such places as clinics and hospitals to deal with their depression, anxiety and physical pain. Mindfulness teachers offer practical tools to reduce patients and clients level of stress. Some mindfulness teachers stay truly dedicated to public service. We must make a very clear distinction between such important developments in the West for the application of mindfulness and the neutered forms of mindfulness offered in far too many large corporations.

Entrenched in a conservative view, workshops for business offer a safe, non-challenging approach rather than serve as a spearhead for change. These workshops and conferences on inner change function as a useful appendix to corporate strategies for self-promotion. Corporations need to sit up and take notice of the Buddha's noble eightfold path and his encouragement to question authority and investigate harmful belief systems. Mindfulness/psychology functions like a trendy product that corporations have hooked onto, enabling them to continue unfettered consumption with a mindful, happy public face. Workshop leaders need to ask themselves whether corporate bosses exploit their skills to make staff malleable to various goals.

The skilful use of language enables a transmission of a wide body of teachings without over simplification. There is the danger of offering a narrow teaching when facilitators repeat, ad nausea, the importance of being in the here and now, as if nothing else mattered. There is even a widespread belief that the Buddha primarily taught being in the now as the path and goal of practice. It is far from the truth.

The Buddha never gave teachings to be *here and now* a very loose translation from the Pali of *ditthe dhamme*. *Ditthe* means *view* and *dhamme* refers to Dharma, namely everything we view. *Ditthe* does not mean *here* and *dhamme* does not mean *now*. The Buddha told people to view what arises and resolve the suffering with what arises.

Religious Beliefs

Real change comes through going deep into the collective psychological structures and policies. This approach shows a mature responsibility.

There is a moral imperative to investigate life. The factory and the office provide a supportive environment for those with questioning minds. We need genuine networks of mindful people working together with equal emphasis on inner and outer change.

A liberating wisdom confirms itself through our capacity to work with others, develop together the skills to create change and the capacity to stay steady in the face of events.

9. THE PRIVATISATION OF SPIRITUALITY

Go into any major bookstore in the High Street, browse bookshelves at airports. Look online. You will see a wide variety of books for sale on spirituality/mindfulness/psychology/mind/body and spirit tailored for businesses. Numerous leaders/coaches/facilitators and teachers in these fields offer a range of courses/workshops/retreats and training programmes for business leaders/ management/marketing consultants/sales staff and office workers.

Books for businesses like to adopt spiritual themes from the East including relaxation, meditation, mindfulness, loving kindness, the sharing of experiences and being in the present moment. Some books simply have a spiritual title with little or no reference to spiritual inquiry in the text. You must read the book to see whether the title and content bear any real relationship to each other. Here are the titles of some of the books available:

- *Business and Spirituality. Exploring Possibilities for a New Management Paradigm*
- *Climb a Different Ladder. Self-Awareness, Mindfulness and Successful Leadership*
- *Coming to our Senses. Healing Ourselves and the World Through Mindfulness*
- *Creating Affluence*
- *How to Apply Mindfulness to Business Relationships*
- *Mindfulness at Work. How to Avoid Stress, Achieve More and Enjoy Life*
- *Spirituality in Business: The Hidden Success Factor*
- *Spirituality in Business: Theory, Practice and Future Directions*
- *Starting a Spiritual Business*
- *The Invisible Hand: Business, Success and Spirituality*
- *The Palgrave Handbook of Spirituality and Business*
- *The Seven Spiritual Laws of Success*
- *The Tao of Business*
- *The Tao of Leadership*

- *The Tao of Sales*
- *The Tao of Trading*
- *The Tao of Warren Buffett*
- *Zen Entrepreneurship. Walking the Path of the Career Warrior*
- *Zen of Business Administration*
- *Zen of Social, Media, Marketing*

At home and abroad, low paid office staff/factory workers/cleaners/truck drivers, chauffeurs and others stay excluded from the benefits of these spiritual programmes, even though stress affects all employees from top to bottom.

Common causes for stress for corporate employees include

- *demands to achieve production targets,*
- *Pressure for punctual deliveries,*
- *Bullying,*
- *Harassment*
- *Blame*
- *Threats to fire*
- *Claims of staff wasting company time*

Poor working environments include

- *Too hot or too cold temperatures in the work place,*
- *A crowded factory floor,*
- *Poor seating,*
- *Standing/sitting for prolonged periods,*
- *Poor lighting,*
- *Handling of chemicals,*
- *Use of dangerous equipment,*
- *Unsafe mining, as well as low hourly rates,*
- *Build up increasing levels of stress for employees*

The CEOs, directors and management working in comfortable, spacious offices, with temperature control, on a substantial salary with large bonuses, do not experience many of the causes for stress of the lowly paid, nor care about it. Corporations run like the ancient Indian caste system with the Brahmins claiming all the privileges at the expense of the lowly paid who become the outcaste, the untouchables and the undeserving poor. Stress reduction programmes and spiritual workshops remain the exclusive right of the privileged.

GM (genetically modified) crops and corporate spirituality share a common strategy. GM crops drive out the essential ingredients that support our eco-system and the natural relationship between fields with crops and the local habitat. Similarly, corporations promote a GM brand of spirituality. They drive out the essential ingredients that support the opportunity for everyone for awakening and transformation, while making claims of the profound benefits engineered to meet the corporations' goals. This is the pick-and-choose mentality – regardless of the cost to people and our eco-system.

The privatisation of spirituality in business targets individuals in the office so that they can relax at work, get on with others, and see all problems as personal. An individual working exclusively on herself or himself will not see the causes and conditions for stress, conflict and exploitation in the policies and structure of the company and their treatment of the workers. The privatisation of spirituality lets corporations off the hook. Outside the business world, we see the same privatisation of spirituality in self-help programmes. Authentic spirituality addresses both together, the inner and the outer life, the personal and the public, the one and the many, the person and the surrounding culture.

What does spirituality mean?

There appears to be no underlying definition. You can make it mean whatever you want it to mean. The dictionary tells us that "spirituality" relates to the human spirit or soul as opposed to the material world. We can ask the same question. What does that mean? Others may define spirituality as the search for or the sense of the sacred. What does that mean while working in the office? Others see spirituality as sensitivity, values and respect for the ordinary. Others see the spiritual as a code of ethics or a sense of oneness. Some define spirituality as a certain personal experience deeper than pleasurable sensations. Spirituality is thus an ideal concept suitable for corporate individuals who wish to find some meaning in their life while being slaves to the office. A spiritual sense of life can blossom when a materialistic relationship to life has less significance.

Has the time come to give a sharp and inclusive definition to spirituality? The definition would liberate spirituality from the privatisation of a special experience for the self. For example, we could say that 'spirituality' means:

> *The application of ethics, mindfulness and wisdom, inwardly and outwardly.*

A three-fold definition of ethics, mindfulness and wisdom would contribute to a profound exploration of the legal person called the corporation. Spirituality would then be an instrumental tool in opening Pandora's Box. The dark underworld of certain powerful corporations would enter the consciousness of the body of the corporation. It would mark the end of the gloss, smug and self-cherishing picture that certain corporations have of themselves. They would realise the harm and suffering they inflict on people, animals and the Earth. Businesses would have to make root and branch changes to their policies.

Spirituality has become compliant with the view of an inner experience of the self. This prevents spirituality from expanding to include ethics and wisdom. If so, there is little point in the application of the concept. Karl Marx famously referred to religion as the opiate of the people. We can make the same point today about spirituality. It becomes the opiate of the middle classes.

GM spirituality has become a supplementary industry, an appendix to corporations to promote brand image, increase market share and support the objectives of corporations. Such spirituality for business neglects to draw deeply and expansively from the long history of profound spiritual traditions and the spiritual/religious communities that have evolved.

We need to demand that corporations show respect to their community of workers worldwide and to the impact of corporate policies on rural and urban communities. For example, the major GM seed producers, such as Monsanto (USA), Du Pont (USA) and Syngenta (Switzerland), persuade farmers to be dependent on their agri-business which weakens self-supporting communities. These corporations sell GM seeds that survive for a season, so farmers then must buy seeds from the corporation for the next season. This seed production effectively controls farmers and keeps control over the kind of crops available, while turning organic life into IPR (Intellectual Property Rights) of the corporation.

GM spirituality has little to do with the goal of an enlightened way of living but confirms an unenlightened approach to spirituality. There is a dark underworld in powerful businesses that mindfulness leaders need to address rather than ignore.

For example, some of the world's corporations, governments and political parties hire private and clandestine intelligence firms and collaborated with government intelligence agencies to spy on non-profit organisations, groups and activists. The Centre for Corporate Policy in Washington, D.C. says that as many as one in four activists could be spies for corporations. This corporate abuse of power undermines democracy and the important work of non-profit organisations and activists campaigning for social and environmental justice. Organisations, campaigning journalists and whistle-blowers endeavour to hold accountable, corrupt practices of corporations.

Corporations will collect information about workshops to report whether the facilitator engages with staff in inquiry in any areas of questionable corporate practice. Facilitators, who dare to mention ethics, will find the corporation politely ends any further invitations to lead workshops.

A small but growing number of influential voices within the corporate world recognise that something seriously is amiss in corporate policies, structures, and belief systems with all its harmful consequences. These thoughtful advocates know the necessity of a major root and branch change so that corporations live respectfully for the welfare of society and the environment. Though currently very rare, these voices point to a radical change in values and vision.

We need to give them every encouragement to speak up against the ongoing policies that ride roughshod over people, infrastructure and habitats. Spellbound by their selfish policies, corporations consistently live in denial of the harm they cause. These advocates know the difference between the willingness to develop a spiritual awareness of inter-connectedness and superficial public relation exercises. The Buddha's message to the powerful that live in delusion is simple. "WAKE UP!"

Promises. Promises. Promises

In the past 50 years, we have had countless promises that spiritual /psychological practices/explorations would change the consciousness of countless numbers of citizens and organisations, from the lowly paid factory and office workers to the CEOs. These approaches towards change include:

- *Advaita (Non-duality)*
- *Buddhism*
- *Emotional Intelligence*
- *Humanistic Psychology*
- *Insight Meditation*
- *MBSR (Mindfulness Based Stress Reduction)*
- *Meditation*
- *Mindfulness (various forms)*
- *NLP (Neuro-linguistic Programming)*
- *Non-violent Communication*
- *Taoism*
- *Transcendental Meditation (TM)*
- *Vipassana (as in Buddhist monasteries)*
- *Yoga*
- *Zen*

Numerous influential corporate voices report that they have received help from reading the books of various spiritual teachers. Many have attended the public talks, workshops or retreats of teachers speaking about the transformation of consciousness. These corporate leaders listened to their teachings on a DVD or watched them on YouTube. The old patterns/habits/karma, however, seem to carry on in much the same way with profit and power still at the forefront of consciousness of the corporation.

In the past 50 years, the popular spiritual teachers/psychologists/religious leaders in the Anglo-American corporate world include:

- *Abraham Maslo*
- *B.F. Skinner*

- *Daniel Goleman*
- *Deepak Chopra*
- *Carl Rogers*
- *Carl Jung*
- *Eric Erikson*
- *Eckhart Tolle*
- *JB Watson*
- *Jon Kabat-Zinn*
- *Ken Wilber*
- *Krishnamurti*
- *Osho*
- *Thich Nhat Hanh*

These approaches, spiritual and psychological, have generated waves of interest, rising and falling, until they find their natural place in the flow of things. All look to bring awareness into daily life, both in the office and at home. Some influential voices, like B.F. Skinner and J.B. Watson, had considerable influence on business for years despite their methods and their conclusions. We still wait for signals of a revolutionary change of attitude encompassed in spiritual values based on co-operation rather than exploitation.

Spiritual movements have the potential to be an active force for change. An enlightened approach campaigns for real change. This needs insight, courage, risk taking, initiatives, vision and a commitment to policies stating the necessary changes needed. Spiritual and religious leaders of all faiths tend to speak in generalities, rather than name in clear specific terms the greed, violence and delusion among powerful political and businesses leaders. The co-operation of social media and political analysists has a significant impact on influencing the way people think and vote.

Spiritual leaders appear to have gone along with GM spirituality with its emphasis on confining spirituality to certain kinds of inner experience, bearing no active relationship to the policies of the corporation or the world that we inhabit. It may not even occur to spiritual teachers that they have submitted to the privatisation of the self at the expense of radical change, near and far, that points to a liberated and compassionate way of life.

The public sector might seem to be a more constructive avenue to express something spiritual. Many of those in the public-sector work for the common good – despite modest income, media attacks, fear of redundancy and regular salary/pension cutbacks, even for the lowest paid workers. Education, health care, local government, public services, transport, media, police, the judiciary and the millions of supporting charities, foundations and non-governmental organisations work for the welfare of people, animals and the environment. Committed to providing a public service, many people in the public sector, express something spiritual about their values.

High levels of stress exist in the public sector as well, hospitals, schools, clinics, prisons and local/national offices of governing bodies. Pressure arises due to efforts to achieve targets. Doctors and nurses may have to perform a certain number of operations per day. They may have to see many patients per day or offer appointments within a certain period, no matter how many requests there are from patients. Stress also arises through the restraints of tight financial budgets and insufficient equipment that needs urgent repairs or modernisation. With such pressure, staff can lose the sense of offering a compassionate service and feel like automatons running from one task to another. Many of the same thoughtful people may be suspicious of being identified with the spiritual since spirituality often sounds vague, wish-washy and other worldly.

A key feature of spirituality includes forms of service for the welfare of others.

Religious Beliefs

It is unfortunate that a superficial spirituality has become yet another brand label covering up the deep issues of love and transformation, as well as the search for meaning and connection. There is a deception here though. Spirituality finds itself trapped in the self. Self-help, self-confidence, self-inquiry, self-improvement, self-esteem, self-love, self-realization, and self-compassion… Such explorations may offer immense benefit. We can keep the hand on the centre of our chest for periods of self-healing.

Yet, we must not forget that self, self, self increasingly creates distance from the outer. These programmes of the privatized world of spirituality rarely generate outer change that contributes to so much personal suffering. It is hard to find any evidence of social change through any one of these self-help programmes. We need a genuine Sangha of mindful people working simultaneously for inner-outer change.

Narrow Expressions of Spirituality

Owing to the misinterpretation of the Eastern traditions, enlightenment then refers to a state of mind having an experience of *Being, Oneness or the Now*. The 19th century Anglo-German period of poets and Romanticism made much reference to these experiences. A person who has an experience of *Being, Oneness* or the *Now* may honestly believe that he or she has reached the final goal of full enlightenment. Enlightenment refers to deep inquiry, fundamental change and an emancipating vision. We know an enlightened life through her or his actions, not through a single experience or state of mind.

GM spirituality supports such views which actively discourage deeper inquiry. Teachers of narrow expressions of spirituality tend to treat thought as the primary hindrance to enlightenment; hence, naïve practitioners exclude a thoughtful analysis of harmful social/corporate/political policies.

Stress certainly appears from excessive thinking but to react against thought, making thought the villain; this shows violence against thought. These same spiritual gurus tell us to go beyond thought, beyond the mind and abide in *Being*. This is what spiritual leaders say because of what they think! Wisdom recognises the value of thought, of skilful reflection. Wisdom discerns beneficial thought from problematic thought. Wisdom does not reject all thought.

These experiences of *Being, Oneness, the Now* have a value in offering some expansion of consciousness and change in perception. These experiences come and go. They can become goals, which have no direct bearing on a liberated wisdom. They become forms of psychological imprisonment through the chasing after or grasping onto such unitive kinds of experiences. Elevation of these temporary experiences into an ultimate reality inhibits inquiry into action, love and wisdom. We need a wise and compassionate response to the suffering that our primary institutions cause. This response matters far more than the desire to rest in the experience of so called *Being*, the *Now* or Oneness.

Seven examples to show the limits of Being, The now and Oneness:

1. *If Being always stays the same and is the only ultimate and true reality, then there is no point in any kind of action since it would make no difference.*
2. *If Being reveals itself as everything changing, there would be no point in doing anything because everything is changing anyway.*
3. *If there is Being which always stays the same and, simultaneously, there is constant change, then what is it that always stays the same and what is it that changes?*
4. *If Oneness always remains the same and is the ultimate and true reality, then there is no point in action since action makes no difference to Oneness.*
5. *If Oneness reveals itself as everything changing, there would be no point in action since every outcome would change.*
6. *If the Now always stays the same and is the ultimate reality, then there is no point in action, since actions will not make any difference.*
7. *If the Now is the only Truth and the Real, then memory and plans become false and unreal. There is no point in reflection on the past or making plans.*
8. *If the Now includes the past and views of the future, and everything else, there is no point in doing anything because it is all in the Now.*

The grasping onto *Being, Oneness or the Now* lends itself to passivity, submission and blind acceptance. The reliance on *such experiences* for awakening rejects the necessity of the non-acceptance of greed, violence and delusion. The ability to rest in *Being* constrains wise action. There is no authentic relationship of Truth to *Being* since seeing the Truth of a situation makes possible new eventualities.

Being in the Now or feeling at one with everything becomes a habitual condition of a mind that resists change. Liberating truth sets the course for fresh happenings. The adoption of the spiritual viewpoint of resting in *Being* or the *Now* reveals already a lack of inquiry into the Dharma of unfolding processes. Those who grasp onto such experiences as the ultimate reality show an unwillingness to make judgments resulting in a failure to act to make radical changes, inwardly and outwardly. The judgment of non-judgment shows naivety in the name of spirituality. Such views perpetuate suffering and do not resolve suffering.

The Secularisation of Spirituality

Secularism places priority on the absence of religious and spiritual practices. A purely secular culture places emphasis on science, education, career, money, personal success, obeying laws and public service. There is an absence of the spiritual, mystical and transcendent in secularism. An authentic spirituality explores deep experiences outside the norms of secularism. Transformative insights offer a dedication to a non-violent and non-exploitive way of life free from submission to the powers of the nation state. There is a growing interest among a small percentage of people in secular culture to the opening up of consciousness, to develop alternative ways of living, meditative depths and to realise a meaningful existence.

Orthodox secular spirituality often rejects the religious life of monks, nuns and priests, as if they had no relevance in contemporary society. Some people see the religious life as the best opportunity to develop wisdom and live a noble way of life. We need to appreciate their calling to ordination, not undermine their renunciation of secularism. If we are hostile to religion, then we, who have moved away from religion, need to ask ourselves (in alphabetical order):

- *Are we changing these ancient teachings to maximise personal popularity?*
- *Do we believe that there is no baggage in secular spirituality?*
- *Do we believe that we never suppress our desires?*
- *Do we claim that we teach without baggage?*
- *Do we water down teachings leading to awakening?*
- *Do we feel let down by religion?*
- *Do we put down people of faith to build up our sense of self-worth?*
- *Do we reject offering teachings on a donation basis?*
- *Do we, the teachers of spirituality, use spirituality to develop a career?*

- *Do we think religious people are naïve?*
- *Do we think secular teachers abide with clarity?*
- *Do we, the spiritual teachers, charge exorbitant fees for our teachings?*
- *Do we realise high fees for workshops and retreats turns people off spirituality?*

We express concerns about the militant voices of religious fundamentalists in all the major faiths, East and West. We can also express equal concern about liberals. With their lack of passionate conviction, the liberal minded spiritual/religious intelligentsia spend far too much time living in ambiguous perceptions and indecisive views. They inhibit the movement towards profound change as much as the fundamentalists. The position of the liberally minded intelligentsia has little to offer to the way of real change.

They keep to a climate of silence on consumerism or offer unhelpful views such as: "It could be like this or it could be like that." The Buddha described such liberals as 'eel wrigglers' since they want to wriggle out of any dispute with authority. Far too many liberals seem to have trained their minds to say little with passionate conviction. Western Buddhism attracts many such liberals. Agnostics can show a humble attitude in admitting not to experience a response to the deep issues of life yet. It would be a pity though to give up on inquiry and settle for the norms of secular conventions.

There is often a terror of saying anything that might remotely appear to be controversial. The desire to please others obstructs a clear, unambiguous view about the causes and conditions for suffering. Right View, the first link in the Noble Eightfold Path of the Buddha, matters. Fearful of sounding judgemental, far too many Buddhists express little in the way of real concerns about some of the critical issues of our time, such as climate change, survival of our species, the world refugee crisis and the never-ending wars. They fear to state that certain governments, corporations or powerful figures need censure. Spiritual practitioners experience some resistance of sounding judgemental. The Buddha disagreed with a passive response. He encouraged those who have examined a situation to speak up and to offer thoughtful criticism of harmful actions.

Agents of change in the Buddhist world increase but very slowly. Western Buddhism belongs to the selfie culture.

We might think that the Buddha said the first link of the Path is No View or Wishy-Washy View. Some liberals would rather the planet died than allow themselves to speak up with passion and conviction and reveal their flawed humanity. Religious fundamentalists and liberals advocating spiritual practices and insights, have little to offer in the way of making changes to the political/corporate ideologies that cast a dark shadow over our daily lives.

Some secular Buddhists in the West show little regard for Buddhist monks and nuns even though these secularists have no experience whatsoever of the life as a monk, nun or priest in the West. The ordained Buddhists face daily challenges to maintain an austere way of life with little understanding from consumer culture. Monasteries, ashrams, churches and synagogues have a vital function in our culture.

The Sanghas of the faithful, of believers in religion, often work to support each other, the local community and organise supportive programmes for those who suffer. We need the wise counsel of those who have renounced much of the material world to concentrate on spiritual/religions matters including service to others. Proponents of GM spirituality need to examine their prejudices against monks, nuns, priests, rabbis and people of faith. We need to develop the humility to learn from the wisdom available in such religious traditions.

The shadows of religions, including Buddhism, show in patriarchy, narrow-minded views, resistance to change and intolerance. We have the same shadows in secularism. For example, certain influential monks with far-right views in Myanmar reveal prejudice and deep-seated aversion towards the Muslim community in the country. They contributed to making the life of 700,000 Muslims unbearable.

Corporate Cathedrals

Major corporations build huge business cathedrals for self-glorification with opulent splendour stretching up into the sky, while their executives look down from the top floors on churches, mosques, synagogues, monasteries and the civic society. The Church has sold off unused churches to the business world to convert into nightclubs, bars, pubs, coffee shops and markets. Money has become a form of the holy communion to gain access to the churches of shopping malls, supermarkets and online sales.

The desire to increase the number of goods confirms the mental sickness of our age focussing around the desires of the self. The ending of one desire gives rise to another desire. There is a relentless pressure to gain, to succeed and to possess. This is a collective pathology. Corporations, governments and citizens live in the spell of this life destroying mentality. The following are core questions that spiritual leaders could ask business leaders/management running businesses accumulating vast wealth:

WHEN WOULD YOU SAY?

- *Are we addicted to profit and success?*
- *Do we suffer from a mental dis-ease?*
- *Enough is enough.*
- *Our business has lost its way*
- *Desire, greed and exploitation occupy the mind*
- *We have let down our workers and our customers?*
- *We have produced enough of these products?*
- *We overcharge for our products*
- *What is the point working in these corporate cathedrals?*
- *What would it mean to bring a spiritual revolution to our entire business?*

The world of religion/spirituality/mindfulness/psychology has failed to question the unhealthy attitudes and lifestyles of our corporate popes and cardinals. The belief in the Church of Consumerism shows a serious degree of delusion that requires urgent spiritual and psychological treatment. This belief in consumerism sustains violence upon people and resources. We can hold corporate leaders accountable as well as governments who support their greed.

The Shadow of Businesses over Western Retreat Centres and Western monasteries

To an alarming degree, the pursuit of profit by business controls every aspect of social life, including religious institutions, retreat centres, and the ability of people to meet to explore inner and outer change. We do not live in a period of state control but of corporate control due to the submissive attitude of Western governments towards corporations.

Religious devotees and Dharma practitioners make immense efforts with money, time and energy to establish, support and sustain facilities for spiritual/religious practices. You would find it hard to see selfless dedication in the corporate world. Spiritual centres, monasteries and places for devotion find themselves in a constant struggle to raise the funds to keep such facilities running. Building regulations, health and safety policies, along with building requirements (down to the tiniest details), ensure the grip of business over spiritual centres and monasteries.

Local government inspectors have the power to go to any spiritual/religious establishment and enforce dramatic alterations, including widespread refurbishment, heating, plumbing and insurance. If trustees do not comply, inspectors can issue a centre or a monastery with orders for closure.

The inspectors warn about the consequences of ignoring legislation, neglecting bylaws and rejecting building regulations in places where people meet. The chances of a catastrophe in a mindful retreat centre, monastery or building for prayer are very remote. The obsession in the political/corporate world to control every area of our life impacts on every citizen. Such control keeps the economy moving and facilities under control of the authorities. The demands to meet with regulations, and the growing cost involved, ensure that the daily rates of retreats keep going up and up every year.

This forces people to work harder and longer to cover the costs of attending a retreat. Trustees and teachers find themselves powerless to say "No" to these demands on such centres. Staff in centres want to be paid a salary. They do not wish to live on donations. The costs of a weeklong insight meditation retreat in the USA can range from $500 to $1500, plus an appeal for donations for the teachers at the end of the retreat.

To take some examples:
- *A retreat centre in Massachusetts, USA, had to spend around $750,000 to refurbish major wings of the centre to satisfy health and safety demands.*

- A centre near Bonn, Germany spent €30,000 to fit a new kitchen. Health and safety inspectors condemned the previous kitchen, even though retreats had been held at the centre for 340 days per year for more than 20 years. Nobody had become ill from the meals served at breakfast, lunch or in the evening. Under hygiene laws, the health inspectors then banned the cooks, staff and teachers from eating their meals in the new kitchen. The staff could only use the new kitchen to cook meals.

- Health and safety inspectors closed the main meal marquis of a much-loved festival in the U.K. There were no reports of anyone getting sick from the nutritious diet provided in more than a decade of the annual five-day festival. The marquis served as a major source of income to ensure the financial stability of the alcohol free, drug free festival, popular with parents and children.

- In Australia, insurance companies put up the cost of insurance against fire and accident in retreat centres to a level that made the daily rate unaffordable for low income meditators.

- In the U.K., regulations for so-called historic buildings meant that the costs of renovation, such as a new heating system and maintenance, inside and outside, spiralled the annual costs upwards. Teenagers, single mothers, students, unemployed, low income and pensioners, can no longer afford to attend the retreats held in an historic building.

- A California centre endeavours to raise $18,000,000 for a dramatic expansion of their centre. Architects, local government and building regulations ensure such exorbitant costs. The desire to provide an elevated level of comfort for meditators contributes to the inflated cost of accommodation.

Along with other teachers and managers, I taught our annual Bodh Gaya retreat in the Thai Monastery between 1975 and 2013, and in Sarnath, North India since 1999. The retreats employed a team of five cooks to prepare breakfast and lunch for the 100 participants for two 10-day retreats. Owing to our health concerns, we had to apply an elevated level of mindfulness for the welfare of the participants. I told our cooks in Bodh Gaya on the first day in 1975 that they had to wash their hands every time they used the toilet (squat toilet, no toilet paper, left hand applied). I asked the cooks why people got sick. The cooks discussed the matter in Hindi between themselves. They all agreed: "Karma," they replied. They initially obeyed my hand-washing rule, because "Guru-ji had spoken," not through understanding the health hazard between the use of the toilet and preparation of food.

I would never ever condone such questionable conditions in a kitchen in the West. The skilful application of mindfulness, skills and knowledge contributes directly to the welfare of people. Mindfulness offers support and protection even in the most trying of circumstances.

Teachers, managers and cooks work mindfully together every year in India to ensure that we uphold the best hygiene practices, despite 'rock bottom' cooking facilities. To our knowledge, no group of meditators has suffered from stomach problems due to polluted food or drink on our retreats attended by thousands since the mid-1970s. We offer rice, dhal, curried vegetables and salad, plus boiled water to drink. The cooks use an open fire to cook, prepare chapattis on a mat on the floor, not on a table, and use large bowls to wash the vegetables from the local market to make salad. Plenty of participants had come to India directly from the West for the first time with stomachs used to the elevated levels of hygiene and yet remained healthy on our Indian retreats.

The chemical business, health inspectors and advertising propaganda have brainwashed our society into a personal obsession about hygiene. The same could also be said for the obsession about needing each kind of insurance. Daily advertisements on the television and other media claim that their toilet cleaner kills 99.9% of all known germs! It is another form of corporate control, a profit-making enterprise, a lack of trust in people to be mindful in matters of hygiene, health, and safety. We can apply the principles and practices of mindfulness in centres and religious institutions to ensure that all participants enjoy nourishing and healthy food, a safe environment, well maintained facilities amidst simple living conditions.

The Buddha spoke of the raft to cross over from *Samsara* (the realm of fearfulness and suffering) to *Nirvana*, (the realm of fearlessness, of liberation from suffering). Various retreat centres have become spiritual hotels. Instead of a raft to cross to the other shore, these centres have become more like five-star ocean-going liners, a pure environment, spotlessly clean not unlike the most modern hospitals.

Meanwhile, the hearts of human beings have become polluted with greed, violence and delusion while living in fear of sickness, bugs and allergies.

Application of Spirituality

We see the compartmentalisation of society into religion, science, education, business and culture. This atomisation into these institutions exposes a problematic separation, a naïve separation of co-dependent events making up daily life. The Buddha's teaching place mindfulness in all directions so that we become clear about the consequences of our actions whether personal, corporate or political. He pointed to the emptiness of obsessing with self-existence since everything relies upon everything else.

A Dharma inquiry/reflection/investigation names the unhealthy views used to reify self-existence. The Buddha said: *"Dharma is taught, by way of inquiry; the four applications of mindfulness, inner and outer towards body, feelings, states of mind and Dharma, are taught by way of inquiry; the noble path is taught by way of inquiry. Thus, Dharma is taught by way of inquiry."* (SN 3.96).

As a key feature of the Buddha's teachings, Dharma inquiry safeguards us from submission to harmful authority, corporate, political, religious and secular.

Corporate Consumerism and the Buddha Dharma

Corporations or spiritual coaches will promote Tibetan lamas, Thai Ajahns, Zen Masters, Taoist adepts, Indian gurus and charismatic Western teachers of Eastern spirituality to add a little mystique to their company and the product. The market consultants can then sell a company or product as having an exotic image. The Buddha Dharma offers a different world view from corporate/consumer capitalism and strategically placed Buddha images to promote products:

As previously said, far too many founders of so called spiritual movements have marginalised profound teachings of awakening, quietly excluding anything remotely controversial, to curry favour with businesses to gain approval, status and income. Regardless of the original sphere of influence, GM spiritually restricts mindfulness to a personal practice, rather than inner-outer circumstances and empowerment to act. Business has rebranded spirituality to obscure dark policies, rather than apply spiritual exploration to change the DNA of a corporation.

The Cult of Corporations

While I was in India in February 2014, some friends who work as mindfulness teachers sent me a brief clip from the Wisdom 2.0 conference in San Francisco. A panel discussion had begun titled *3 Steps to Corporate Mindfulness the Google Way* when a handful of activists entered the packed hall of corporate mindfulness leaders. They secretly gained entrance to dissent against the frequent eviction of low income residents from their homes, so landlords could make much more money from well paid employees of Google and other corporations in the area. Rents near Google bus stops rose 20% in a year affecting local tenants struggling to make ends meet.

Rather than listening to the real concerns of the activists, a senior manager at Google, Bill Douane, recommended the audience to "check in with your body" and "feel what it's like to conflict with people with heartfelt ideas that may be different from what we're thinking." As he spoke, Google security guards were engaging in an aggressive tug of war with the activists to pull down their banner *Eviction Free San Francisco* they had unfurled at the edge of the stage. Then Douane told the audience "to take a second and see what it's like." The audience dutifully obeyed rather than listen to the grievances of the dissenters. It would have been more mindful for the audience to hear what eviction feels like. But that is not the Google Way.

When I first saw this clip, I thought it was a Monty Python Sketch. The clip turned out to be an actual event exposing the shallowness of corporate mindfulness. As viewers of the clip, we would have to assume that the security guard's eviction of those voicing dissent gave a clear example of the 'Google Way' of mindfulness, namely the exclusion of dissent. Wisdom 2.0 cut the live feed and deleted the interruption from their video. Fortunately, someone filmed the two-minute scene on their private device. Readers can see the Google clip on *YouTube: Wisdom.20. Eviction.*

Spiritual workshop leaders working with business men and woman lack the inner empowerment to inquire deeply into corporate values. We should not expect them to be engaged in the work for deep change in corporate policies. Sadly, some spiritual/mindfulness leaders appear caught up in a triumphalism and personal hubris around their courses, as if these courses will transform capitalism. They have fallen into the same trap as businesses of converting their spiritual programmes into a marketable commodity.

Leaders sell the product of spirituality/mindfulness/psychology for a high daily rate. Sadly, far too many spiritual teachers working in the business world have taken on board with unquestioning obedience the expectations of corporations. Mindfulness belongs to Dharma Inquiry.

Dharma Inquiry (*Dharma vicaya*) includes:

- *Causality*
- *Emptiness of I and mine,*
- *Global ethics*
- *Right action and their results*
- *Right livelihood*
- *Sustainability*

Popular teachers of *Being*, such as Jon Kabat-Zinn, Eckhart Tolle, Adyashanti and others resident in North America, offer useful reminders and supportive practices for being calm, peaceful and in the present moment. This is a commendable start.

Their words do give the impression that they seem to believe that their teachings on *Being* are in accordance with the Buddha's teachings. These Western teachers might equate abiding in *Being* as enlightenment. The Buddha taught liberation from taking up experiences of Being as enlightenment. He made it clear on numerous occasions that nothing is worth grasping onto including deep experiences of *the here and now*.

An enlightened life bears no relationship to adopting such a single experience as enlightenment. The calm witness with a sense of being has made useful steps along the road of dharma inquiry to an enlightened way of life.

Apple – the Uncool Corporation

Some corporations exploit a blend of commercial power and spirituality to promote a product. Apple Inc., the Californian based consumer electronics corporation, marketed their CEO, Steve Jobs (1955 to 2011) as a Zen Buddhist, with an austere monk-like appearance, who spent six months in India in 1974 and practised meditation until his early death, aged 56. The marketing of Jobs as a successful hippy type offering cool products neglected to mention his personal wealth of a staggering $8.2 billion. It might be worthwhile to repeat the sum.

His personal wealth was 1000 x one million dollars x 8. Instead the Apple publicity department boasted that the corporation only paid Jobs $1 a year. Forbes made him the 42nd wealthiest American in a nation of 300 million citizens. Whether Jobs was a practising Buddhist, Christian, Jew, Hindu, Muslim, or born-again secularist has no real bearing on his powerful role as CEO of Apple.

There is nothing cool about Apple Inc. It is a brutally aggressive company. Presumably, Jobs acquired much of his staggering wealth through his corporation selling overpriced computers, overpriced iPhones and overpriced iPads, inflicting punishing factory conditions on Chinese factory workers and avoiding paying corporation tax as much as possible.

Our hearts reach out to Jobs, his family and friends, due to his long and losing struggle with pancreatic cancer. His desire to gain such personal wealth, however, running into several billion dollars, reveals another type of pathology, namely the accumulation of staggering wealth. This pathology reveals a more serious condition than pancreatic cancer owing to the wider consequence on the poor in the USA, Chinese employees and elsewhere. Jobs died in early October 2011. Two weeks after his death, his authorised biography became available. The story of the life of Steve Jobs, his rise to so-called success in business and his interest in Buddhism and spirituality, proved to be the biggest selling book on Amazon for 2011, even though the book only came out in late October of that year.

The marketing of Steve Jobs (the promotion of the corporate cult of personality) successfully obscured the fact that Steve Jobs ran a worldwide corporation obsessed with success regardless of sweatshop labour, unethical business practices, the use of dangerous chemicals, environmental destruction and tax avoidance. The massive promotion of their CEO obscured inquiry into the business model of their corporation. Apple Inc. is not cool. It is cold, ice cold. There is no indication of real empathy for those employees living in hardship or for those suffering due to the environment impact on citizens in subsidiary companies of Apple.

The US Senate Committee reported that Apple Inc. cut their U.S. corporate income tax by an average of $10 billion-a-year for the past four years. This money could support around 50 million desperately poor people in the USA surviving on food stamps. They are three million people or more living lonely lives on the streets or in squalid housing conditions of US cities. Apple Inc. and their CEO never had any interest in the plight of the poor since the price of their products are far out of reach of those people relegated to the gutters of society.

Liberals tend to nod with approval of the so-called success story of Jobs. Personal and corporate greed and the Buddha-Dharma remain utterly incompatible. The money driven globalisation of corporate/consumer capitalism means that CEOs of corporations neglect compassion for their own employees at the bottom of the wage scale and the desperation that far too many experience. It would be better if more Buddhists found inspiration on their meditation cushion to develop insightful ways to press corporations, such as Apple, to change their aggressive behaviour in the obsession with power and profit. Our relationship to the past and to the future matters as much as the present moment.

There is the capacity for a significant truth to emerge out of a situation, out of an event, including past and future, as well as present. The discovery of such insights and realisations of truth can set the course for fresh priorities and vision. Wise judgments emerge from such insights.

Voices of Dissent

We need to explore deeply the Dharma of liberation, a theology of liberation and a spiritual tradition of social inquiry and social justice. This takes bold men and women to implement change. A few small birds can change the direction of a mad elephant.

Indian society did not have a large dependency on slaves for its economic output as was the case with the Greeks, Romans and the Persian and Egyptian civilisations. In the last 500 years, the British Empire and the Spanish Empire engaged massively in slave trade to serve as the backbone of running their Empires. Today we witness Western nations employing cheap labour often in harsh working conditions, indoors and outdoors, to serve the interests of the political corporate empires' ambitions and voracious appetite of consumers to maximise pleasurable sensations through the sense doors. We live today in a society of beggars at the sense doors at the expense of millions of lowly paid factory workers who have become the modern slaves.

Mindfulness practices, inquiry and spiritual explorations have the potential to change the culture of a corporation from the bottom up and the top down. These voices know that it requires a determination to make explicit the areas to address. Research and inquiry, often through the work of thoughtful campaigning organisations can provide the material and the evidence to address the dark side of corporate priorities. Authentic spirituality addresses the light and the dark, the known and the hidden, the beliefs and the denials. It may well be important to leave behind religious rituals, canon law and ancient ceremonies. These voices of change need to be mindful of creative and wise steps to implement change. Office buildings replace churches, office meetings replace church services and CEOs replace religious leaders. We need to question authority and bring democracy to corporations, so workers elect the CEO and the directors.

Authentic spirituality belongs to a bold and liberated exploration. Who will take a big step forward in the corporate world for its transformation?

10. WISDOM, DEMOCRACY AND CORPORATE RULE

When the ocean swells, the great rivers. When the rivers swell the tributaries swell. When ignorance swells unhealthy formations swell. When unhealthy formations swell, consciousness (under their influence) swells. (SN 11.11)

While ancient Greece struggled to establish a form of democracy, the Buddha created the world's first democratic institution in the form of the Sangha. He advocated collective responsibility, agreement and the freedom to adapt for the welfare and benefit of the individual and the collective. It was a radical movement away from the authoritarian control of the political power of the Kings of nations of India 2600 years ago, the authority given to the Vedic texts, the Brahmin priests, and the gurus. These forms of authoritarian rule demanded deference and devotion from their subjects and followers. People were expected to submit to the will of authority.

The Buddha swept authoritarian rule aside and introduced democratic processes. To make democracy effective, the Buddha advocated tolerance of views, conflict resolution, compassion and the resolution of suffering as the foundation of his democratic principles. Because of the Buddha's initiatives, the Sangha is the world's oldest institution.

Wisdom addresses suffering, the causes for it, the dissolution of suffering and the skilful means to dissolve suffering at the personal, social and global level.

In the Buddha's last discourse (*Maha Parinibbana Sutta*), the Buddha taught seven conditions that support the development of a true democracy of dialogue, co-operation and wise settlement of differences. The application of these conditions enables the continuity of an assembly for centuries, including the Sangha of the ordained. He listed the seven conditions as:

- *If Dharma practitioners assemble often and in large numbers*
- *Meet and disperse peacefully and attend to the affairs of the Sangha through proceeding in accordance with the spiritual disciplines (vinaya)*
- *Show respect towards the wisdom of the elders*
- *Not to fall under the grip of desire and the becoming of the ego*

- *Cherish the outdoors and nature*
- *Establish themselves in mindfulness and awareness*
- *Practice to live in peace with each other.*

These seven conditions lead to everyone's welfare. He made it clear that participants in the Sangha and its democratic values can expect the growth of the Sangha through giving equal attention to all the conditions. Twenty years after the death of the Buddha, the Sangha held its first Council with a reported 500 people in attendance to agree on the most skilful means to preserve and disseminate the teachings. With its values and practices, the Sangha travelled all over Asia to disseminate the Dharma including Afghanistan, Japan, Burma, Nepal, Thailand and Sri Lanka, as well as throughout the sub-continent of India, from the Himalayas to the tip of India. They kept to the democratic vision of the centres for Dharma practice *(dharmasalas)*, endorsed responsibilities of householders and mendicants with a way of life free from authoritarian rule. This vision established the Buddha-Dharma through the wisdom and organisational skills of the Sangha. Living a way of life of a certain austerity, the Sangha could devote its attention to inner transformation, community living and the responsibility to support those in need, both homeless mendicants and householders.

Democratic principles underlined the Sangha, so everyone knew they had a voice. At that time, the Sangha only referred to the Buddha as the Teacher. They did not even confer on those who shared their wisdom the title of a 'teacher' but were simply known by their first name and insights beneficial to others. Ananda was known for his personal attention to the Buddha, Sariputta was known for his understanding of the Buddha's teachings. Maha Kassapa was known for his austerity. Maha Kaccana was known for his wisdom.

Yogis, Brahmins, gurus, priests, spiritual teachers, householders, seekers and practitioners from other traditions would come to the dharmasala with questions, concerns and curiosity. The democratic and egalitarian attitude drew immense interest from both secular and religious culture. The Buddha offered freedom of exploration in contrast to the authoritarian rule of political and religious leaders.

Authentic Democracy

Authentic democracy does not depend upon the antagonistic voices of disparate groups of people, often engaging in hair splitting arguments in a public forum, but on the ethics, values and clarity of the electorate. A person may have little or no formal education, as often the case in ancient India, yet can articulate his/her concerns in a public debate. The pursuit of knowledge through formal education certainly can contribute to such values, but formal education can also feed dogmatic views, intolerance and the identification with an ideology in which access to power matters more than the resolution of suffering.

Since democracy is concerned with the true welfare of all its citizens, near and far, then democratic governments have the task of skilfully issuing the promotion of non-exploitation, conflict resolution and right livelihood to set up a sense of community on a large scale and at the local level. A thoughtful and caring electorate can see beyond the narrow limits of self-interest. Then democracy has much to offer in terms of the welfare and freedom of everyone. If democracy becomes overshadowed by authoritarian control and manipulation of the public mind, it will become mediocre, shallow and subservient. There are alarming signals of this trend today.

Wisdom explores in practical ways a way of life of non-violence, no exploitation and sustainable values. Mindfulness, meditation and dialogue contribute to wisdom to liberate human beings from a contracted and imprisoned life. Society does not offer an education that includes the ethics of non-violence, non-harming, mindfulness, meditation, spiritual inquiry, compassion and awakening. The mind of contemporary society has not evolved in 2500 years. It might well have regressed. Technology, gadgets and modern weapons become extensions of the selfish, violent and fearful mind. Nothing much has changed.

Many current values remain far removed from the Buddha's seven factors that contribute to the real growth of the community, including the nation state, union with other nations and the global community. Modern day democracy contributes to the decline of democracy and the increase of corporate/political control over our lives. People, who vote or do not vote out of fear, habit or blame undermine democracy and the fabric of society.

Democracy becomes a precious institution when citizens have the knowledge and the skills to move away from unhealthy and destructive habits, develop contact and friendship with others and participate in groups, networks and organisations for meaningful change. Society needs to take notice of the real alternatives in education that support the whole community and address all the needs of the child – emotional, mental, physical and spiritual – and the child's relationship with other children, adults, animals and nature.

The Buddha invited men and women to dedicate themselves to a depth of inner work and community life for both adults and children, without cost. He brought householders and the nomadic sangha together to explore wisdom teachings. We have very, very few examples of this in the West.

Living community life, practitioners entered into a non-formal agreement with householders in a mutually beneficial exchange. Unlike society, where the exchange shows as money for services or goods, the Sangha shared the Dharma with householders in exchange for the four requisites of food, clothing, accommodation and medicine. Wealthy benefactors would provide *dharmasalas* that also served as simple residential facilities, sometimes in parks in cities, or rural environments, for the homeless mendicants to practice and for householders to go there for practice and to receive teachings on the variety of Dharma themes including ethics, meditative concentration, love, wisdom and liberation. The number of centres grew throughout northern India as interest in the Buddha-Dharma grew.

It required initiative, inspiration and co-operation to set up the dharmasala. The assembly of practitioners employed a foundation of spiritual discipline – the *vinaya* – a Pali term that means "leading away from" unhealthy habits. These disciplines included mindfulness and respect for activities of body, speech, and mind as well as the decision-making process. For example, the Sangha observed a discipline of keeping a noble silence after an assembly came to an agreement rather than backbiting on the decision with a view of undermining the credibility of the agreement. If the practitioner did not attend the meeting, then he or she might enquire about the decision without voicing judgemental reactions against it.

In his final discourse, the Buddha went deeper into the psychology that enables a community and democracy to flourish. He then touched upon another seven conditions that serve the interests of the Sangha and society.

- *Trust in the power of the Dharma and the practice*

- *Regret over errors of judgement*
- *Apprehension of unhealthy tendencies or reactions*
- *Commitment to learning from history and the present*
- *Be resolute and determined*
- *Be mindful*
- *Be wise*

In the company of others, the Buddha said that practitioners train themselves, openly and in private, in a "virtuous way of life, spotless, appreciated by the wise." Without the exploration, as outlined in the above seven conditions, there is the danger that democracy loses its substance as a form of wise assembly where all have a voice. In today's democracy, there is very little left except a ritualistic vote for two or three major parties.

Has democracy given way to Corporate Control?

In DN 11.13, the Buddha gives an example for not seeing what is happening around us. There were heavy torrents of rain, flashes of lightning and thunder that killed two farmers, who were brothers, and four bulls. Even if near to the event, it could be that one does not see what is happening even though one is not asleep.

Modern day societies ensure the withering away of democracy in front of our eyes. As citizens, we lose our participation in meaningful political, social and economic change. Capitalism permits power and wealth to be in the hands of corporate regimes unaccountable to the people.

In the United States, Forbes 400 provides information about the 400 richest people in the country. In 2009, the bottom 60% of the U.S. households owned only 2.3% of the total U.S. wealth. India boasts about a new billionaire every month – in a country of 1100 million people with 75% living in abject poverty in rural and city environments. Capitalism endorses the unfettered accumulation of personal wealth regardless of the cost elsewhere. CNN Money reported that the CEO of a corporation in 2011 earned around 340 times per annum the income of one of his workers.

In the 1980's, CEOs earned around 40 times the income of workers. The CEO of Viacom, the American media conglomerate, earned

1990 times as much and the CEO of Oracle, a US computer technology corporation, earned 750 times of the workers' wages. The gap between CEO's and staff gets bigger and bigger every year.

It is easy to secure such information – simply google such figures to bring up the information.

Major corporations constantly seek ways to squeeze money out of their customers. Watchdogs to protect customers from exploitation remain toothless as business finds new ways to increase their profits.

I rented a dongle, a small gadget from the Orange telephone company to download my emails while abroad. When I returned home from Australia I received a bill from Orange for £2250.00 for the use of the dongle for less than 90 minutes. The EU Commissioner described these charges by mobile phone companies as a "rip off."

I regarded the size of the bill as a violation of the U.K. Unfair Contract Terms, 1977 for a fair and reasonable contract. Downloading or streaming a 30-minute video could be anything between 100 megabytes and 300 megabytes. That would add £800 to £2,400 to your bill, depending on your provider. The cost to a telephone company is believed to be around three pence per gigabyte. Yes, per gigabyte. There are 1024 megabytes to a gigabyte.

I downloaded my emails on the first day or two, as well as looking at news websites at the beginning of a three-week period of Dharma teaching in the rainforest. After two days, the retreat manager told me that Wi-Fi was available. It had not been available in previous visits. My use in the forest could have cost me £25,000 - £75,000 if I had used the dongle around an hour or so a day for the month of my stay in Australia. I appealed to the Watchdog who told me that I had made the contract with Orange and had to pay up. I wrote to my Member of Parliament who wrote to the CEO of Orange who then said that I had to pay the full amount for the Orange bill.

The size of my Orange telephone bill made the main story in the local newspaper, main story of an inside page of an evening newspaper. I spoke on a local BBC consumer affair programme. In the local radio office, four out of five staff told me of their dongle and smart phone bills between £75.00 and £825 for their use overseas. I read that Orange had merged with the T-Mobile phone company in an £8.2 billion deal.

It cost Orange around £600 -£800 million to integrate a 28 million customer base, mostly in the U.K. and Germany. Orange and T-Mobile had set out to recoup the cost of the merger from its customers. Their lawyers ensured no outlet from the telephone contract, even though I signed nothing. It was hard to find on the Orange website the warnings about downloading information on a dongle or smart phone. Overseas charges for the use of a dongle or Smartphone contributed to the merger. The company refuses to disclose the profit margin on downloaded information. I changed my provider to Zen Internet.

Corporate exploitation of customers will continue if the systems for greed remain in place. It would require revolutionary change if corporations were to adopt the Buddha's model of participatory democracy. To democratise corporations, it would mean:

- *The dissolution of the present status quo*
- *The corporation would become a community*
- *Leaders would be democratically elected*
- *Bosses and workers would decide on the product*
- *Enabling creative initiatives to make the product sustainable*
- *The business would consult with the local community*
- *And an end to the huge wage disparity between the board and the workers.*

Backed up with the governments and the police, the corporate world has slowly and systematically taken control over the lives of millions to the point of echoing features of an authoritarian regime.

We live in a pernicious system that enslaves people to an immensity of stress at work, endless hours of employment to make ends meet due to the treadmill of debt. The government and business pump out the language of freedom and democracy to obscure the reality. Freedom only has any meaning for citizens who engage in a participatory democracy at work and in their local communities, as well as their capacity for freedom of being and doing. The freedom of the rich and powerful treads heavily on the majority, on the 99%.

Banks and corporations have high-jacked the word "freedom". They demanded and got freedom from regulation causing the loss of peace of mind for untold numbers of debt ridden citizens. The concept of the "free market" has become a euphemism for brutal competition and the hiring and firing of staff to consolidate a position. The so-called free market capitalism and authentic democracy are incompatible due to wealth and power concentrated in the hands of the few, namely billionaires and multi-millionaires. Corporate rule wields an immense influence on governments, democracy, workers and the environment. It is not enough for governments to make critical comments about corporations and bankers unless their words follow up with legislation to ensure support for the poor and middle classes.

20 Examples of Corporate Rule

1. *Corporations control our elected representatives through large donations. Corporations in the USA and elsewhere find ways to give substantial sums of money to their chosen political party. The U.S. Supreme Court and the Court of Appeals, ruled that Political Action Committees (PACs) are now allowed to accept unlimited donations from corporations and unions provided the money does not go directly to the campaign. Is there an attempt by these corporations to buy the election for the Democrats or Republicans? In the end, just 100 individuals or companies accounted for more than half of the disclosed donations to Super PACs, according to OpenSecrets.org. Politicians seeking office become subservient to companies that exploit the data available on social media. The data enable these companies to target groups of citizens in order to swing an election in one direction. It only needs five or six people or less in every 100 to change the outcome of an election. The new government then cultivates a favourable business culture above all other considerations, regardless of the needs of the citizens. Far too many politicians advance the interests of their investors, who got them into office.*

2. *Capitalism prevents a meaningful participation of citizens in the affairs of the state. Powerful corporations exploit the trust of millions of people who use social media. They swamp users with advertising, allow powerful political organisations to gain access to the profiles of groups of people and engage in constant surveillance of the use of social media. Citizens find they unwittingly ratify the interests of powerful political/economic groups. Political candidates have become dependent on the financial support of corporations directly and indirectly. Politicians then wave a finger of mild concern at big bankers and corporations for their huge salaries and bonuses, but take no real action against their paymasters.*

3. *Corporations control workers. Major and Asian corporations rely upon cheap labour to maximise profits. Workers in poor nations receive a pathetically low monthly income, barely enough to support their families, and often work in conditions that violate health and safety concerns. Around 3.5 million factory workers in China earn around $7*

or $8 per day often working around 15 hours per day for around 50 cents per hour. They live in minimalist conditions and crowded sleeping quarters. Industrial accidents, sickness and sheer exhaustion make a significant impact on the workforce. Western workers find themselves working as much overtime as possible to pay off debts, match earnings with outgoing daily expenses, pay monthly rents/mortgage, student loans, car bill and credit card debts. Certain corporations will employ young citizens for days or weeks, on trial for a job, without paying them any salary, with the excuse of giving them "work experience." Young people believe that working in a coffee shop, store or office will help them get a job. They are there serving as free or cheap labour.

4. *Corporations influence legislation.* Major corporations endorse lower taxation to make themselves better off and to get people to spend more rather than pay taxes for the welfare and support of the poor. The corporate world enjoys major tax breaks for the wealthy. Some of the superrich use tax havens worldwide to avoid the retribution of a reasonable percentage of their wealth for those in need. Corporations exploit natural resources of land, forests, water, air, oil and gas regardless of the consequence for present and future generations. They employ an army of lawyers to avoid paying compensation or offering a minimum payment, and for getting away with causing environmental destruction.

5. *Corporations control what appears on our streets.* They advertise their products in posters, billboards and neon lights. There is no permission for local communities to invite their artists to display freely their art on billboards and highways as well as our streets in villages, towns and cities. Statues on our streets primarily consist of powerful leaders, warlords, and monuments to those who faithfully served and died for their leaders. British warlords include Winston Churchill, Admiral Nelson and Oliver Cromwell. The occasional displays of graffiti reflect the small gestures of dissent.

6. *The corporate world controls the arts.* Corporations determine the availability of the arts since they control much of the funding. Advertising agencies extensively promote corporate businesses on the cinema screen, including alcohol, cigarettes, junk food and junk drink with all the devastating health consequences. Around 90% of all films (movies) show actors in the film smoking a cigarette or making comments about smoking. Tobacco companies target films for young people, said the American Legacy Foundation. Around 480,000 people die in the USA every year from smoking related diseases and 16 million

Americans live with a disease that smoking caused (Centres for Disease Control and Prevention USA).

7. Corporations control sport. Corporations pay huge sums for sports stars to advertise their products. Sports stars must sign contracts to tie them completely to the product. They are not allowed to dress or use in public equivalent items of another company. They have reduced sport to a marketable product. Sport stars and their teams must refrain from expressing any political or social views, no matter how compassionate. Any political views from sport stars might affect sales as their views might turn off potential customers with different political views. Billionaires buy up major sports clubs for their personal entertainment. Sportsmen and women have become modern day gladiators for wealthy CEOs.

8. Corporations target the young to make them into consumers. They promote their brand image to the very young to wear their designer labels, buy their junk food and watch their television programmes funded through their advertisements. Parents find themselves regularly tormented by their children to buy products of certain companies. Companies will increase the price of their garments with their brand name on the garment.

9. Corporations target sex to promote their products. You will find overt sexual innuendos to sell every product from cars, to food, to clothes, to about everything. Porn is the biggest industry on the Internet. Intensification of desire around sex for men and women reflects in dress, magazines and social life. Gambling is high up there as well. The gambling industry depends upon the addiction of their customers for their profits. They make a fortune from the rich and poor alike driving customers into despair over their losses.

10. Corporations and the Media Empire control the streets. Using the law, the police ensure that street dissents start and begin within times and locations agreeable to the authorities. The police regularly act with violence to provoke violence so that the newspapers the following day report about the violence rather than the reasons for the dissent. Media empires marginalise dissent through hostile reporting thus keeping the streets clear for shoppers. Our streets do not belong to us but to the government, businesses and the police.

11. Corporations control the media who disseminate information. Aside from the occasional column, the questioning of capitalism, corporations and democracy virtually remain off limits. Why? Newspapers depend

on businesses for advertising. Newspapers cannot afford to lose their clients. So, they very rarely challenge specific corporations who buy advertising space in their newspaper. The media offers a narrow debate on economic ideology and the consequences of capitalism. Those who campaign for the redistribution of wealth and an economic system based on justice remain marginalised because that would reduce profit margins. Dissent against big banks, corporations and the concentration of wealth and power are tolerated in the short term and then the police move in. Governments and the police tolerate dissent on the streets for a few hours and then disperse the crowds.

12. Corporations control education. Schools, colleges and universities function to meet the needs of corporations, the media, industry and the market. Corporations monopolise television stations, journals and scientific research. Through their lobby groups, they put increasingly more pressure on governments to control the freedom of the Internet to suit their terms. Children and young people spend an increasing amount of time studying in schools and at home to meet corporate demands upon leaving school or university. The demands of government and business rob children and young people of their chance to play, have fun and a happy emotional life. Children exist as consumers of the future.

13. Corporations determine diet. Supermarkets and fast food chains have a substantial influence over a nation's diet. There is an epidemic of obesity caused more through the actual food eaten than the amount of food. Around 40% of adults in the US are obese and 20% of children (National Centre for Health Statistics, USA, 2017). Food experts appealed to the food industry to mark their products with three traffic light symbols. Red would show elevated levels of salt, sugar and fat. Amber would show medium levels. Green would show low levels of salt, sugar and fat. The cartel of the food industry blocked such regulations as it would reduce dramatically the consumption of fast food. Fast food leads to a faster sickness and faster death.

14. Hospitals are full of people hospitalised due to what they put in the mouth. The food industry does not care. They refuse to take responsibility for their junk food, their advertising playing on people's vulnerabilities and their utter disregard for exploitation of land for their own gain.

15. Corporations control medicine. For example, corporations determine the health policies for the World Health Organisation (WHO). The WHO

has determined that AIDS, smoking and birth control take priority. Although these are important health issues, it ensures that the WHO has moved away from its original vision of aid for the desperately poor and sick adults and children living in poor nations in Africa and parts of Asia. The current WHO priorities serve the interests of the West. Administrative costs take a toll on the budget. Medical students listen to lectures on the relationship of diet and health from a single lecture in four years to a total of 60 hours in four years of training to be a doctor. Some medical students never listen to lecture, nor receive any training, to know about the impact of, fattening food or food with chemicals/additives and processed food and on the health of patients. Doctors work as agents of the pharmaceutical industry. The medical profession can only provide a leaflet for a healthy diet to patients addicted to food that slowly kills them.

16. Corporations provide all the necessary equipment for surveillance. Governments buy surveillance equipment for the military, for the streets, shopping malls and the DNA database. The U.K. House of Lord Constitution Committee said that U.K. citizens lie in a surveillance society. The Committee said that growth in surveillance by both the private sector and the State risked threatening people's rights. The U.K.'s DNA database is the "largest in the world", the report concluded. Police in England, Wales and Northern Ireland can take DNA and fingerprints from anybody arrested on suspicion of a recordable offence. The police can hold samples; they can hold indefinitely whether people are charged or not. The U.K. has the highest number of cameras in public places (more than 40,000) per population in the world. Powerful sections of the media have engaged in phone hacking and illegal surveillance in Britain on certain citizens to obtain stories to create a scandal to sell to the newspapers

17. Corporations control the economy of countries in severe debt. Corporations welcome the immense opportunities that arise when a country finds itself in a massive debt crisis. The World Bank and the International Monetary Fund (IMF), both based near the White House, Washington DC, tell debt ridden countries to sell off to the private sector their public assets such as land, forests, reservoirs, ports, airports, railways, gas, electricity and roads. They will order debt ridden governments to cut salaries and staff in the public sector, eliminate social programmes and dramatically reduce the range of public services. Billionaires control aid.

18. Corporations benefit from the launching of a war and seeing it continue. A war provides one of the greatest opportunities for business. It allows the so-called defence industry to create and manufacture more weapons paid for by taxation. It supports the military efforts to destroy the weapons of another country and thus create another market at the end of the war. The longer the war continues the greater the number of contracts with the government. Politicians use tasteless metaphors such as 'theatre of war,' 'collateral damage' and 'opening salvoes' to describe the deliberate slaughter of people. It allows the use of new weapons on the enemy as well as providing countless jobs to private contractors. On the defeat of the enemy, it means new markets open as the West installs obedient governments, ensures the privatisation of all resources, and converts citizens into consumers.

19. Corporations encourage debt. Corporations tell customers to purchase a product this year and pay for it next year. Customers are persuaded to buy two items and get one free. Customers are told of big discounts when the prices were made high in the weeks before the sale. Corporations hire psychologists, use focus groups and various strategies to get customers to buy. The alcohol industry spends $2 billion per year on advertising, mostly beer with revenue spent for television. (Citigroup Research). The industry targets young adults, middle aged people, the elderly and those with alcohol problems.

20. Corporations control taxes. An army of corporate lawyers and accountants receive substantial sums of money to dig out every tax loophole imaginable to avoid paying taxes. They effectively decide how much state money can go to support the young, elderly, sick, unemployed, single mothers and low-income groups consisting of millions of citizens.

Previous generations of citizens have had to resist Fascism, Communism and other authoritarian regimes. We now have Corporatism, an authoritarian regime – exploitative of citizens worldwide and consuming natural resources at terrifying speed. Freedom is limited to a choice of consumer goods and saying what you like if Corporatism stays in control. Corporate rule controls far too much of our lives. We can find the wisdom through a collective inquiry into the cause and conditions that places power into the hands of the few and away from the many.

Data Collection on our Lives

The US Government collects data on medical and financial histories, monitors e-mail, wiretaps under a generic warrant and searches homes without a warrant. The police can label a non-violent activist of any faith or no faith with all the fearful consequences. In January 2012, the National Defence Authorization Act authorised the US military to detain indefinitely, without charge, anyone they regard as a suspect. The Act also permits the interrogation of U.S. citizens and non-citizens, which denies them their legal rights, as stated in the Constitution. The government with its massive networks of surveillance and the corporate world with its huge industry produce surveillance equipment targeting citizens, groups and demonstrators. Government agencies, as well as infiltrated networks (are installed/act/are there) to ensure that nobody thwarts the aims of the nation state.

While holding people accountable for their actions, the Buddha explained the inner conditions that give rise to unhealthy states of mind and their widespread consequences. Born into inherited privilege and royalty's power of life and death over its citizens, the Buddha examined the inner process that leads up to the "whole mass of suffering."

The repetitive contact with the object gives rise to a certain sensation. This sensation gives rise to a desire. This desire gives rise to clinging. This clinging gives rise to its inflated existence in the present and what can become in the future.

The Buddha explained that this sequence keeps repeating itself incessantly due to a major blind spot in the mind, namely a constant ignoring of the spell of impressions and projections. Contact conditions the sensation, the sensation conditions the desire, the desire conditions the grasping, and the grasping conditions the existence of the problematic mind. Unless resolved, the problematic mind continues.

Many people constantly live ensnared in this narrow, conditioned state of mind dependent on sensations to sustain it. It is a small consciousness living in a small sphere of action. Wealth, property, yachts, private planes and diamonds, only confirm the degree that consciousness remains painfully tied to a small world of a handful of aims and objects that the self has invested with foremost importance.

Just as the repeated cycle imprisons the rich and powerful, it equally imprisons the middle classes and the poor. In that respect the rich, middle and poor alike have much in common besides going through, without exception, birth, ageing, pain and death.

The problematic mind exaggerates the status and possessions but when things start to go wrong, the greed collapses and gives rise to fear. There is contact with the object, a painful sensation, desire not to lose what one has, grasping onto the object fearfully and terror of the future. Greed and fear follow the same inner trajectory. Contact-sensation-desire-grasping-existence-becoming leads to suffering. There is an ignorance of this process and an ignorance of ways to live freely while being fully engaged with the unfolding process of life without being bound to the unsatisfactory sequence of causality. Wisdom confirms the ending of ignorance through skilful application of alternatives to greed, anger and fear.

On the first page of Andrew Sorkin's book *Too Big to Fail*, he reported the fear and panic when the Chief Executive of the J.P. Morgan Bank, the third largest US bank, suddenly realised that his client, Lehman Brothers, the fourth largest investment bank, was on the very verge of collapse. "We need to prepare for Lehman Brothers filing. And for Merrill Lynch filing. And for AIG filing. And for Morgan Stanley filing."

The book relays the wholesale terror on Wall Street in boardrooms, offices and the stock exchange due to the calamitous scale of the collapse. The desperate CEOs, board members and major investors made frantic phone calls. The terror and the rage ran through the minds of the powerful in the corporate world as their corporations started to crash all around them. The loss of control sent CEOs, investors and traders into a state of desperation; some felt suicidal as their financial world collapsed. Fittingly, the cover of Sorkin's book shows a dinosaur.

Merrill Lynch, a brokerage firm and branch of the Bank of America, lost $19.2 billion between July 2007 and July 2008 due to pathetic and irresponsible management decisions through selling risky mortgages. The share prices of AIG (American International Group) fell by 95%. Lehmann Brothers became bankrupt in 2008. They lost $13.2 billion in the space of six months. Morgan Stanley engaged in global wealth management with assets of $779 billion. Their business collapsed. Morgan Stanley borrowed $107.3 billion from the government during the 2008 crises, the most of any bank. All those involved displayed fear, greed and terror – expressions of states of mind needing therapy and counselling.

In 2007, Goldman Sachs profited from the collapse in subprime mortgage bonds by short-selling subprime mortgage-backed securities.

This investment company and securities corporation made a profit of $4 billion by "betting" on the collapse in the sub-prime market. Goldman Sachs also benefitted from the bankruptcy of some of their competitors. This investment bank wields enormous influence with some of its former executives placed in the US Treasury as well as European governments. It leaves democracy under the influence of the corporate world, especially Goldman Sachs. Greed, anger and terror show mental illness.

People who make much money, especially quickly, will find themselves to be less generous, less hospitable, and likely to indulge in destructive habits such as smoking, drinking and eating junk food. Making money becomes their primary relationship with less and less time for loved ones. Their lifestyle shortened their lives by years. Greed is not good for you as it eats away happiness and health.

In the 1985 film, *Wall Street*, directed by Oliver Stone, Gordon Gekko proclaimed that "Greed is Good." Many Wall Street gamblers on the money markets approved of the proclamation. They showed little or no concern when companies crashed and about the impact on the lives of workers around the world who lost their jobs, and in some cases their lives, due to market speculations.

From the Buddha's psychological analysis, the CEO's executives, economists and financial experts lived for years in a state of ongoing collective delusion. Part of the delusion included the belief that the marks and signs of figures on their computer screen represented something different from greed, blame and delusion. Greed, blame and delusion reveal significant signs of a problematic mind. A person becomes caught up in the cycle of contact, sensations, desire, grasping, existence and becoming. This leads to unhappiness, despair and mental health issues.

The grasping impacts on the inner life produces certain addictive sensations to form greed. All the carefully constructed mathematical models of economic growth made a laughing stock of economists and financial experts. Naïve presidents and prime ministers claimed in the 1990s that the era of 'boom and bust' had ended. What rises will fall. What the foolish perceive as steady reveals itself as unsteady, fragile and vulnerable to collapse. Then the grasping impacts on the inner life to produce sensations of fear and terror at witnessing the collapse of all that had been built over the years. All the mansions, private planes, yachts and other displays of success mean nothing when you know you are a total failure in your own eyes and in those of your peers. You are imprisoned to the existence of power, status and name, and its absence or loss.

The Buddha concluded that the wise know the arising, the passing, the satisfaction, the misery and the stepping out of whatever leads to grasping. (D.1.21). If this is understood it would change the world and end corporate greed. Far too many men and women in big business live in the realm of the hungry ghosts, namely those depicted with a big stomach and a very small mouth. Hungry ghosts can never get enough of what they want and live in envy of others.

Our democracy and freedom seem far from the democracy and freedom that the Buddha and the Sangha had in mind. It is not only issues around inner depth, values, right livelihood, democracy and freedom that belong to the issues of the vast way. Scientists tell us of their real concern about the ongoing reduction in oil, depletion of groundwater, washing away of toil soil, pollution of land, water and air, toxic contamination of sentient life, including humanity, the threats to biodiversity and climate change.

The Buddha warned repeatedly of ignorance and self-delusion. Freedom from greed, fear and delusion functions as the open doorway to a wise response to personal and global issues. Freedom to know the reality shows through a direct and undistorted experience of what presents itself.

The corporate world has a lot to answer for.

SECTION THREE – The Sangha and…
11. TEACHINGS FOR ALL KINDS OF SANGHA

The word *Sangha* means *Assembly, Association, Collective, Community* or *Gathering*. In the East, the word Sangha often refers to the order of Buddhist monks and nuns. This is a limited use of the word. A Sangha shows itself whenever two or more people gather together in supportive and skilful ways for each other and others elsewhere.

The Sangha can draw upon the teachings and practices that the Buddha outlined in his discourses. A noble person in the Sangha, the company of the wise, experiences immense confidence in the Dharma with its application to the variety of circumstances of daily life. The roots of the Dharma express as a non-violent, non-exploitive, non-deluded way of life.

The task of the Sangha includes knowing the difference between who has taken responsibility for harmful actions and who has not caused any harm. The Buddha made regular reference to those t0 be held accountable and those who caused no harm.

The Sangha develops the capacity to listen to the voice of the wise. At times, the wise may censure, hold accountable and criticise others. With wise support, we can engage in undertakings to make changes and experience the benefits of those changes. The wise praise those who engage in actions which lead to the welfare and happiness of others (AN 3.65).

Conditions for the Welfare of Society

King Ajatasattu had decided to conquer and occupy Vajjia, a neighbouring country. The Vajjian people had come to happiness and prosperity through practising the Buddha's seven conditions for the welfare of society (AN iv 17). They were:

- *To hold frequent public meetings*
- *To meet to make decisions and carry them out in concord*
- *Uphold traditions and honour agreements*
- *Respect and support the wisdom of the elders*
- *Respect the wishes of women*
- *Pay respect to people*

- *Support and protect the wise and noble ones.*

The Buddha pointed out that in matters of human experience what we experience, others also experience. He gives examples:

- *I wish to live and do not wish to die.*
- *I wish for happiness and am averse to suffering.*
- *I do not wish to have someone take my life.*
- *I do not wish for thieves to rob me.*
- *I do not wish another to engage in abuse of sexual relationships*
- *I do not wish to be lied to and deceived.*
- *What is displeasing and disagreeable to me is displeasing and disagreeable to others as well.*

How can I inflict suffering on others, desire their death, steal, sexually abuse or lie to those who also find it displeasing and disagreeable?

Having reflected on what we and others have in common, one abstains from bringing suffering, harm and death to others.

This approach brings praise from the wise and brings purity to our heart and mind. One lives a life of wise behaviour. The wise see no need for any criticism in such an approach, said the Buddha (SN 55:7).

The task includes a reflection on views and the intentions that might follow on from the views. If we plant the bitter neem seed in moist soil, water the plant, then the seed will eventually become the bitter neem fruit. The views that we adhere to will affect our mind, speech and body (actions) owing to our volition and tendencies. If we plant the seed of a sugar cane in moist soil and water it, it will lead to a sweet fruit. As we sow and water a seed, so the fruit will come (AN: 10.104).

As a dedicated father, the Buddha explained to his son, Radula, the importance of reflection on the impact of his actions upon others. The key question is: "Will the actions lead to any harm to people?" The same principle applies to oneself. "Will my actions bring harm upon myself?" The Buddha regarded social responsibilities as important as personal reflection.

In the teachings, the act of giving requires reflection as well. The Buddha listed eight considerations regarding giving. Those who give large sums or small sums need to reflect upon their intentions. Self-interest may have a major influence on donations. This requires some exploration in terms of wise counsel.

Reasons for Giving that Require Reflection:

1. *From Desire. A person or organisation wants to offer money without knowing the intentions and views behind the desire. The desire stops the reflection behind the desire and examination of the consequences.*

2. *From Blame. A person gives a nasty gift or a miserly payment to show cynicism and to display revenge. A government or corporation offers free weapons for use on the enemy*

3. *From Manipulation: A person imagines their gift of money etc. is for the good but it may produce more harm than good. A gambling industry offers a free start of £10.00*

4. *From Delusion: A company keeps offering cut price deals on unhealthy food harming men, women and children.*

5. *From Fear: There is fear of disapproval or rejection. A corporation cuts prices out of fear of going bankrupt.*

6. *From the family habit: A person gives simply because the family expect it in certain ways.*

7. *From Religious reasons: A better rebirth.*

8. *For self-interest. The mind becomes peaceful and happiness arises.*

9. *For an ornament. Giving equips the mind to impress others. (also see in AN.33).*

Five Reason for Giving from a Noble Person:

1. *Gives out of confidence and trust. A person has looked at the motives and the benefits for the beneficiary and gone ahead.*

2. *Gives out of respect. A person gives to another out of appreciation and respect for what they do.*

3. *Gives at the right time. A person sees the need to give and knows it is the right time.*

4. *Gives with a generous heart. A person with a warm, open heart wishes to share with others.*

5. *Gives without putting oneself or others down. The act of giving matters more than putting oneself or others down. (AN 5:148)*

The Buddha spoke in the highest terms of the importance of giving.

If people knew, as I know, the results of giving and sharing, they would not eat without having given, nor would they allow the stain of miserliness to obsess them and take root in their minds (It 26).

The gift of food provides others with a long life, beauty, happiness and strength (AN 4:57).

Noble Ones who abstain from the destruction of life give people and animals an immeasurable freedom from fear, blame and affliction.

One who offers such freedom can know the same freedom as well (AN: 8.39). Such a great gift to others is "primal, long standing, ancient and uncorrupted", said the Buddha.

The Buddha also addressed the importance of speaking the truth in all situations. He referred to the Sanghas in the social, political, religious and business world, such as a council, an assembly, a guild, a court and a family meeting. A person acts as a witness. "Tell me what you know."

He explained that the wise *act as a cow herdsman, who prods, taps and pokes the cows with a stick, so they don't get themselves into dangerous territory. The wise poke and prod those who get into suffering or cause suffering* (MN 19).

The witness then states to all those present "I do not know" or "I know" or "I do not see" or "I see." He or she does not consciously speak falsehood for his own ends or for another's ends or for some trifling worldly end.

The Buddha referred to points in speech that are important to bear in mind:

- *Abandons chatter*
- *Abandons divisive speech*
- *Speaks at a proper time*
- *Beneficial*
- *Courteous*
- *Goes to the heart*
- *Promotes concord*

- *Reasonable*
- *Speaks to support discipline*
- *Speaks on the Dharma*
- *Speaks the truth*
- *Speaks what is beneficial*
- *Succinct*

Mind, speech and body then link with the truth of situations, the truth of responsibility and concern for others.

In summary, the Buddha said: *"This recognition enables a depth of love to emerge – an all-encompassing love, abundant, immeasurable, without hostility and without ill-will. This love, friendship and loving kindness liberates a person from the limits of any karma to reveal a dwelling with God (Brahma Vihara).*

The same emergence applies to liberation through appreciative joy, compassion and equanimity, a capacity to stay steadfast amidst any circumstance. *"The making of merit for a better future does not equal a 16th part of liberation through love. This liberation shines forth, bright and brilliant."* (MN 99; It 27)

The Sangha consists of a group of people exploring an insightful way of life. The members of such a Sangha look at the condition of their mind and the mind of others. The practices include noticing how strong certain patterns of behaviour and their impact upon oneself and others are.

The Buddha takes anger as an example, which he says has a 'poisoned root' and a 'honey tip.' The poisoned roots indicate what infects and erodes friendship and love. This erosion seeks to make others feel bad about themselves, rather than enabling a person to know themselves and their behaviour.

He referred to three kinds of anger:

Anger etched in stone. The person is angry frequently and the anger has been arising for a long time.

Anger etched in the ground. Anger arises but does not persist long. Weather conditions can quickly change the face of the earth.

Anger like a line on water. the reaction does not last even when spoken to roughly and harshly.

Governments, politicians, various organisations and individuals often act from resentment/blame which blinds them from considering other responses from the harmful behaviour of others. We examine resentment in both directions:

Do our words and actions contribute to the resentment of others?

Do their words and actions contribute to our resentment?

Ten Grounds for Resentment:

1. *They acted for my harm*
2. *They are acting for my harm*
3. *They will act for my harm*
4. *They acted in the past to harm somebody I care for*
5. *They are acting now to harm somebody I care for*
6. *They will act in the future to harm somebody I care for*
7. *They acted on behalf of somebody else who is problematic*
8. *They are acting on behalf of somebody who is problematic*
9. *They will act on behalf of somebody who is problematic*
10. *Another person becomes angry without a reason. (AN 10:79)*

Those who threaten us take comfort with our anger. Seven things gratify those who threaten us. Those who dislike us will enjoy knowing that we are angry. Why?

1. *We appear ugly*
2. *We cannot sleep*
3. *We cannot succeed in getting what we want*
4. *We have to spend a lot of money to defend ourselves*
5. *We lose our standing in society*
6. *We lose our friendships*
7. *We live in misery and engage in harmful acts of body, speech and mind. (AN 7:64)*

The Buddha offered five ways to dissolve resentment towards another or others:

1. Develop kindness
2. Develop compassion
3. Develop equanimity
4. Give no attention to the person
5. Know that the person(s) own their karma, are) heir to their karma and have) karma as the cause of their resentment. (AN. 5.161)

A practitioner might choose one of the above five approaches and cultivate it daily for 40 days and 40 nights to see if the resentment will have dissolved.

A man claimed that the Buddha had "abused and reviled him with rude, harsh words." He then abused the Buddha.

The Buddha replied: "*I do not abuse anyone. Your abuse still belongs to you (SN. 7.2).*

A person engaged in discussions needs to understand whether he or she is fit to talk.

The Buddha lists the primary considerations. The person can:

1. Offer a categorical answer
2. Can make distinctions
3. Can offer a counter question
4. Can set aside a question, if necessary
5. Can stand firm in the view
6. Stands firm in his strategy
7. Stands firm in his assertion of what he knows
8. Stands firm in the procedure.

If a person is asked a question, and speaks evasively, tries to divert the question, shows anger and bitterness, this person is unfit to talk.

If the person who asks the question overwhelms the questioner, crushes him, ridicules him and seizes upon a slight error, then this person is not fit to talk.

One who lends an ear (on everything said) has a supportive condition. One with a supportive condition:

1. *Fully understands one thing*
2. *Abandons one thing*
3. *Realizes one thing.*

Directly knowing, he reaches a fulfilled liberation. This is the goal of the discussion, the goal of the supporting condition and liberation through non-clinging (AN 3:67).

Four Qualities of a Good Friend

1. *Helpful*
2. *Shares happiness and suffering*
3. *Points out what is beneficial*
4. *Shows sympathy. (DN 31)*

A person obsessed with greed and ambition will experience mental suffering and dejection (AN 3.54).

Four Kinds of People in the World

1. *One who lives neither for the welfare of others nor of himself*
2. *One who lives for the welfare of others*
3. *One who lives for his own welfare*
4. *One who lives for the welfare of both others and himself.*

The one who lives for the welfare of others and himself is the best, the preeminent, the supreme and is the finest of these four kinds of persons.

The best kind of person works to remove the greed, anger and delusion of others as well as from oneself.

What way is a wise person of great wisdom? The Buddha replied: "He plans for his own welfare. He plans for the welfare of others. He plans for the welfare of both. He plans for the welfare of the entire world (AN 4:186).

Sanghas consist of communities. A business is a Sangha. An intentional community is a Sangha. An organisation is a Sangha. A religious faith is a Sangha.

A deep community is not restless, not vain, not rambling in talk, well established in mindfulness with clear comprehension, concentrated, restrained in the application of their senses. The deep community is foremost (AN 2: 42).

Seven conditions for the non-decline of an organisation
1. As long as everybody holds frequent assemblies
2. As long as everybody assembles in harmony and adjourns in harmony
3. As long as people do not claim what has not been claimed and do not abandon what has not been abandoned
4. As long as there is respect for the guides and wise leadership
5. As long as people do not fall under the control of desires and demands of another
6. As long as people live in moderation
7. As long as people establish mindfulness to those present and those to come (AN 7:23).

The Buddha said to King Pasenadi. "Suppose you were at war and a battle was to take place. A young man from the military caste would arrive untrained, unskilled, inexperienced, frightened and quick to flee. Would you employ him as a soldier?

"Surely not, said the King.

The Buddha then asked: "Or would you accept a person from another caste?"

"A king intent on waging war, would employ a youth skilled with the bow, who has strength and who is not a coward – even if he is from a low caste.

The Buddha said: "So one should honour the person of noble conduct, a sage regardless of caste."

A Sangha of nomads lived together in harmony. The Buddha saw the men blended together like milk and water and looked upon each other with kind eyes. "How do you abide thus?" he asked.

"The one who returns from the village first sets out the water for drinking, for washing, places refuse bucket in place. The one who arrives last eats the remaining food. He puts away the seats and the water for drinking, washing, and the latrine. If some items are too heavy, he waves others to help. We do not need to break into speech. Every five days we sit together all night discussing the Dharma. This is how we abide diligent, ardent and resolute." (MN 31).

How Does One Earn Respect and Esteem from Others?

- *He does not presume intimacy when it is mere acquaintance*
- *He does not distribute things he does not own*
- *He does not make friendships in order to sow divisions*
- *He does not whisper in the ear*
- *He does not make demands or excessive requests.*

These qualities earn a person respect (AN 5: 111).

Sakya asked the Buddha a question:

"Why do people harm each other?"

The Buddha replied:

"Owing to the bonds of envy and miserliness."

Why is there envy and miserliness?

Due to likes and dislikes.

Why are there likes and dislikes?

Due to desire.

Why is there desire?

Due to too much thinking.

Why is there (too much) thinking?

Due to proliferation of thoughts and projections (DN 21).

On Quarrels and Fights

Why do people quarrel, fight and kill each other?
Why do rulers quarrel with rulers?
Why do the powerful quarrel with the powerful?
Why do the religious quarrel with the religious?
Why do householders fight householders?
Why do parents and children quarrel?
Why do brothers and sisters quarrel?
Why do people attack each other?
Why do they inflict suffering on each other?
Why do they kill each other?

The Buddha responded:

"The cause for all these quarrels and wars is the desire for pleasure." (MN 13)

What includes Pleasure?

- *The pleasure of getting what one wants*
- *The pleasure of getting attention*
- *The pleasure of getting one's own way*
- *The pleasure of feeling superior*
- *The pleasure of defeating another*

Issues rooted in Desire (Wanting, Craving, Pursuing, Neediness, Demanding).

In dependence on desire, there is:

- *Going after*
- *Gain*
- *Judgement*
- *Desire for more*
- *Inflation of importance*
- *Inflammation of a situation or experience*
- *Possessiveness*

- *Meanness/tightness*
- *Control over*
- *False speech, divisive speech*
- *Threats*
- *Use of weapons*

The Buddha told the story of the King of Savatthi who invited several blind men to touch an elephant. The King asked the men what they touched.

Your majesty, it is a:

- *Water jar*
- *Basket*
- *Ploughshare (after touching the tusk)*
- *Pole*
- *Storeroom.*

The blind men got into an argument. Every man claimed he was right and the others were wrong.

The Buddha said that disputes arise through seeing differences in the meaning and the phrasing.

He encouraged people to take the view in a dispute: "It is a mere trifle that I shall be troubled, and the other person will be hurt. The other person is angry and hurt because he or she is attached to his/her views and relinquishes them with difficulty."

"If I can make that person emerge from the unwholesome and harmful view, then it is a much greater thing. One cannot realize Nirvana unless one overcomes bitterness, dejection and conflict."

There are Six Roots of Dispute:

- *Holds to a view tenaciously*
- *Angry and hostile*
- *Acts without respect for the wise*
- *Ignores the training towards wisdom*

- *Leads to the harm and suffering of others*
- *Relinquishes views with difficulty.*

Who is a difficult person to change?

- *Dominated by harmful desires*
- *Praises and defends himself and disparages others*
- *Angry and resentful*
- *Resists feedback*
- *Gives feedback to the one addressing his issues*
- *Prevaricates*
- *Unwilling to account for his behaviour*
- *Deceitful*
- *Adheres to his/her own view*

An easy person to change does not display these kinds of views and attitudes.

One needs to review oneself in these areas as well as others, said the Buddha.

Four Kinds of Marriage

A wretch lives with a wretch

A wretch lives with a Goddess

A God lives with a wretch

A God lives with a Goddess (AN 4.53)

Who is a wretch?

A person who destroys life, takes what is not given, engages in sexual abuse, speaks falsely, indulges in addictive substances, negligent, lacks ethics, harmful character, tight and abuses others.

Who is a God and a Goddess?

A God and a Goddess live with virtue, wholesome character, dwell at home with a pure heart and do not revile or abuse others.

The God, Goddess and wretch can manifest out of the same person.

(Bullet point list for the four types? All in italics??)

Six Ways to develop Wealth while "seeing the danger of it."

1. In ethical and virtuous ways
2. Without violent demands
3. Creates happiness and feels pleased
4. Does not feel tied to it
5. Not infatuated with it
6. Shares the wealth (AN 10.91)

On Social Status

"I do not say one is better because of:

One is better off, because one is from an aristocratic family

One is worse off, because one is from an aristocratic family

One is better off, because of beauty

One is worse off, because of beauty

One is better off, because of great wealth

One is worse off, because of great wealth

I do not say that all people must be served

I do not say that none are to be served

One should not serve if one ends up worse

One should serve if one becomes a better human being.

If ethics, learning, generosity and wisdom increase in service, then he should serve.

A Brahmin said to the Buddha that priests, the military, the merchants and the workers should keep to their prescribed tasks as their wealth. He said the Brahmins prescribed this view without the consent of others.

The Buddha rejected this view. He said that the application of the transcendent Dharma is the true wealth of a person (MN 96).

Caste or Class is Convention

If a Brahmin, soldier, merchant (businessman or woman) or worker prospers in wealth, then their wealth puts them outside of the caste. Being wealthy, there are no differences between them.

If a Brahmin, soldier, merchant or worker lives an ethical and virtuous way of life, then there is no difference between the four castes.

If a person robbed and abused others that person would face) execution. There would be no differences with regard to the castes.

The statements of the Brahmins (to confine people to their caste) are mere words to the world.

Corrupt Leadership and the End of the World

When the minds of Kings (Presidents, Prime Ministers, CEOs) are corrupt

Their ministers, directors and managers will be corrupt.

When the priests and householders are corrupt

Then the people in the cities, towns and countryside will be corrupt.

The sun and moon will proceed off course.

Then the seasons and the years process off course.

The winds blow off course.

The Gods (forces of nature) get upset

Sufficient rain does not fall.

The crops ripen irregularly.

The people become short-lived, ugly, weak, sickly.

The entire world rejoices if the King (Queen, President, Prime Ministers, CEOs) live uncorrupted lives (AN 4:70).

For the Welfare of People

- *Distribute grain and fodder for those who cultivate crops*
- *Assign proper wages to those the state employs*
- *The business community give money to support the poor*
- *Then those intent on their own occupations will not cause harm.*
- *Revenues from the people will be great.*
- *The land will be tranquil.*
- *The land will not be beset with thieves.*
- *The people will know joy in their hearts.*

- *The people will play with their children.*
- *Families will dwell in open houses.*

12. THE WISDOM OF POLITICAL ACTION

In the space of two generations, Buddhism in Asia, as a force for tolerance, non-violence, kindness, and wisdom has declined significantly. Civil wars, authoritarian rule, violence and economic plundering have had a major impact on traditional Buddhist culture. The Chinese government has impacted upon the religious culture of Tibet while modernizing its mediaeval infrastructure. As Buddhism takes some form of rebirth in the West, it faces as great a challenge for renewal and revitalization as in the East. Many Buddhists, East and West, remain noticeably mute on issues such as climate change, war and cultural and environmental destruction.

Nevertheless, there are signs of health and vigour within the Buddhist tradition, East and West. As men and women explore the depths of Buddhist meditation practices, they find ways to express their insights and wisdom in daily life. They come to a real understanding of the significance of the Buddha's teachings and the significance of causes producing consequences. Noble men and women are emerging as a force for wisdom and compassion to the realities that we face in our life on Earth. It is a credit to them all.

The Dalai Lama, religious leader of the Tibetan people and Nobel Peace Prize winner, must rank as one of the most beloved human beings on this Earth. He has brought the importance of tolerance, kindness and understanding towards oppressors to the world's attention.

Buddhism matters immensely to many Tibetans in exile and among Mahayana students worldwide, but faces the challenge of finding its place in the contemporary world. Younger Tibetans and progressive Dharma students feel that many Tibetan masters and lamas are out of touch with democratic values, egalitarian attitudes, gender equality and post-modern thinking that doubt the narrative of major religions and political organisations. Some Thai Ajahns, Tibetan lamas and Western practitioners live in three different realms with different narratives – all of which deserve our interest.

In Kampuchea, the late Ven. Maha Ghosananda, nominated for the Nobel Peace Prize five times, led Dharma Yatra walks across his country, still littered with countless anti-personnel landmines. The country and Buddhism still slowly recover from the Kampuchean holocaust of 1975-79. Venerable Ghosananda has been a beloved friend of mine since we lived in the same Vipassana monastery of Ajahn

Dhammadharo, in Nakornsridhammaraj, southern Thailand, during the early 1970's. In 1997 he told me, as we were engaged in a dissent about landmines, seated on the steps of the Senate in Washington DC that he was telling the Cambodian soldiers to "kill the hate inside of themselves, lay down their arms, and rebuild our country."

Ven. Thich Nhat Hanh, a saint and Nobel Peace Prize nominee, gives support to the people of Vietnam. His Dharma teachings rank among the most respected in the West. In Thailand, Sulak Sivaraksa, twice nominated for the Nobel Peace Prize, has been an outspoken voice in his country, which he only refers to as Siam. Thai Buddhism, though, withers under the impact of capitalistic values and relentless thirst for profit.

In Sri Lanka, Dr. Aryaratna received the prestigious Gandhi Peace Award for his devoted and loyal work for the Sarvodaya Movement to improve the values, culture and economic realities of village life in his country. In Sri Lanka, a savage civil war continued until May 2009 between Sinhalese and Tamils. Both sides denied it was to be a religious war, yet their respective Buddhist and Hindu beliefs separated both sides rather than helping them to bring about reconciliation. War and hatred replaced Buddhist practices on dialogue and reconciliation. We may not necessarily agree with all the views, attitudes and conditions affecting such loved exponents of the Dharma, but all share an authentic voice of concern and stay true to it. We need such inspiration.

In 1989, I met with the Abbot of the Temple of the Tooth in Sri Lanka for meetings as a board member of the Buddha Peace Fellowship. He told me: "As a Buddhist monk, I uphold the first precept of not killing. But we Sinhalese must defend ourselves and our nation against the Tamils." Such views were not helpful.

Compassionate voices in the Buddhist tradition show a depth of calmness and often astonishing cheerfulness, despite what they witness and what they know. Their Dharma wisdom safeguards them from becoming dragged down into frustration and despair as they attempt to dissolve powerful and destructive forces. They provide a voice of vision willing to challenge and confront the abuse of authority regardless of any risk to themselves and their supporters. The best of the Buddhist tradition extols wisdom and compassion as a natural outcome of clear, unprejudiced seeing of a situation.

Some Buddhist leaders, like others committed to similar values, endure the cynics and the disillusioned that have lost trust in the power of communication, and instead support war as something unavoidable. The Buddhist view on these matters is simple. The time for dialogue is today rather than waiting into the indefinite future for men, women and children to die before political and military leaders have said: "Enough is enough."

Dharma practice calls upon practitioners to stay true to the deepest values as an authentic way of life regardless of personal attacks, naïve idealism and ridicule for not supporting the objectives of the nation state. Dharma teachings have a natural leaning towards decentralisation of authority, as well as wise authority. This shows itself in the sheer frequency with which the Buddha questioned the authority of kings, Brahmins, gurus and traditions, as well as his analysis of authority in the *Kalama Sutta*. Liberation from authority of the self, within or without, lies in the heart of the Dharma. That does not mean that we ignore the wise council of others, who are knowledgeable and insightful in their respective fields. The mindful practitioners take care not to invest all authority in one single individual. We must take responsibility for our lives, listen to the wisdom of others without projecting images onto others.

The Buddha said that there are four things conducive to the growth of wisdom:

- *Association with the wise*
- *Listening to the Dharma*
- *Wise attention to what matters*
- *Dharma practice.*

He added: "These four things are an immense help to a human being." (AN IV 246). Dharma practice includes going into areas of conflict. The Buddha once walked between two armies about to launch into a battle over land. He picked up a piece of rock and asked the Generals and soldiers whether a piece of rock was worth more than a single drop of blood of the family and friends. The generals resolved their conflict through dialogue.

A Priority for the West

Dharma in the West must evolve into an authentic and relevant instrument for change, a liberation movement, a network of men and women committed to not only witnessing change but also willing to make changes, inwardly and outwardly, as an outcome of direct insights and wise action. Meditation functions as a remarkable tool for inner depth, a building block of Dharma practice, but it can become an escape, a passive response. In a teaching on liberation, there is a major step from knowing the necessary action and to then taking the action. From knowing to action shows one expression of a liberated and fearless life. Meditation can contribute to clear knowing, inwardly and outwardly.

There is a long-standing history of passivity in Buddhist countries - Mahayana, Theravada and Zen - enabling brutal regimes to exercise terrible power over a submissive Buddhist population. The West can too easily inherit that same shadow from the East. Spending an excessive amount of time sitting on the meditation cushion watching sensations or chanting may inhibit direct compassionate action.

Crippled with ideology, the West believes strongly in competition, success and achieving the aims of the nation state. There is a blind refusal to explore a different inter-action with daily life with an emphasis on empathy, co-operation and a sustainable way of life. The minds of citizens absorb vast amounts of information from various sources, much of it utterly irrelevant. Painful personal, social and media information gradually enters the deeper layers of our mind increasing levels of anxiety about the present and future. This information glues together as a weight on consciousness' healthy response or has it become a weight on consciousness inhibiting us from authentic engagement with life? People get depressed with the weight of suffering for themselves and for others.

The practitioner sits in the driving seat with the ability to look at the mirror to see what is behind needing attention and to see the way ahead. Mindfulness of the past, present and future matter along the way. Positive and negative views, hope and fear, tell us more about our attitude than about unfolding events. The present moment could become an escape from a wise response to concerns and consequences of the past and future. Practice engages in a fully participatory way in these three fields of time: past, present and future.

The depth of clear awareness sees the signs of possible unintended consequences. The Buddha referred to three signs or marks for discernment, namely arising, persisting and passing (AN 111.47).

Each of the Three Characteristics of Existence deserves reflection:

- *What has arisen?*
- *What persists?*
- *What passes?*
- *What needs to change in terms of what arises?*
- *What needs to change in terms of what persists?*
- *What needs to change in terms of what passes?*

This requires the capacity to listen, inwardly and outwardly, to sense and to comprehend. The experience of the deepest truths and realities shed light on the movement of life. This enables the capacity to stay true to events while expressing a wisdom to deal with what reveals itself.

An Original Voice

Authority, author and authenticity share a similar meaning. Based upon 13th century French, these words carry the sense to originate, to increase and stay true to something. An authority makes something happen originating from an original voice that benefits others through staying true to the seen and known. The Zen tradition has employed the term over the centuries of the "original mind" – not as a foundation of the mind shared by all, as some orthodox Buddhists would have us believe. Our original mind creates fresh insights, new ways of responding, for example the capacity for imaginative ways to respond to situations.

The power to express love and compassion demands something different from within, original and bold. The destructive logic of the mind can sabotage an original movement towards a dynamic expression of love and insights. Excessive thoughts can shackle consciousness. This inhibits the opportunity to take steps into the unknown. Can we make a change of direction regardless of the "if" and "but" of our own thoughts and the thoughts of others?

The one who enjoys and the one who suffers depend upon habitual ways of believing and thinking. These two inner voices act as shadows over an original voice. The authentic practitioner releases creative energy trapped in the shadows, which challenges the belief that the self acts as the agent of actions. We must cease to be who we think we are; to listen, explore and act in unfamiliar ways. We are not who we think we are. We do not link authenticity to the enjoyer or the sufferer. Practice dissolves this shadowy self, a constructed view that life revolves around enjoyment and suffering.

The boundaries devised to protect individuals from any kind of vulnerability can become the blocks that inhibit communication towards a great liberation. Listening to discourses, reflection and meditation serve as a catalyst for change and the vitality to implement change. One significant insight for the Dharma practitioner, one flash of light, can save a thousand hours of the self struggling with itself on the meditation cushion, just as one picture can say more than a thousand words.

Shankara, the great sage of eighth century India, reminded his students to be indifferent to the transitory so that they can give full attention to the Immeasurable. He encouraged them to treat the relative world of impermanence as *maya*, as false and deceptive. His teachings point directly to what the yogi has not realised through imparted knowledge. Shankara aimed to transform the consciousness of the listener. It is not an easy task since students often struggle with a range of mental hindrances that hinder access to deep realisations.

Referring to the five hindrances to liberation, the Buddha described the:

- *pursuit of sensual pleasure* – *like coloured dye in the water*
- *anger* – *as boiling water*
- *laziness and dullness* – *as algae over the water*
- *restlessness and agitation* – *as churning/ripples in the water*
- *doubt/fear* – *as muddy and clogged water*

(SN. 46.55)

The Buddha said that the mind caught up in any of these hindrances "cannot know or see clearly what is." When stuck in a hindrance, those memorised chants will not recur to the mind, let alone those that have not been recited." said the Buddha in a rebuttal of dependency on chanting. "One can easily remember chanting when the mind is calm and clear," he added.

The Buddha said: "Let him see each arisen state. Let him know that and be sure of that." (MN 131)

Application of the Dharma

The Sangha of practitioners keeps faith with insight through experience, through insights from skilful and unskilful situations. It is sometimes a bit scary, and sometimes ruthlessly challenging to face what arises. The torch holders of the Dharma, the collective network of practitioners, stretch themselves to the limits, and then go further.

If the opportunities arise, the Sangha loves freedom of movement, to travel, to go on pilgrimage. It prefers hardship to comfort, the tent to the villa. Authentic Buddhist monks and nuns have a precious role since they set the example of renunciation, but they need to be fearless in their criticism of the opulence of far too many Buddhists who practice Buddhism as a hobby, a method of stress management, a self-improvement programme or a satisfying cosmology around karma and rebirth. Some feel concern that the Dharma in the West has become a path for personal contentment through the application of a handful of tools stripped of its original purpose: a revolutionary way of life that is neither materialistic nor theistic.

The Sangha offers the specific attitudes and tools to make real change possible.

With love and appreciative joy for a modest way of life, the renunciation of the superfluous comes effortlessly giving support (to what??). Our lifestyle then contributes to a sustainable world. We learn to travel more lightly on our journey through life. Renunciation of self-indulgence is an indispensable feature of the path, so that there is no clutter whatsoever in the mind, nor tendency for the self to latch on to 'this is mine!' or 'I want it!'

The Buddha commented (AN Iv 23):

By comprehending the world,

Just as it has become.

From all the world he is released.

In all the world, he clings to nothing.

He added in a later discourse:

By walking, one can never reach
The end and limit of the world.
Yet there is no release from dissatisfaction and suffering
Without reaching the world's end.
He no more longs for this world,
Nor for any other.
(AN Iv 45)

The above words of the Buddha deserve attention, a single pointed meditation in which the meditator addresses every line to see what inner response, if any, emerges from the depth of being. On first reading the lines of the verses may seem incomprehensible. What is the world? What is the end of the world? The world the Buddha referred to is the world of name and form, self and other, mind and matter, consciousness and objects. 'I' and 'my' finds itself imprisoned into this inner world. In seeing and knowing the end of this world, without looking for a heavenly world, the immeasurable reveals itself simultaneously.

It is not unusual for dissent to appear in the Sangha on sensitive issues such as ethics and renunciation. Honest dissent enriches the Sangha. Clear comprehension draws from the wisdom of the conservative tradition and moves into areas of progressive development that conservatives resist. The conservative and radical values of Buddhism can support each other through respect for the insights of the past and respect for the creative expressions of the Dharma for the present and future.

The Sangha questions deeply the problematic values of conventional life while remaining free from any obligation to feel loyal to the nation state and its political and economic imperatives. The renunciation of grasping unhealthy belief systems points humanity to an awakened state free from the wasted energy and violence needed to grasp onto the nation as self-important and then defend it.

The Sangha lives in a different state altogether – without boundaries of any kind. There is a shared responsibility for the turning of the Dharma Wheel. Countries consist of lines on the map, often against the will of millions of people.

With an Eye to the Future

Like all the other major world religions, Buddhism often adheres to the past rather than having eyes to the present and future. Authority in Buddhism lies in the hands of men. There is little indication in the East of any shift in authority to show that gender free wisdom. Countless numbers of thoughtful women and men keep Buddhism at arm's length because they cannot see a scrap of difference between the authoritarian manners of the male Sangha of Buddhism, and the likes of rabbis, priests and imams of other religions. Ordained Buddhist leaders make politically correct statements about the importance of women in the Dharma and yet fail to re-introduce full ordination for women. Devotees nod their heads in agreement as an act of deference to authority. The same senior monks retain their grip on authority, their power and their intransigence.

The Buddha himself appeared resistant to supporting the voluntarily chosen homeless way of the Dharma life for women. His stepmother and aunt, Maha Prajapati, with hundreds of women, asked to join the homeless Sangha and the Buddha said: "Do not ask." His aunt took no notice and she and other women shaved their heads, put on yellow robes and tracked the Buddha down. He still refused.

Ananda, his attendant, asked the obvious question: "Do women have the same potential as men for full awakening?" The Buddha acknowledged that they did have that equal potential. The Buddha initially refused to ordain women, because he felt that society was not ready for this step. He may have felt concern for the safety of women living a nomadic, and sometimes, solitary way of life in remote places. Finally, he granted women the opportunity to take full ordination. This radical step in ancient India enabled women to renounce the householder's life and join a free-spirited, nomadic movement.

In the 11th century CE, Moghul invaders attacked northern India and destroyed the monasteries and Buddhist libraries. They killed many monks and nuns or forcibly disrobed them, the *bhikkhuni*s of Buddhist nuns virtually disappeared. Since then, senior Buddhist monks have clung to a view passed on from one generation to the next that for women to take full ordination a monk and five fully ordained nuns must be present. This effectively blocked full ordination for women. Taiwan became the last bastion of women's full ordination. Taiwanese Buddhism, a non-Theravada country, became the key to full women's ordination. It was a liberating step for women who felt tied to the role of being a housewife.

In early 1998 a Taiwanese Abbot and some Theravada monks participated in a bhikkhuni ordination for 20 women in Bodh Gaya. I recall being a supporter for the women's monastery in Sri Lanka. It was not easy for women seeking full ordination, but supporters had made a start. There are now small numbers of fully ordained nuns in Theravada countries though the leaders of the established monastic Sangha do not always recognise them. The full ordination of women does not give equal status to the men as the rules as women are expected to show deference to monks.

Whether as householders, living a nomadic way of life, or as monks and nuns, they all have a key role in Dharma life in the West. The West needs monasteries where men and women can take refuge from the pathology of consumer culture and go deeply into the Dharma with an ethos of mutual respect. Monasteries provide an environment free from the external pressure of sexual needs and imagery. Advertising and the mass media assault the senses with the result of distortion of perceptions through sensual desire. Buddhist monasteries offer rare and precious environments for conscious people.

Hierarchy comes from the Greek word *hieros* meaning *sacred*. *Archos* means *ruler*. A true hierarchy nourishes all in the hierarchy to expand and develop as human beings. This is the second duty of a leader. The hierarchy in the Sangha includes the role of teacher, seniors in practice, voices of wisdom and experience, and those who are new or relatively new to Dharma practice. An authoritarian voice refuses to allow for dissent, exercise influence in a narrow way and dissuades others from pursuing a wider exploration. The dumbing down of authority shows an unhealthy viewpoint. Some people fear hierarchy whatever their place is on the ladder reacting with cynical views.

It is not always easy in the West to reconcile the apparent paradox of discipline and freedom. Discipline, the exercising of restraint or the act of giving up seems to inhibit our freedom to go after what we want. Dharma discipline contributes to a fully awakened life, a happiness not determined by acquisitions and status. A child gives up her or his three-wheeler when he or she has the confidence to mount a two-wheeler bicycle. An experience of effortless renunciation comes through such a change in priority.

The Sangha differs from an army of soldiers engaged in unquestioning obedience to orders. Some Buddhist teachers insist on strict adherence to certain methods and techniques. A practical method proves beneficial in a retreat. While this may be necessary in an intensive retreat, it produces harmful consequences (sectarianism, cults, submissive behaviour, and loss of natural autonomy) when the Buddhist teacher absolutely insists that the practitioner must give or be ostracised. Some schools and teachers insist that their students do not practice with other teachers. Such traditions can tell students to stay away from meditating with others of a different practice.

There are various rationalisations for the imposition of such restrictions – 'you will become confused,' 'you can't mix practices, 'others won't understand unless they join our programme'. Serious practitioners need to be aware of such attitudes and stay mindful of any restriction of freedom to inquire or share their experiences. People who belong to a sect or cult often live in denial of the diversity of ways of meditation. It is important to listen to those with a diverse range of experiences in the spiritual life conceiving priorities and those who equally disagree.

Dharma teachers with years of experience need to ensure continuity through establishing a solid Sangha of teachers, facilitators and organisers. Some long-standing teachers feel inhibited to invite one of their students to teach in case it gains the disapproval of their own teacher. Teachers take responsibility for sustaining the tradition. This is an important aspect of our authority as Dharma teachers.

To cherish the ideals of total selflessness inhibits the spirit of being a spiritual teacher. Men and women can place too high an expectation on themselves. Some teachers report that they never felt very ready to teach. There is always more practice while some teachers move effortlessly between teaching and being students of other teachers. If expectations of others or ourselves are too high, no potential teacher will feel ready to share the Dharma with others or sense that anybody else is ready to teach either.

If that ideal is clung to, nobody will ever be ready to teach. I have spent my life moving in religious/spiritual/service orientated groups and networks and have not found one completely selfless individual.

The Buddha does not offer such a romantic ideal. He teaches liberation from suffering so that we understand ourselves and others.

Vigilance is necessary to safeguard Dharma teachers from getting caught up in a mode of relationship involving the misuse of power, intentionally or otherwise. Dharma teachings are a constant encouragement to explore through different teachers, practices, lifestyles, meditation, yoga, psychotherapy, trainings and forms of service. In any authentic exploration, teachers will meet strongly differing views from others. Some teachers, both religious and secular, remain determined to sustain the accepted moral order refusing to perceive a morality outside of it. Codes of morality, precepts and vows have worked in the past; people have observed them, they claim. These teachers see any questioning of a fixed moral order as a rationalisation for questionable behaviour.

Others will claim that the old moral order of right and wrong is repressive, self-righteous and leads to punitive and reactionary treatment of those who defy the order. Some authority figures in the Dharma state the need to explore human relationships, to allow interaction to take place, so that the authoritarianism of the old order dissolves. This allows for greater freedom of expression with each other.

Adherents of the old order and those exploring an evolutionary shift may find it hard to experience a common ground of understanding. There is a moral certainty among the traditionalists, free from ambiguity of right and wrong. Those engaged in an unfixed, non-absolute Dharma standpoint may find themselves coming across cautiously on ethical matters. Their position stands in stark contrast with those who strongly advocate the old order. It is easy to end up on the defensive if you find yourself inquiring into ethics without knowing a conduce view, with neither a defined set of absolutes in morality, nor the certainty of the old order.

The old order sanctions those who adhere to fixed norms in some areas but often ignores other areas of ethics. Adherents will privately and publicly rebuke or excommunicate those who act differently. The danger of the old order is the rush into judgement without considering the causes and conditions that determine action. Fearful of coming to a judgement about unwise action and its consequences, the liberals in the Dharma end up clinging to a moral relativism. Such conservatives and liberals offer little in the way of insight and inspiration.

Authentic teachings show us the way to look at actions and results of actions. We develop the capacity to inquire into the specific conditions that bring about a specific result. Dharma teachers give support enabling people to stand on their own two feet, so they know how to develop deep ethics, unambiguously and intelligently. For this to take place, Dharma practitioners need to explore communication for months or years. The employment of the divine power of friendship and insight expresses a noble way of life.

The Buddha said that the noble ones experience empathy with others. In terms of leadership, it requires that teachers make themselves approachable and accessible for the sharing of knowledge and direction. A Dharma leader can offer not only knowledge but also enthusiasm through his or her dedication and personal exploration.

The leadership of Dharma teachers matters significantly if the Dharma is to take root in the West. This includes the immense task of not only sowing seeds in the hearts and minds of individuals and society but also contributing to a revolution of consciousness. Wise counsel with others gives support to teachers.

Wise application of authority, friendship and vision ensure that the West adapts to the Dharma, not the other way around, so that the Sangha remains true to authenticity and dedicated to a liberated and compassion way of life.

13. DISSENT AS A FORM OF HEALING

Dissent is a form of healing since it empowers the dissenter who chooses to act rather than living under the weight of submission or numbness. The act of dissent has the potential to be a truly liberating process. Dissent consists of one person or a group questioning the authority of another. Authentic questioning carries a deep ethic as it aims to reduce causes and conditions for suffering found in the policies and views of the ruling group. The willingness to campaign to reduce suffering confirms the act as being one of compassion.

At best, the dissent carries a discerning judgement – a determination to apply wise principles to the heart of any expressions of corruption in the political/corporate establishment. Dissent belongs fully and directly to a contemporary Dharma way of life. The Buddha spent much time dissenting about greed, hate and delusion. It is important to keep alive the long tradition of dissent. There is a common view that dissent exclusively means involvement in a demonstration. It is one expression. One can ordain as a Buddhist monk to dissent against consumerism or live a simple, nomadic way of life in the East or West to dissent against the demands, the voracious appetite of society. Dissent can offer the first step towards inner-outer change and for some the everlasting step.

The word 'protest' often has a negative flavour, because it has become heavily loaded with anger and associated with street violence on demonstrations. An angry attitude makes little or no difference to changing the views of those who abuse power.

Meaningful Political Action

People can change profoundly through meaningful political action, as much as through inner change and working on themselves. Direct action to change circumstances that generates suffering empowers people. Outer change gives support to inner change and inner change gives support to outer change. One important change does not precede the other. The world will have fallen into pieces if people wait to dissent until they deem themselves happy, peaceful and emotionally well-adjusted human beings. Yet, if people think that changing the political/financial system without inner change matters most, then such people need to become students of history. One regime will replace another; one oppressive system of government can give way to another. Inner-outer abides as an inseparable relationship. It is easy to be spellbound with a myth that our inner life is a self-existent entity, bound to its past, independent of society and environment. This is the privatisation of the self.

Many Buddhists begin work on themselves through mindfulness, meditation and inquiry. As they develop and mature as human beings, they treat with equal concern the outer as much as the inner. Action matters. It is the movement from despair to empowerment, from the restrictions of the self to a wider vision, from the individual to the collective. The Buddha said: *"It is actions that distinguish beings."* (MN 135)

To dissent against injustice and exploitation of the individual or group expresses an ethic. The ethics of valid dissent to stop suffering serve the deep interest of the one who engaged in dissent, as well as the rest of society. Authentic empowerment contributes towards the transformation of the structures, timetables and demands upon the lives of individuals.

Practical Ways towards Changing the World

1. *Acts of compassion*
2. *Attending and organising public meetings*
3. *Boycotts*
4. *Conflict resolution, use of judiciary*
5. *Constructive engagement,*
6. *Personal contact with opposition*
7. *Consumer awareness*
8. *Dialogue groups, facilitation*
9. *Generosity, service, voluntary work*
10. *Imaginative initiatives to gain the attention of the media*
11. *Letters, petitions to the media, politicians and corporations*
12. *Mass gatherings*
13. *Meetings at home*
14. *Memberships of campaigning organisations*
15. *Non-violent dissent, street demonstrations*
16. *Posters, leaflets, articles, essays, books*

17. *Reaching out to social media, networks and caring people*
18. *Taking risks*
19. *Telephone, e-mail, Flickr and website*
20. *Use of the arts and creativity*
21. *Workshops, weekly meetings*
22. *Yatras (pilgrimages), peace walks, vigils*

In 2007, thousands of Buddhist monks and nuns joined courageous laypeople in Rangoon to dissent against the Burmese military government, the doubling of bus fares and fuel bills on an impoverished nation. Senior Buddhist monks overturned their begging bowl to stop senior officers in the military regime from placing alms in the bowl thus keeping the bowl for the worthy ones. By doing so, the monks denied the army officers the opportunity to make merit. It constituted a very bold dissent.

Mercifully, these brave monks and nuns did not spend weeks or months or more on the couch of the psychoanalyst encouraging them to look at their feelings. Action matters. It is the same with the courageous monks and nuns in Tibet protesting against the occupation of China. Palestinians engaged in regular protest against Israel's occupation of their country. These actions keep the humanity of dissenters alive and free from despair.

Psychotherapists, psychologists, and meditation teachers need to do much more to show clients and Dharma practitioners the way to make practical, effective, and empowering dissent on social/political issues that damage the lives of their clients. Unlike dissent marches to reinforce prejudice, the act of dissent has the capacity to be therapeutic. A commitment to non-violence, a willingness to listen to others and participation in meetings and street march will contribute to inner empowerment. Authentic dissent supports those who in need and develops a sense of one's inner worth.

The concerns and passion that lead to dissent can show a healthy emotional and compassionate response. The client, who only wishes to unburden their feelings, may show a lack of respect for themselves and for others through a passive response to citizenship and neglect of a liberating empowerment. Can an awakened life ignore the realities of the nation state, political belief systems, armaments, the corporate world, health care, debts and so on?

The street is the natural home of those who wish to voice their concerns. A collective dissent on the street offers the sense of belonging, a sharing of an ideal, a vision. Undeterred by rejection, ridicule and personal danger, those who engage in this form of dissent express the power for transformation, an urge for change. The refusal to accept the rhetoric and tyranny of the old provides the potential for an evolutionary leap of consciousness.

Those who live away from the cities must find ways to make their voices heard, too, through local campaigns, demonstrations, support of local groups, social networks and correspondence.

The symbolic act of the walk, or the occupation of a section of the city, as the act of dissent, represents far more than the sum of its parts. It is about change – both root and branch in the corridors of power. The Walk becomes a valid vehicle to empower people, as well as to dissolve the indifference that numbs consciousness. The Walk is the movement and determination of one mirrored as the many. Dissent is a significant step to real change.

Authentic empowerment includes contributing towards the transformation of the structures, timetables and demands upon the lives of individuals. Healing develops when people speak up for other people. Advocacy is an important aspect of healing. For example, a social worker often acts as the guardian angel for families and individuals struggling to keep their lives, if not their sanity, together. As skilled professionals, social workers handle extraordinarily well the immense personal problems of individuals, families and communities.

The army of professionals in the caring professions, need to encourage their clients to act against injustice as well as help them to handle their emotions. Without action, without dissent, it can lead to a deafening silence and collusion with social oppression. "I suffer. Therefore I am." Dissent is a valid form of therapy, a valid form of Dharma practice, too. The healing power of dissent shows that those who suffer should not bear all the responsibility for their suffering. Therapists can help empower their clients to struggle for change. Contemporary therapy sees listening, plus perhaps a few personal exercises, as the only response to abuse.

There are extensive writings bringing together psychology, spirituality, religion and philosophy. There are schools of thought attempting to integrate consciousness with the various sciences. It is a well-meaning vision. Yet these schools of thought ignore the undeniable influence of politics, party and non-party politics, upon consciousness. Contemporary psychologists/philosophers and pundits have frequently marginalised political consciousness from their inquiry, even though political decisions and indecision, affect life. How can there be a visionary view excluding political analysis?

The Buddha taught personal and collective responsibility

We have to find ways to change the structural suffering in governments, businesses and organisations. This requires policies that open the doors to what has been hidden from colleagues in the workplace and from public view. There is the dissent of the whistle-blowers. It takes courage to speak up at the risk of losing one's job.

The Buddhist traditions have tended towards a view separating the application of the Dharma from the structural suffering in institutions, big and small. Some Buddhists believe that the Buddha declined to engage in any social criticism or had any interest to change society. Some Buddhists have the impression that the Buddha only created an order of monks and nuns without the need to address genuine issues of concern in society. The Pali texts show something very different.

For example, the Buddha devoted the lengthy Sigalaka Discourse to the responsibilities of householders. He explained the dangers of harmful actions, dangers attached to addictions, haunting the streets, gambling, bad company, poor friends and outlined true friendship. He met a young Brahmin, a householder, named Sigala taking a morning ritual bath, saying his prayers and bowing in the six directions, north, south, east and west, above and below following the request of his late father. Sigala followed the request of his late father.

The Buddha then defined the six directions as six important kinds of relationships - one's relationship with our parents and children, teachers and students, friends, colleagues — employees/supervisors, husband or wife, and spiritual counsellors. The discourse showed that a wise and loving relationship in all six areas contributed to healing, meaningful change as well as departure from the old ways of relating.

He voiced his concerns to the major powerful influences in society and gave some clear advice on their responsibilities as well on seeking change in common beliefs. He also addressed:

- *Animal sacrifice and the protection of all sentient beings*
- *Consumerism – namely the pursuit of pleasure as the primary reason for existence*
- *Practices and privileges of Brahmin priests*
- *Religious beliefs, including widespread belief in a personal God*
- *Rulers, kings and authority figures*
- *Spoke of the importance of ethics beginning with a commitment not to engage in killing*
- *The application of non-harmful livelihoods and lifestyles*
- *The caste system, humanitarian values*
- *The dependency on charismatic figures, reason, tradition and books*
- *The responsibilities of the rich to share their wealth*
- *The significance of love and compassion in all directions*
- *Yogis for engaging in extreme, self-punishing practices widespread in India*

The Buddha did not reject society but engaged in the transformation of society as well as speaking in depth to his nomadic Sangha. His voice struck a strong chord with growing numbers in society who realised that the old system of authoritarian rule and imprisonment in the caste system could change. He established the world's first major network for women to live a nomadic way of life. He pointed to a liberated way of life for women, mindful and peaceful, as well as free from duties as wives, mothers, and daughters.

It is one thing to recognise the limits, if not the foolishness, of those in power whether locally or nationally. No shortage of people expresses a critical view during a discussion. It is another matter altogether to develop skillful means to change the status quo. It is this movement toward co-operation and action that shows a genuine awareness of the reality of a painful situation, not just finding fault. The Buddha commented that we are known by our actions.

One person can make a difference. Are you the one?

14. THE DHARMA THAT IS DIFFICULT TO SEE

In one of the Buddha's discourses, called the Noble Search (MN 26), the Buddha stated that the Dharma is "difficult to see."

Immediately after the night of awakening and in the weeks that followed, the Buddha engaged in reflection. "I considered," said the Buddha, "this Dharma that I have attained is profound, hard to see, hard to understand, peaceful and sublime, unattainable by mere reasoning, subtle, to be experienced by the wise."

"This generation delights in worldliness. It is hard for such a generation to see this truth, namely specific conditionality and dependent arising. It is hard to see this truth namely the stillness of formations, letting go, the end of desire and Nirvana." He added that if he had to teach this Dharma, "others would not understand me, and it would be wearying and troublesome."

After his awakening, the Buddha said that he "would find it hard to teach for it will never be perceived by those caught up in attraction and aversion. They will never discern or understand this obtrusive Dharma which goes against the worldly stream, subtle, deep and difficult to see." This was his first response to what he had realised.

People easily take their view of the world for granted. This view states: "There is myself and there is the world. "Events touch us. It reinforces the view that I am here and the event, near or far away, is there. That is the reality of things, we claim. This repetition of this form of language strengthens the view to be the true reality as a matter of course, day by day. Naturally enough, human beings have consistently reacted against this, as it is imprisonment. Humans have endeavoured to find views to undermine, change, or shake up that view. Some truth seekers look for a higher purpose. They construct something metaphysical, such as God or the Beyond; something outside of the worldly order of things, to transcend the conventional worldly view. Some adopt two views with equal conviction. "I am living in the world" as one view. There is *That* which transcends the word as the second view.

The metaphysical often goes together under the general language of religion and spirituality. The belief in the transcendent helps people to cope with worldly views and all the stress and insecurity that go with them. The transcendent view gives a higher purpose to existence. Some refer to their belief in God with a promise of an afterlife. Devotees of God may refer to people as sons and daughters of the Divine. The adoption of a transcendent view gives a different feeling to life, a consolation for ageing, sickness and death. Believers committed to the belief in non-transcendence identify with the view "I exist in the world. One day I will no longer exist."

The belief in the existence of the transcendent or its non-existence belongs to those who have neither knowledge nor experience of the middle way. Reaction against non-existence shows itself in the desire for continuity which can make the transition into death easier through the promise of an afterlife in some form, whether rebirth or heaven. Human beings have consistently felt secure or insecure in the worldly or religious view or both. The desire for continuity and the views of non-existence after death ends up as a tricky situation to resolve, as if we had no alternative to either view.

From his experience, the Buddha understood worldly and religious views. There is a clear recognition of some of the values of worldly life through moderation in lifestyle, ethics and social concerns. Wise application of social concerns in the worldly framework relieves suffering. Tragedies on a personal level or large-scale invite an immediate response so that this suffering does not happen again. What are the steps to protect people? People in society form an inquiry to investigate painful events. What happens in personal and natural catastrophes? The Buddha endorsed any inquiry to end suffering through taking steps to see the causes and conditions that triggered a situation. Nevertheless, worldly life alone is not fulfilling.

Some share a deep interest in deep spiritual experiences that do not fall into any religious category or language. Dharma teachings recognise the valuable role that spiritual experiences and the accompanying language play in human life. There is no rejection or undermining of such experiences. The Buddha designated and described the range of important depths of the spiritual experience. He referred to some of these experiences as deep absorptions (*jhanas*) or as formless realms (*arupa ayatana*). Deep love or sudden expansions of consciousness show two kinds of spiritual experience. These spiritual experiences can arise inside or outside of meditation.

Happiness and joy suffuses a person so he or she knows a freedom from the problematic mind at such times. One feels remarkably light, grounded, centred, happy and untroubled. A genuine sense of a spiritual experience opens the mind to a fresh awareness of life.

These experiences show no indication of attraction, aversion or agitation. Boredom, anxiety, fears and other unwelcome states of mind have no presence at such times. A person can say with validity during these spiritual experiences, "I feel incredibly free." There is an authentic freedom in those times. This freedom relates to the form of meditation, the form of communication or the form of creative expression. Regular meditation can trigger such experiences, sometimes to be life-changing. An absence of spiritual experiences indicates an undernourished life. Any time of the day or being in the nature can trigger such experiences. It would be a very poor life that does not have regularly authentic spiritual experiences.

Four profound experiences to change our way of looking at the world

- *The Realm of Infinite Space*
- *The Realms of Infinite Consciousness*
- *The Realm of Infinite No-thingness*
- *The Realm of Neither Perception nor Non-Perception*

Some step further and experience the formless realms of spiritual experiences. One formless meditation experience arises as the extra ordinary sense of spaciousness, an infinite spaciousness, an incredible sense of expansion. In that spaciousness, one feels one can accommodate everything. There is no wanting, nor desire in this sense of vast openness, no need for anything, inwardly and outwardly. Some people have formed the view that this experience is the ultimate experience.

Infinite Space

A deep sense of infinite space finds its way into our being. We know a truly spacious way of being. The view of self and other, me in the world, finds itself replaced with infinite spaciousness, a vast, unlimited formless realm. Some people would take the view that a deep experience of infinite spaciousness reveals the transcendent, the ultimate state, because no divisions manifest in this experience.

Yet, there is access to deeper experiences that an infinite spaciousness.

Infinite Consciousness (

At a very subtle level, the purest condition of consciousness arises. This infinite consciousness:

- *Accommodates space as well*
- *Appears as the self of one revealed as the same self of all*
- *Can reveal anything internally and reveal everything externally*
- *Functions as the great container*
- *Is infinite in its capacity*
- *Seems to be the essence of who I am*
- *Seems to be the true self*

Consciousness seems infinite with no way to measure it, or to limit it. The view may arise that consciousness with a capital C is the true nature of things. All is Consciousness. Only Consciousness can confirm inner and outer life. Consciousness is the supreme element. This view is not born from reasoning, nor from cerebral ideas, but born from depths of meditative presence, the well-being of the person and a receptivity to a sense of the infinite.

Infinite No-thing

In authentic and genuine ways, these experiences change people's lives, priorities and values. They put into a proper perspective the material world, selfishness and egotism. The important experience of the realm of infinite consciousness can shift to an even more subtle level. There is the experience of the real realm (??) of infinite no - thing. We realise we do not live in a world of things, in a world of multiplicity, sentient and insentient. This is not a state of nothingness. Pali word is *akincina* - no-thing. This worldly view claims that every 'thing' is different from every 'thing' else. This is the conventional worldly viewpoint. This view ceases to be the reality; we recognise it as one common perception among human beings. In this realm of experience, the meditator might mistakenly conclude that the world is an illusion. The experiences of these four formless realms might reveal that:

- *Infinite space embracing Oneness of everything*
- *Infinite consciousness, as intelligence throughout the universe*
- *Infinite no-thingness, as the infinite and that is it*

- *Neither perception nor non-perception shows the deceptive nature of perception.*

These realms of perception can change to the everyday perception, which sees everything as different from everything. The universe appears full of different things. Every object is different from everything else. No two snowflakes are the same. We rely upon perceptions to claim the true reality.

Infinite Space, Infinite Consciousness and Infinite No-thingness In Oneness, the view of differences fades away. All is One. Everything absorbs into everything else.

Neither Perception nor Non-Perception

Realizations may arise that show the unreliability of any perception to reveal the truth. Perceptions remain vulnerable to the variety of conditions that give support to the perceptions. Any change in those conditions impacts upon the perception. We can perceive something with certainty one way in one experience and switch to perceiving it in another way, radically different, with the alteration of the perception.

Yet, we cannot claim that there is no perception. In his very subtle experience, the meditator realises that we cannot rely upon these formless realms of experience. These experiences can feel mystical, spiritual, religious or spontaneous. Once again, the range of such experiences expands our way being without offering a single experience to rely upon.

These kinds of experiences do not fall into the category of worldly views. The Buddha encouraged the exploration of these four types of experiences so that we have an immense potential to see and know the diversity of ways we can know life beyond ego and consumerism. We can know a deep value to these wondrous shifts in perception; awe and wonder spring from such shifts.

In his discourses, the Buddha gives tremendous encouragement to develop, utilise them and counteract the common view of self and the world as the only reality while dealing with attraction and aversion. The worldly view is an imprisonment. The exploration of such experiences with deep meditation enables seeing in a dramatically unusual way. Mind-altering plants and drugs seem like kindergarten experiences compare to knowing intimately the formless realms. It is easy to elevate these experiences as ultimate, as an absolute of the way things are.

The Buddha never sanctioned the range of secular, religious, spiritual and mystical experiences as ultimate. He never proclaimed that everything belongs to the relative. He teaches liberation through seeing and knowing what has become. He never states that you experience Nirvana and then go on to something else, as if Nirvana functioned as a stepping stone to something else.

The Notion of Absolute Truth

In the Dharma, there is no such thing as the absolute truth. The reason is simple. If there were an absolute truth, then we would have to start naming what that absolute truth is. Once we start to engage in the naming, it will bring duality. Others will have a different absolute truth. This sows the seed of worldly, religious or spiritual conflict. If the Buddha reduced everything down to relative truth, there would be no point in implementing initiatives for liberation and Nirvana.

All experiences, worldly, spiritual and mystical, share something in common. Every experience arises, stays for a while and then passes. Each experience can give a different viewpoint, a similar viewpoint or a hierarchy of viewpoints to dispute. The yogi can experience a profound sense of Oneness, a deep sense of an Infinite Consciousness that accommodates everything or an extraordinary sense of Infinite Space, free from limits. The experience then fades. The feeling quality fades.

A view may form that it is the ultimate experience, a spiritual experience or just another experience. Some will long for the experience again to reconfirm its significance. After a deep experience, a person may feel dissatisfied. "I am now back into my old mindsets and my old views and opinions. I have to deal again with the world. I must deal with worldly issues in daily life. I want to get back to that transcendent and transformative experience in my life."

People move backwards and forwards between diverse kinds of experience. The Buddha recognised and appreciated the worldly experience as a valuable resource for insight and understanding. He also recognised religious beliefs and the power and support that they can give human beings. The Buddha also brought in a fresh discourse that included the religious, spiritual and worldly, but which were not limited to these categories. He changed the priority and the language. He stated: "This Dharma is profound, hard to see, hard to understand, peaceful, sublime, unattainable by mere reasoning, subtle, to be experienced by the wise."

The Buddha placed the priority on a profound understanding of dependent arising, the contingency of all experiences. Conditionality acts as the unshakeable thread that runs through the whole body of the teaching, subtle and deep. This teaching deserves exploration of the range and depths of human experience. It is the keen exploration of causes and conditions that forms the main body of the teachings, inwardly and outwardly, until the unconditioned stands out as obvious as light does to a person with good eyesight.

Living in Relationship with Others

One person reacts to another person, whether friends, loved one or political leader. This reaction gives selfhood to her or him – that means fixing the person in a certain way. Due to the reaction, the view places the person in a category, a box: "You are like this. You did this." Positively or negatively, the projection distorts perception. That is the signal. The more substance is given to the reaction, the more it reveals the strength of the projection. There is no inherent self in the person. There is no inherent truth to the reaction. If that were the case, then the reaction and the object for the reaction to land upon could never change. If there were a real, permanent self, a fixed self of the other person, it would mean that the person. It would mean that the person dwells independently of the causes and conditions that make her or him up.

The Dharma recognises expressions of the worldly, spiritual and religious experiences and their functioning for human life. The Dharma also endeavours to liberate us from holding to an experience to confirm something transcendent. The wish for a transcendent experience is very strong. The Buddha acknowledged this. Take an example. A person says to me: "Christopher, I have this very deep longing inside of me. I have sat retreats with you, practised in a monastery, been to India, and attended Dharma workshops. I have sensed something. I have tasted something. Yet, I feel something is not complete, not fulfilled."

It is not unusual to experience a deep longing in the fabric of the being. There is a knowing that longing does not have to have any ego in it. The longing just arises, stays and passes at various times. There is longing in the spiritual/religious life and secular life. That longing may manifest in diverse ways such as longing for a deep communion with another human being. There is longing to be with God, for a profound experience or longing for enlightenment or liberation.

The human being feels the gap between the longing and that longed for. The gap ends. The person may say that which I really longed for has touched me. I really know now what I longed for. I really felt that experience. That does genuinely happen. The longing can find fulfilment. There is no guarantee that longing will find any fulfilment. The longing can stay through the life arising with intensity throughout life.

From the Dharma standpoint, it is not essential to fulfil the longing. It is not a problem. Like everything else, longing constitutes a dependent arising. We do not have to make a problem out of longing. This shift in the view liberates longing from frustration and disappointment. There is an understanding that longing comes because the conditions are there for longing to arise. A fulfilment after a longing, either in the short term or in the long-term, feels precious and profound. We learn to love the gap between our longing and what we long for. A fulfilled longing emerges due to the presence of certain causes and conditions.

People give voice to their fulfilled longing. The movement called longing and the completion of the longing confirm dependent arising. The Buddha's Dharma goes back to his very first words after those weeks under the tree reminding all how difficult it is to see clearly and understand the nature of dependent arising as a liberating element. Longing and fulfilment are dependently arising. It is not a matter of trying to complete or fulfil our longing. This is a central feature of the teaching. The exploration has precious elements since it allows many expressions of freedom.

Dharma does not advocate an absolute truth to attain; this movement reinforces the idea of an 'attainer.' I want to reach this absolute truth, which reinforces the "I" that wants to attain it. Once named and described, this absolute truth finds itself in conflict with another absolute truth. To settle for relative truth feeds the same problem of conflict with another. The teachings avoid dividing truth into absolute and relative.

The Buddha said: *"Whatever is seen, heard, smelt, tasted, touched or clung to, people know as the truth. Among those entrenched in these views, one holds none as true or false."* (AN 4.24).

There are infinite ways of a full freedom to explore the past, present and future. Excessive thinking and the exaggeration of thinking about the past does two things. Too much thinking generates stress. In a stressful attention to the past, the thinker cannot see the past clearly or understand any event. It places the thinker out of touch with the potential to see the causes and conditions for what happened. He or she will not understand the way perceptions of the past, present or future influence their lives due to the spell of excessive thinking (*papanca*). The mindful person does not hold to the view that the past is an illusion. The Buddha did not proclaim this kind of view.

In verse two of the *Mulamadhyamakarika*, Nagarjuna wrote that there are four specific conditions for what arises, not five. Whatever arises depends on the conditions to arise.

The Buddha has not placed these four conditions into a single formation, but the Pali words do appear in the Sutta. These are the first four specific conditions listed in the Abhidhamma:

- *Hetu*. A causal condition. Striking a match is the causal condition for its lighting. Pressing computer keys is the causal condition for words on screen.
- *Arammana*. Supportive Conditions. A match is the supportive condition. The computer is turned on etc.
- *Samanantara*. These are the factors leading up to the immediacy of the situation. The process leading up to includes the bringing of the match and the side of the box together to make a flame. In the second example, these are the factors leading up to the reading of the words on the screen.
- *Adhipati*. Maintaining after. A flame is emitting from the match. Words appearing on screen are the dominant condition (what does that mean?).
- It would be worthwhile for people from every social class to remember these specific conditions, meditate on them and reflect on them.

A person might ask:

- *Causal Condition. What you do see as the cause for this experience?*
- *Supportive Condition. What do you see as the supportive conditions for it?*
- *Leading up to Condition. What led up to it and show in the immediacy?*

- *Maintaining Condition. What is the dominant condition supporting the experience now?*

Nothing arises from itself or from another specific thing. This does not mean to say that nothing arises, but nothing can arise from itself or exclusively from some*thing* else. It is always worthwhile to bear in mind all four essential conditions. There is no fifth condition.

Any change in the dependent conditions changes the dominant condition.

Owing to *papanca* from certain memories and feelings, we can trigger anxiety about the future that reveals more about the inner life than the causal connection between the present and the future. Distorted perceptions colour the future, sometimes strongly enough to make the perceiver of the future forget the importance of the relationship to the future. Projections and excessive thinking distort the capacity to attend wisely to the outcome.

Too many conditions can dependently arise that alter significantly an anticipated outcome. Conditions form together to produce an outcome. If people possessed all available knowledge of conditions, the person would be able to see and know everything that will happen. He or she would be omniscient.

If you spend a minute or two giving mindfulness to a single flower, you will connect with its petals, leaves, the name of the flower, the plant, root, earth and the conditions that bring about the flower. You will feel closer to the flower arising from causes and conditions. You will know, naturally and easily, that the flower does not have its own self-existence. You will know that it needs light, water, earth and air. You can offer clear acts of kindness to the flower for it to grow.

It is not an illusion, nor a flight from the present, to consider the future. Insights into the present, may give me some indication of what might unfold in the future. You may be able to see the past and the present to know what is not going to lead to happiness or suffering in the future. The undistorted freedom to look at yesterday, today and tomorrow confirms a wise attitude. Freedom stands out in the presence of dependent arising. The wise know that changes in the conditions lack the inherent power to add or reduce freedom. This freedom, this liberation for the wise knows no conditions. Freedom, the unconditioned, emptiness and Nirvana confirm different words for the same truth.

The Buddha summarised this extraordinary sense of dependent arising as:

> "When there is this, that comes to be;
> with the arising of this, that arises.
> When there is not this, that does not come to be;
> with the cessation of this, that ceases."
>
> *(SN 12.61)*

The exploration of causation, of dependent arising reveals the emptiness of I and my, of egotism and the superficiality of self-aggrandizement.

An enlightened life reveals itself through seeing, knowing and understanding the dynamics of dependent arising

15. CHARTER FOR LIFE ON EARTH

We think of life as only about self and other, and sometimes self against other. This viewpoint shows itself from the personal to the political. When the Communist bloc dissolved at the end of the 1980's, the West found another 'other,' namely the Arab world. Our shadow is everything we do not see about our self. We project fear and blame onto others.

Western leaders and Western military could not endure the EDS (Enemy Deficit Syndrome). The end of the Cold War led to the War on Terror. Instead of mutual co-operation, the West built up yet again the self-other syndrome, us and them. The dark projections of Western leaders landed on Islam and Arab culture. Islam and Arab responded in like. US Military bases in Muslim countries, 9/11 and military invasions intensified the differences unleashing death and destruction.

Tied to the beliefs in the differences between self and other, a destructive morality targets the 'other'. Until people on Earth engage in a depth of soul searching on this core problem, the tyranny of the self and other continues. We fail to understand why the West continues to trouble the rest of the world. The West identifies itself with a social Darwinism view of existence – survival of the fittest, superiority of the Western "civilisation" and a distorted theory of evolution that believes that the West shows the pinnacle of evolution. We have come to widely accept this view as the Truth, as the reality.

Such views feed notions of us and them, superiority and inferiority.

The Consumers and the Goods

The self and other principle equally applies to consumer goods. Consumers invest into goods giving them a significance far beyond the merit of the items in question. A clear signal of exaggerated significance to goods shows it*self* when the item fails to live up to its promise – despite a bewildering number of pages in the manual! The relentless campaigns of governments and businesses convert citizens into consumers. This becomes the primary aim of politicians, the corporations and economists running the nation state. Do the aims of the nation state and big business determine our lives? Have we submitted to this priority way (unclear to me) with unquestioning obedience?

Advertisements tell us that the ownership of the latest consumer goods will make us happy – happy individuals, happy families and a happy nation. We may see between 4000-5000 ads per day. Businesses use every conceivable space to bombard us with products to buy. Yet, millions live unhappy lives owing to debts, dysfunctional families, obesity, despair and daily medication to reduce the pain in body and mind. We need a revolution to change the warped values and the painful consequences on the emotional, mental and body life, as well as on communities and the environment. There is an exaggeration of the importance of owning expensive goods from the big houses, luxury yachts and fast cars.

Love, peace of mind and insights dissolve the self - other divide, whether it is oneself and other people or oneself and consumer goods. Based on such clarity, we can work for social change. The dissolution of self and other makes a fundamental shift in consciousness, thus freeing life from such a dichotomy. To see the emptiness of this duality releases fresh levels of love and a wise response to events.

The Darwinian belief in struggle, competition and survival gives way to a fresh sense of cooperation, sustainability and compassion as an authentic way of living. Us and them, self and other obscure clarity and wisdom. Me and my possessions, me and what I want to own ensure a narrow way of life with little vision.

- *This Charter for Life gives support for all sentient beings and the Earth.*
- *This Charter offers an outline for a fulfilled life, free from conflict born of belief in self-other.*

We require wise attention and direct action, two of the key features of Dharma practice. We need to enter into a dialogue to reduce competition and instil co-operation for the true welfare of all. Competition breeds conflict. Co-operation for change develops wisdom. Drawing on the wisdom of the Buddha-Dharma, this Charter contributes to the protection of all sentient beings, while giving support to diversity and sustainability.

A CHARTER FOR LIFE ON EARTH

Listed in Alphabetical Order

1. *Right Action:* Join and support organisations and political parties dedicated to the welfare of the Earth. Dissent skilfully about war, environmental destruction, economic targets and corruption in governments and corporations affecting the lives of people and animals. Dissent about harm and destruction of natural resources, land, water, and air. Engage in ethical investments and support worthwhile projects. Support and develop, as fully as possible, spirituality, religion, arts, science and philosophies that support the Earth and all its occupants.

2. *Right Conservation:* Save energy. Use less oil. Conserve water. Wear more clothes at home and work out to keep warm rather than turning up the heating. Examine every area of your home and the rest of your life to see where you can save energy. Apply the principles of conservation to every area of your life. Campaign for switching off lights and energy at night in government and business offices, large and small.

3. *Right Diet:* Let go of eating anything with a face - animals, birds or fish. Meditate on feelings of pleasure and pain, since people and creatures have such feelings in common. Find out about the methods of the meat industry from start to finish. Arable land produces far more food for humans. Buy organic food to protect the environment from the destructive effects of intensive agriculture, support local farms and local shops. Use as much as possible, fair trade imported goods. The Internet offers a wealth of information on the impact of diet, food and drink on humans and animals. Use medication from the pharmaceutical industry as the very last resort.

4. *Right Letting Go:* Let go of your car. Or, if you believe you must have a car, then try to keep to one car per household and share your car with others. Drive sparingly and conserve fuel by staying well within speed limits. Only use the car for very necessary journeys. Make the same modest sized car last over many years. Use public transport or walk as much as possible.

5. *Right Mindfulness:* Practice keeping to basic requisites of food, clothing, accommodation and medicine. Make things last. Refuse to live with excess. When you go to the shops carry shopping bags from home and do not accept plastic bags. Keep packaging to the minimum. Give to charity shops and buy from them. Be mindful of what you wear in terms of the ethics of shops and clothing factories. Avoid companies that are known to sell goods made in

'sweat-shops' in developing countries. Be mindful and informed about all points in this Charter.

6. *Right Renunciation:* Let go of desire for a bigger or better home. Have a spring clean in your home and see what you can give away or recycle. Support and develop love of minimalism and enjoy the outdoors in all weathers. Avoid shopping malls. Buy only necessities. Avoid impulse shopping. Keep out of debt. Offer dana (in the form of donations, time, and energy) to worthwhile projects and individuals.

7. *Right Sustainability:* Be well informed about recycling; compost waste food and recycle paper, plastic, metal and glass. Develop and support local community initiatives and social networks that work together for the welfare of people, animals and the environment in the area where you live. Support complementary medicine, mindfulness practices, exercise and a sustainable lifestyle. Check ingredients in food, shampoos, and so on. Avoid junk food, cigarettes and all recreational drugs.

8. *Right Travel:* Only use air travel, if at all, to serve others or to go to new destinations to change one's life such as the monastery, the ashram, retreat centre, the rainforest, a pilgrimage, a visit to sacred places and through direct contact with nature. Use flights to reconnect with loved ones. If wealthy or the most senior of monks, still turn right when you step on board the plane and use economy class! Go camping or walking and take vacations in your own area. Minimise holiday hotels, beach resorts and flights for the pursuit of pleasure.

9. *Right Co-operation:* Organisations and institutes need to co-operate together in the task of inquiry into all the key areas that make up our daily lives, such as those mentioned above. The vision of life from conception to death needs fresh perceptions and exploration so that, as a collective, human beings live a loving and adventurous life, and form groups and networks to look at all the essential areas impacting on us all.

10. *Right Communication:* Develop initiatives within the local community and political processes to respond fully to the ongoing crisis on our Earth, due to the politics and economics of self and other, us and them, competition and conflict. Communication involves human beings taking a deep, daily interest in the capacity to co-operate to change the current mode of competitive thinking.

The Charter reminds us to apply the deep significance of contemporary forms of renunciation that contribute to a mindful life. Our acts of renunciation for the welfare of people, animals and the Earth, show the power of loving kindness to shape our priorities and values. The application of loving kindness to countless situations confirms a wise way of life.

Knowledge, with love and liberation, support the real welfare of everyone. This is the priority.

In Conclusion

Life constitutes a steady stream of unfolding events. Most of these events sail past consciousness with merely momentary interest as we move through the day. Out of the emergence of these unfolding events, we experience that certain situations make an impact upon us – for better or worse. The impact may arise due to any of the four conditions or a combination of them, seen or not seen.

- *Inner interests*
- *Latent tendencies*
- *The strength of outer circumstances*
- *A combination of inner and outer conditions.*

The combination of circumstances may be obvious or hidden to us, but the impact demands from us our full attention. Love is the willingness to give a quality of attention to that connection with the depth of our being. Love has an important function, not to possess, nor control the object of interest, but has the capacity to relate with heart and mind to events. Love serves to bridge the divide between the inner and the outer.

Love reveals a worthwhile encounter with a person, a group, a species, a habitat or a profound insight or vision. While acknowledging the convention of forms, disciplines and social agreements, love also speaks and acts outside the limits of convention. Original minds can show acts of dedicated love that baffle and mystify others who are operating within their limited personal frames of reference.

Genuine love confirms the presence of Truth since Truth and love point to the recognition of what we share, as well as the acknowledgement of what keeps us apart. We know the beauty of love and the transcendent power of love through our way of being in the world, not through adopting the views of institutions and ideologies that support us and them. The transcendent power of love and equanimity means that we stay steady, like a mountain in a hurricane, regardless of fluctuating circumstances. True love endures right through life. We have this remarkable ability to stay steady, non-violent and dedicated to meaningful change, regardless of what happens.

The jewel of love becomes sacred through a willingness to stay true to a love that remains free from wanting, let alone demanding, anything from the other. Presence or absence of the other has little, or no relevance, for real love. We sustain a loving encounter with a person, place, or way of being even when it defies common sense and logic. The erosion of such a deep connection occurs through placing this love in the pressure cooker of personal desires.

The nature of the loving rapport given through words, gestures and touch, actualises the cells of our being. The need to be loved generates a psychological climate of frustration and an inability to offer love. Love returns love. There are hundreds of ways to show love. We can use our imagination to offer love to another. The true challenge to love depends upon our perception of differences and the apparent realness of those differences.

The experience of oneness, of unity, will not withstand the impact of the perception of differences upon consciousness. We might live a very calm and harmonious life, but we will still have to the face the feelings of differences and attend to them. We might hold to the view that oneness embraces all differences. If oneness embraces all differences, then we could experience oneness by itself without any reference to differences.

We cannot experience oneness independently of differences. The wisdom of oneness and differences, of unity and separation, acknowledges both sides of the duality. Oneness and differences equally belong to the field of worthwhile and valid experiences. If we elevate oneness into a metaphysical construct, we will perceive oneness as the answer and differences as the mundane perception. From a spiritual standpoint, we do not have to pursue a profound experience of oneness, but endeavour to explore every side of perception and non-perception.

The experience of oneness is precious, eye-opening, and insightful but we do not have to regard the experience as the answer to our prayers. The experience of differences is not true reality either. The unitive experience certainly serves as powerful reminder that all of nature shares much more in common than what separates. We also realise the daily experience of differences functions as one way of perceiving the other, the world. We do not need to adhere to a view that life is one or life is two.

Accompanied with wisdom, the power of love concerns itself with the plight of the human situation, the full range of perceptions and feelings, without grasping onto one expression of perception above another.

Love then becomes the confirmation of our humanity. The love that fills our being confirms our living presence in the world, while the corrupt patterns, such as greed, violence and fear, inhibit our inner wealth. Authentic teachings and practices join love and wisdom. We draw upon the depths of our inner experience and engage in the application of our insights and wisdom for the benefit of all.

We integrate the inner with the Universal, the relative with the Ultimate and love with a liberating wisdom. An enlightened life embraces ethics and action while seeing and knowing a profound liberation.

APPENDICES
Outline of the Discourses (Suttas) of the Buddha

MN – Middle Length Discourses of the Buddha (Pali: Majjhima Nikaya)

DN – Longer Discourses of the Buddha (Digha Nikaya)

SN – Connected Discourses *of* the Buddha (Samyutta Nikaya)

AN – Numerical Discourses of the Buddha (Anguttara Nikaya)

Sn – Sutta Nipata

Dhp – Dhammapada

It – Itivuttaka

Ud – Udana

Vin – Vinaya. Five Volume. Book of the Disciplines. Translated by I.B. Horner. Pali Text Society

The Number behind the letters of the discourse indicates the exact discourse. For example MN 29 refers to discourse number 29 in the Middle Length Discourses or the same location, for example M i 192.

The Suttas are grouped into various collections

1. The Middle Length Discourses of the Buddha translated by Bhikkhu Bodhi from Majjhima Nikaya. Wisdom Publications, Massachusetts in 1995.

2. The Long Discourses of the Buddha translated by Maurice Walshe from the Digha Nikaya Wisdom Publications, 361 Newbury Street, Boston, Massachusetts 02115, U.S.A. in 1995.

3. The Book of the Gradual Discourses translated by E.M. Hare from the Anguttara-Nikaya. 5 volumes approximately 1400 pages published by Pali Text Society and Unwin Brothers Limited, The Gresham Press, Old Woking, Surrey in 1978.

4. The Connected Discourses of the Buddha translated by Bhikkhu Bodhi from the Samyutta-Nikaya, approximately 2174 pages publication date, November 2000. By Wisdom Publications, Boston, Massachusetts, Pali Text Society, London in 1980.

5. The Sutta-Nipata with Commentary. Translated by Bhikkhu Bodhi. 1500 pages. Pali Text Society, Oxford, England.

6. The Dhammapada (423 verses) translated by Acharya Buddharakkhita, introduction by Bhikkhu Bodhi the Buddhist Publication Society, Kandy, Sri Lanka.

7. The Udana and The Itivuttaka, translated by John D. Ireland, Buddhist Publication Society, Kandy Sri Lanka.

8. The Book of the Discipline. Vinaya. Five Volumes. Translated by I.B. Horner. The Buddha's discourses on ethics, precepts, laws, Sangha and society.

Books by Christopher Titmuss

1. Spirit for Change
2. Freedom of the Spirit
3. Fire Dance and Other Poems
4. The Profound and The Profane
5. The Green Buddha
6. Light on Enlightenment
7. The Power of Meditation
8. The Little Box of Inner Calm
9. An Awakened Life
10. The Buddha's Book of Daily Meditations
11. Buddhist Wisdom for Daily Living
12. Transforming Our Terror
13. Sons and Daughters of The Buddha
14. Mindfulness for Everyday Living
15. Meditation Healing
16. The Mindfulness Manual
17. Poems from the Edge of Time
18. The Buddha of Love
19. The Explicit Buddha
20. The Political Buddha

Books to be published in 2018 and 2019

- *The Spiritual Roots of Mindfulness*
- *The Daily Life Handbook*
- *The Buddha in the West*
- *The Questioning Mind of the Buddha*
- *Ten Years and Ten Days* (Memoir from letters/diaries. Traveller, Buddhist monk etc. from 1967 – 1977)

Websites. Blog

www.christophertitmuss.net

www.insightmeditation.org

www.mindfulnesstrainingcourse.org

www.dharmainquiry.org

www.dharmayatra.org

www.meditationinindia.org

www.christophertitmussblog.org

MAY ALL BEINGS LIVE WITH LOVE
MAY ALL BEINGS LIVE WITH INSIGHT
MAY ALL BEINGS LIVE AN AWAKENED LIFE

Printed in Great Britain
by Amazon

45858259R00136